ReFocus: The Films of Richard Linklater

ReFocus: The American Directors Series

Series Editors: Robert Singer, Frances Smith, and Gary D. Rhodes

Editorial board: Kelly Basilio, Donna Campbell, Claire Perkins, Christopher Sharrett, and Yannis Tzioumakis

ReFocus is a series of contemporary methodological and theoretical approaches to the interdisciplinary analyses and interpretations of neglected American directors, from the once-famous to the ignored, in direct relationship to American culture—its myths, values, and historical precepts.

Titles in the series include:

Preston Sturges Edited by Jeff Jaeckle and Sarah Kozloff

Delmer Daves Edited by Matthew Carter and Andrew Nelson

Amy Heckerling Edited by Frances Smith and Timothy Shary

Budd Boetticher Edited by Gary D. Rhodes and Robert Singer

Kelly Reichardt E. Dawn Hall

William Castle Edited by Murray Leeder

Barbara Kopple Edited by Jeff Jaeckle and Susan Ryan

Elaine May Edited by Alexandra Heller-Nicholas and Dean Brandum

Spike Jonze Edited by Kim Wilkins and Wyatt Moss-Wellington

Paul Schrader Edited by Michelle E. Moore and Brian Brems

John Hughes Edited by Timothy Shary and Frances Smith

Doris Wishman Edited by Alicia Kozma and Finley Freibert

Albert Brooks Edited by Christian B. Long

William Friedkin Steve Choe

Robert Altman Edited by Lisa Dombrowski and Justin Wyatt

Mary Harron Edited by Kyle Barrett

Wallace Fox Edited by Gary D. Rhodes & Joanna Hearne

Richard Linklater Edited by Kim Wilkins and Timotheus Vermeulen

Roberta Findlay Edited by Peter Alilunas and Whitney Strub

edinburghuniversitypress.com/series/refoc

ReFocus
The Films of Richard Linklater

Edited by Kim Wilkins and Timotheus Vermeulen

EDINBURGH
University Press

Edinburgh University Press is one of the leading university presses in the UK. We publish academic books and journals in our selected subject areas across the humanities and social sciences, combining cutting-edge scholarship with high editorial and production values to produce academic works of lasting importance. For more information visit our website: edinburghuniversitypress.com

© editorial matter and organization Kim Wilkins and Timotheus Vermeulen, 2023, 2024
© the chapters their several authors, 2023, 2024

Edinburgh University Press Ltd
The Tun—Holyrood Road
12 (2f) Jackson's Entry
Edinburgh EH8 8PJ

First published in hardback by Edinburgh University Press 2023

Typeset in 11/13 Ehrhardt MT by
IDSUK (DataConnection) Ltd
A CIP record for this book is available from the British Library

ISBN 978 1 4744 9382 6 (hardback)
ISBN 978 1 4744 9383 3 (paperback)
ISBN 978 1 4744 9384 0 (webready PDF)
ISBN 978 1 4744 9385 7 (epub)

The right of Kim Wilkins and Timotheus Vermeulen to be identified as editors of this work has been asserted in accordance with the Copyright, Designs and Patent Act 1988, and the Copyright and Related Rights Regulations 2003 (SI No. 2498).

Contents

List of Figures vii
Notes on Contributors viii

    Introduction: Linklater's Itinerant Oeuvre 1
    Kim Wilkins and Timotheus Vermeulen

Part 1 Auteur Cinema in Context

1 'I Think I Still Qualify as a Slacker . . . Just One that's Currently Lucky': The Myths of *Slacker*, Austin, and Richard Linklater 15
   Mary P. Erickson
2 On Being a Vegetarian in Texas: The Incongruities and Politics of Linklater's *Fast Food Nation* 34
   Claire Parkinson
3 The Little Space Between Hal Ashby and Richard Linklater 50
   Rob Stone
4 On Drifts and Swerves: Linklater's Love for Lacunae 67
   Jeroen Boom

Part 2 Genre as Means

5 Richard Linklater and the Field of American Dreams 85
   Timotheus Vermeulen
6 *Boyhood*: Linklater's Testament of American Youth after 9/11 100
   Timothy Shary
7 The (Un)bearable Weight of Gendered Genre: Richard Linklater's Post-*Boyhood* Masculinities 115
   Mary Harrod

8 Stories So Far: Romantic Comedy and/as Space in *Before Midnight* 136
   Celestino Deleyto

Part 3   Style and Meaning

9 Empathetic Effort in *Where'd You Go, Bernadette* and *Bernie* 157
   Kim Wilkins
10 Richard Linklater's Humanism: Moral Primacy, Recency Effects, and *SubUrbia* 176
   Wyatt Moss-Wellington
11 Keeping Time in *Dazed and Confused*, *Everybody Wants Some!!*, and *Boyhood* 194
   Bruce Isaacs
12 Rhythm and the Rotoshop: *Waking Life*, *A Scanner Darkly*, and Rhythmanalysis 210
   Christopher Holliday

Index 234

Figures

3.1	Intervals of flânerie in *The Last Detail* . . .	50
3.2	. . . and *Before Sunrise*	51
7.1	The colonel's pallor in *Last Flag Flying* suggests the U.S. army's waning vitality as a viable social institution	124
7.2	The generic choreography of emotion is embraced by *Last Flag Flying*'s climactic funeral sequence	125
7.3	Tanner Kalina's Alex Brumley is the face of queer fat in *Everybody Wants Some!!*, in a scene where his housemates suggest losing at cards means he must fellate a moose	128
7.4	Finn's costuming in *Everybody Wants Some!!* expresses both the provisionality of identity and generational confusion	131
11.1	Olivia: the unbearable burden of time	204
11.2	Mason and the spectator in a knowing, collusionary exchange	207
12.1	Wiley Wiggins at the train station in *Waking Life*	216
12.2	Wiggins encounters Eamonn Healy	226
12.3	Bob's shifting physiognomy and composite form as he wears the scramble suit in *A Scanner Darkly* contrasts with the uniformity of the audience	229

Notes on Contributors

Jeroen Boom is a doctoral candidate at Radboud University Nijmegen working on cinematic cartographies of precarious ecologies including images of migration and the aesthetics of environmental devastation. His dissertation focuses on disruptive gazes in experimental cinema about European migration, analyzing its visual (de)construction of border spaces and its different imaginaries of the sea. He is also co-coordinator of the research group 'Critical Humanities' at the Radboud Institute for Culture and History (RICH) and teaches various courses on film and visual culture.

Celestino Deleyto is Professor of Film and English Studies at the University of Zaragoza, Spain. He is the author of *From Tinseltown to Bordertown: Los Angeles on Film* (2016), *The Secret Life of Romantic Comedy* (2009) and *Alejandro González Iñárritu* (2010) with María del Mar Azcona. He has published articles on film genre, romantic comedy, transnational cinema, and cosmopolitan theory in *Screen, Cinema Journal, PostScript, Film Criticism* and *Transnational Cinemas*, among others. Celestino is currently researching borders, transnational cinema, and cosmopolitan theory. His most recent publications are 'Looking from the Border: A Cosmopolitan Approach to Contemporary Cinema,' *Transnational Cinemas*, 8:2 (2017): 95–112, 'Performing Cosmopolitanism: Julie Delpy and Ethan Hawke in Richard Linklater's "Before" Trilogy,' *Transnational Screens*, 10.1 (2019), 23–33, and 'The Way of the Dog: *Truman* through the Cosmopolitan Lens,' *Studies in Spanish & Latin American Cinemas*, 17.1 (2020), 51–72.

Mary P. Erickson teaches media studies at Western Washington University. Her research focuses on regional and independent screen media, distribution and marketing, gender, and technology. She co-edited *Independent Filmmaking*

Around the Globe (2015). She has also worked in independent film as a publicist, researcher, and distribution consultant.

Mary Harrod is Associate Professor in French Studies at the University of Warwick. She is the author of *Heightened Genre and Women's Filmmaking in Hollywood* (2021), *From France with Love: Gender and Identity in French Romantic Comedy* (2015), and the co-editor with Mariana Liz and Alissa Timoshkina of *The Europeanness of European Cinema: Identity, Meaning, Globalization* (2015) and *Women Do Genre in Film and Television* (2017, winner of the British Association of Film, Television and Screen Studies Best Edited Collection Prize 2019), as well as numerous articles and chapters. Her first journal publication was on pastiche in Linklater's earlier films and appeared in the journal *Screen* in 2010.

Christopher Holliday teaches Film Studies and Liberal Arts at King's College London, specializing in Hollywood cinema, animation history, and contemporary digital media. He has published several book chapters and articles on digital technology and computer animation, including work in *Animation Practice, Process & Production* and *animation: an interdisciplinary journal* (for which he is also Associate Editor). He is the author of *The Computer-Animated Film: Industry, Style and Genre* (Edinburgh University Press, 2018), and co-editor of the collections *Fantasy/Animation: Connections Between Media, Mediums and Genres* (2018) and *Snow White and the Seven Dwarfs: New Perspectives on Production, Reception, Legacy* (2021). Christopher is currently researching the relationship between identity politics and digital technologies in popular cinema and can also be found as the curator and creator of the website/blog/podcast www.fantasy-animation.org

Bruce Isaacs is Associate Professor in Film Studies at the University of Sydney. He has published work on film history and theory, with a particular interest in the deployment of aesthetic systems in classical and post-classical American cinema. He is the author of *The Art of Pure Cinema: Hitchcock and His Imitators* (2020), *The Orientation of Future Cinema: Technology, Aesthetics, Spectacle* (2013), and *Toward a New Film Aesthetic* (2008). He is currently working on a large research project entitled 'The Making of the Modern Action Film.'

Wyatt Moss-Wellington is Associate Professor in Media and Culture at the University of Nottingham Ningbo China. He is the author of *Cognitive Film and Media Ethics* (2021), *Narrative Humanism: Kindness and Complexity in Fiction and Film* (Edinburgh University Press, 2019), and co-editor with Kim Wilkins of *ReFocus: The Films of Spike Jonze* (Edinburgh University Press,

2019). Moss-Wellington is also a progressive folk multi-instrumentalist and singer-songwriter, and has released four studio albums: *The Kinder We* (2017), *Sanitary Apocalypse* (2014), *Gen Y Irony Stole My Heart* (2011), and *The Supermarket and the Turncoat* (2009).

Claire Parkinson is Professor of Film, Television and Digital Media and Co-director of the Centre for Human Animal Studies at Edge Hill University. Her research interests focus on storytelling and agency; media, culture, and animal studies; eco-media; American cinema; activism; cultural history; and film and politics. Her publications include the monographs *Animals, Anthropomorphism and Mediated Encounter* (2019), *Popular Media and Animals* (2011), and *Memento* (2010) and the edited collections *Routledge Companion to Cinema and Politics* (2016), *American Independent Cinema: indie, indiewood and beyond* (2012), and *Beyond Human: From Animality to Transhumanism* (2012).

Timothy Shary is a professor at Eastern Florida State College in Palm Bay, Florida. Timothy has published extensively on youth in cinema. His books include *Generation Multiplex: The Image of Youth in Contemporary American Cinema* (2002, 2014), *Teen Movies: American Youth on Screen* (2005), and the collection *Youth Culture in Global Cinema* (2007). He most recently authored *Boyhood: A Young Life on Screen* (2017).

Rob Stone is Professor of Film Studies at the University of Birmingham, where he co-directs B-Film: The Birmingham Centre for Film Studies. He is the author of *Spanish Cinema* (2001), *The Wounded Throat: Flamenco in the Works of Federico Garcia Lorca and Carlos Saura* (2004), and *Julio Medem* (2007) and co-author of *Basque Cinema: A Cultural and Political History* (2016). He also co-edited *The Unsilvered Screen: Surrealism on Film* (2007), *Screening Songs in Hispanic and Lusophone Cinema* (2013), *A Companion to Luis Buñuel* (2013), *Screening European Heritage* (2016), *The Routledge Companion to World Cinema* (2017), and *Sense8: Transcending Television* (2021). He is the author of *Walk, Don't Run: The Cinema of Richard Linklater* (2013; 2nd ed. 2018) and he features in conversation with Dave Johnson on the Criterion blu-ray release of *The Before Trilogy* (2018). He is currently writing *Lady Bird: Self-determination for a New Century* (2022).

Timotheus Vermeulen is Professor in Media, Culture and Society at the University of Oslo. He has published widely on cultural and aesthetic theory, close textual analysis of film and television, and contemporary art, including books on Metamodernism (*Metamodernism*, edited with Robin van den Akker and Alison Gibbons, 2017; *Anmerkungen zur Metamoderne*, Textem, 2015), suburban culture (*New Suburban Stories*, edited with Martin Dines, 2013), and suburban film (*Scenes from the Suburbs*, Edinburgh University Press, 2014). He is a regular contributor to *Frieze*.

Kim Wilkins is a Postdoctoral Research Fellow in Screen Cultures at the University of Oslo. She is the author of *American Eccentric Cinema* (2019) and co-editor with Wyatt Moss-Wellington of *ReFocus: The Films of Spike Jonze* (Edinburgh University Press, 2019). She has published widely on indie cinema in numerous journals, including *Textual Practice*, *Film Criticism*, and *Texas Studies in Literature and Language* as well as edited collections. Her current research examines gentrification and contemporary German film and television and has appeared in *Screen*, *NECSUS*, and *Cinephile*.

Introduction: Linklater's Itinerant Oeuvre

Kim Wilkins and Timotheus Vermeulen

In August 2019, Richard Linklater announced a new project. Over the course of the next twenty years, he will film an adaptation of Stephen Sondheim and George Furth's musical comedy *Merrily We Roll Along*. It's an ambitious enterprise, to put it mildly. Though Linklater is uniquely experienced with extended shooting schedules, he has never directed a musical. *Merrily We Roll Along*'s screenplay, moreover, has long been considered difficult to the point of being unfilmable. And, lest we forget: by the time the film is released, the perennially youthful director will be an octogenarian.

And yet, this project would seem atypical to anyone but Linklater. After all, he has made a name for himself doing precisely this: rethinking the rules of film production in general and the relationship between film time and real time especially, moving continuously between and across genres, contemplating the cinematic apparatus, all the while winking knowingly to his audience. As David T. Johnson puts it:

> Whereas other directors have moved from project to project without a clear pattern in mind, Linklater's work offers a particularly satisfying trajectory in this regard, with the choices in subject matter as surprising and interesting as the eventual films into which they are made. Consider that *The Newton Boys* (1998) followed *subUrbia* (1997), or *Tape* (2001) followed *Waking Life* (2001), or *Bad News Bears* (2005) followed *Before Sunset*, and it can become tempting to view the films as not having any discernible relation to one another other than the fact that they all share the same directorial credits in their title sequences.[1]

To be sure, reading Linklater's filmography as a plotted career timeline gives the distinct impression of disconnection—a collection of disparate projects that, at first glance, appear almost random in their selection. However, as Johnson notes, on closer inspection it becomes clear that coalescence is not a particularly illuminating lens through which to view Linklater's oeuvre. Rob Stone instead characterizes Linklater's approach to filmmaking as cubist in manner in that it "rejects a single viewpoint, preferring to fragment a three-dimensional subject and redefine it in a temporal collage made up of several points of view, as though seeing it in a shattered mirror."[2] As Stone writes:

> by definition no cubist portrait can ever be complete because its subject exists in the time that it expresses and is therefore constantly changing, evolving, arriving, and departing. So too is the cinema of Richard Linklater, whose movement between independent film and the studio system, between genres, European and American cinema, politics, and philosophy is a product of versatility and variation. Linklater certainly disproves the assumption of idleness as a defining characteristic of the slacker ethos.[3]

We, too, consider the individual films that comprise Linklater's oeuvre less as stepping stones in a cohesive and conclusive authorial narrative than as different points of departure along intersecting trails, each of which provides a different vantage point from which to view a set of recurring themes centered around American culture and politics, history, filmmaking in and outside of Hollywood, filmic and experiential apprehensions of time, American regionalism, and the complexities of interpersonal relationships—though we will shortly come to suggest an alternative conceptual metaphor to describe this, one to our mind more in spirit with Linklater's persistent empathy and familiarity with his subject matter: that of Ludwig Wittgenstein's "family resemblance." It is the act of traversing the distance between different points of departure, the constant movement along the winding and intersecting paths that connect them—the distinctions and overlaps across each of the family members, if you will—that underpins the twelve essays collected in this volume.

LINKLATER AND THE ACADEMY

The Films of Richard Linklater is the first edited collection dedicated to the filmmaker's oeuvre. This is astounding for—as the above suggests—if there were ever a filmmaker whose work befits the nature of the edited collection, which relies on the inclusion of various voices and positions on any given topic, it is surely Richard Linklater. Why then this curious absence? It certainly was not for lack of material. At the time of writing, Linklater has directed twenty-one feature films, three short films, two television series, as well as an experimental video and documentary over a period of thirty-two years. Neither can Linklater's impressive and diverse output be described in any way as undiscovered or overlooked by industry bodies, critics, or the cinema-going public. Indeed, his projects are consistently mentioned in, among others, *The New York Times*, *Sight and Sound* (published by the BFI), and *The Guardian*'s "best of" lists.[4] Twenty of his feature films have received worldwide distribution, and over half have been nominated for, or have won, significant industry awards. Four years after receiving a nomination for "Best Director" for his breakout film, *Slacker* (1991) at the Independent Spirit Awards, Linklater took home the Silver Bear in the same category at the Berlin International Film Festival for *Before Sunrise* (1995). In 2014, *Boyhood* received six award nominations from the Academy of Motion Picture Arts and Sciences, including Best Picture and Best Director, and won Golden Globes for Best Director and Best Motion Picture – Drama, as well as the Silver Bear for Best Director at the 64th Berlin International Film Festival—a perhaps surprising feat for a meditative portrait of one boy as he matures into a young man, shot at yearly intervals over the course of twelve years.[5] In the same year, Linklater was awarded a coveted Honorary Associateship at the London Film School. In addition to such acclaim for his directorial endeavors, Linklater has established the thriving Austin Film Society, a production company, has been pivotal in developing the careers of numerous Hollywood film stars—and introduced to a mainstream audience cinematic techniques and devices—such as slacker-aesthetics, rotoscope, "slow filmmaking"—that have changed the terms of filmmaking, particularly within the American context. Indeed, so significant is Linklater's impact on late twentieth-century culture that one of his films and concepts—that of the *Slacker*, of course—has come to define an entire generation.

To date, three book-length studies on Linklater's oeuvre have been released: Stone's insightful *The Cinema of Richard Linklater: Walk, Don't Run*, which is now in its second edition; Johnson's volume on Linklater in the University of Illinois Press's Contemporary Film Directors Series, and Thomas A. Christie's *The Cinema of Richard Linklater* from 2011. The first two offer filmography-to-date studies that combine production history, socio-political commentary, and textual analysis informed—to differing degrees—by philosophy, film, and literary theory, while the latter provides a broad strokes survey of Linklater's work via film narrative summaries and accounts of their reception in the popular press. Mary Harrod and Lesley Speed have written impressive essays on Linklater's oeuvre in the context of the aesthetics of pastiche and subversions of Hollywood convention respectively, and Jennifer O'Meara's *Engaging Dialogue Cinematic Verbalism in American Independent Cinema* (2018) successfully examines dialogue in Linklater's feature films.[6]

In addition to these filmographic accounts, clusters of scholarship have formed around specific films, or film-sets, the largest being the *Before* trilogy to which Han Maes and Katrien Schaubroeck's recent collection, *Before Sunrise, Before Sunset, Before Midnight: A Philosophical Exploration* (2021) joins a rich body of literature that includes work by Lilia Kilburn, Peter Lurie, Robin Wood, Celestino Deleyto, James MacDowell, and Maria San Filippo, among others.[7] Smaller clusters have formed around *Slacker*, which has been, correctly or otherwise, heralded as a breakthrough moment in American indie cinema and emblematic of a Gen X politico-cultural zeitgeist; *Boyhood*, which has been examined through the lens of the youth film—most notably in Timothy Shary's *Boyhood: A Young Life on Screen* (2018)—and, owing to its extended shooting schedule, as a study of the relationship between film and lived time; and Linklater's two animated features, *Waking Life* (2001) and *A Scanner Darkly* (2006), which have featured particularly in debates regarding the indexicality of cinema and digital technology, and the affordances of Rotoshop animation.[8] Indeed, with the exception of Lynn Turner's feminist examination of the ethics of recollection in *Tape* (2001), and Katrina G. Boyd's and Wyatt Moss-Wellington's brief but shrewd analyses of *Bernie* (2011), relatively little attention has been paid to Linklater's work outside of these four clusters.[9] Although often insightful and enriching, the grouped formation of this extant literature divulges a tendency in scholarly writing to privilege Linklater's output where a perceived distinction from what is commonly conceived as the trappings of Hollywood is most clear—whether they be the assumed conventions of established genres such as the romcom or youth film, apparent disavowal of linear storytelling, blurred lines between reality, hallucination and dreamstates, or that which may be read in line with a more general "indie" aesthetic.[10]

While the relative lack of attention paid to Linklater's work—and dearth of material on some films—is notable, it is not our aim that *The Films of Richard Linklater* will serve simply as a corrective to this imbalance—even if we have tried to be inclusive and we make a point of treating films generally considered "critical" and "commercial" equally. In this collection, too, inevitably, there remain notable omissions. Though there are chapters dedicated to many of Linklater's less-studied films, including *Fast Food Nation* (2006), *SubUrbia* (1996), *Bad News Bears* (2005), *Last Flag Flying* (2017), *Everybody Wants Some!!* (2016), *Bernie* (2011), and *Where'd You Go, Bernadette* (2019), there is no extended discussion of movies like *Tape* (2001), *Me and Orson Welles* (2008), or *The Newton Boys* (1998). This book further does not attend (not extensively, in any case) to Linklater's non-feature work. Certainly, we hope that this collection achieves a representative account of Linklater's body of work and its various contexts of production, distribution, and consumption. But we readily acknowledge it is not exhaustive.

It seems to us that Linklater's under-representation in scholarly fora is less of an anomaly in view of his critical popularity and generic variability than precisely a consequence of it. With his tendency to switch genres, work in and out of Hollywood, as well as his shifting yet ostensibly unassuming stylistic register, Linklater's is an oeuvre that poses a problem, for instance, to the evaluative nature of classical auteur cinema. Linklater's filmography does not adhere to the criterion of thematic and stylistic consistency that the evaluative criticism of *la politique des auteurs* championed.[11] Although often cited as a filmmaker whose work is preoccupied with conceptions of time—an undoubtedly apt assertion given films like *Boyhood*, *Waking Life*, *Dazed and Confused*, *Everybody Wants Some!!*, and the *Before* trilogy—Linklater's stylistic approaches within the subsection of his oeuvre that formally or thematically attend to this concern vary greatly, from retro nostalgia, walking-and-talking naturalism, to a Rotoshop lucid-dream aesthetic.[12] More tellingly, almost half of Linklater's films (including *Fast Food Nation*, *Bernie*, *Bad News Bears*, *Last Flag Flying*, and *Me and Orson Welles*) appear to harbor little to no interest in this thematic concern at all. Similarly, although Linklater has long advanced a slacker aesthetic across many of his films—an indifference toward, or withdrawal from, the institutions, politics, and social norms associated with American ideals of capitalist, and specifically neoliberal, progress—others, such as *Where'd You Go, Bernadette*, *Bernie*, and *Me and Orson Welles* present different outsider responses to the American socio-political project. And for someone who is associated so unambiguously with the Austin film scene, one would be justified in asking what exactly is so Austinite about the films themselves.

Nor can his films be read—in a (post)structuralist or sociological tradition—as mere products of their time, place, or culture. Indeed, Linklater and his films inhabit ambiguous relationships to both Hollywood and American independent film traditions. Likewise, they speak to but aren't the mouthpiece for the dominant cultural sensibility of the late twentieth century—postmodernism. Linklater is critical of corporate America and yet his restless entrepreneurial spirit reads like a textbook definition of the neoliberal subject. Stone might be right in pointing out that Linklater's work ethic disqualifies him as slacker, but his oeuvre does saunter on the margins of industry and meanders in and out of genres, debates, and sensibilities much like the drifting curiosities of his most famous type—like a flâneur pretending to loiter.

What we are interested in is developing a conceptual idiom through which we can discuss the distinct qualities of the individual films as well as their relationships to each other—the independent to the commercial, teen comedy to existential drama, biographic to collaborative. A jargon that is stable but premised on contingencies, that has an internal logic but is open-ended. Let's be clear: we are not interested in pinpointing a single defining commonality, let alone essence. Like Johnson and Stone, we don't believe there is one. As such, *The Films of Richard Linklater* sees Linklater's films much like Wittgenstein famously conceived of games, or numbers: not a set defined by a core principle or universally shared features but "a complicated network of similarities overlapping and crisscrossing: sometimes overall similarities, sometimes similarities of detail."[13] What we're after here is appreciating the "network of similarities" that appear across films, idiosyncratically but unmistakably, like the recognizable gait of two siblings who otherwise look nothing like one another, or the temperament one of them shares with a second relative but not a third. We suggest that, from *Bad News Bears* to *Tape*, *The Newton Boys* to *Where'd You Go, Bernadette*, Linklater's films together form an oddball family, whereby each film—or set of films—is very different to one another and yet they bear such distinctive and selective semblances: not a signature but a way of holding the pen, say; not a single point of view or interest but overlapping quirks.

LOOKING AFTER AMERICA

It might be difficult, indeed, to our mind impossible (and certainly unproductive), to pin down Linklater's family of films to a single quality or trait. But we can say where they live: America. We don't just mean that Linklater was born in the U.S., or that he lives there, or makes most of his movies there, though these facts aren't irrelevant, obviously. What we mean is that Linklater makes American films, films that reflect what it means to live in and live out America. They communicate an ongoing desire for—and the acknowledged failure of— what can only be described as American foundational values, regardless of their genre, irrespective of their industrial context, and notwithstanding their oft-mentioned European philosophical and stylistic influences: spacious landscapes and tight communities, frontiers and those left or stayed behind, self-perseverance and self-realization, as well, of course, as baseball. To continue the conceptual metaphor: this desire takes on as many guises as siblings have differences. In the celebratory yet fraught Americana imagery that emerges in *Boyhood*, *Dazed and Confused*, *Bad News Bears*, and *Everybody Wants Some!!* it is expressed through speculative, critical nostalgia: the America that could be but never is, exactly. The desire for America takes on more vicious form, however, in the dehumanized exploitations of capitalism in *A Scanner Darkly* and *Fast Food Nation*: this is what America has become, in spite of its promise.

One could point out, of course, that this double-coded concern with America is precisely what has underpinned demarcations of American auteurism from Classical Hollywood—Orson Welles, Howard Hawks, and John Ford—to the 1970s movie brat generation of auteurs, credited by Noel King, among others, for temporarily creating an artist-led politically engaged American cinema within the commercial confines of Hollywood.[14] Certainly, Linklater's own generation of indie auteurs can be characterized as continuing this line with a similarly reflexive American cinema culture.[15] America's answer to America, the joke goes, is still America—just seen from a different perspective, or concentrating on different people and stories.

This argument is especially persuasive if we take into account Linklater's "identity politics": as Stone has noted, Linklater shares with Classical Hollywood but also New Hollywood and the nineties' indie scene a concern with an America that is predominantly white, mostly middle class, and more often than not, male. Linklater's films document white communities and white baseball teams, suburban disaffection and lower middle-class worries, male comradery, and *Boyhood*. Classical Hollywood aside, it is by now well documented that, despite the countercultural, sexual revolution, and racial equality clout attributed to the New Hollywood, this coveted period in Hollywood history too was almost uniformly dominated by white male filmmakers, whose output largely showcased and investigated the decade's socio-political tumult and generational disillusionment from their privileged position.[16] The indie auteurs championed as either the second coming of the descendants of these New Hollywood mavericks collectively share a similar demographic make-up—and perhaps also unsurprisingly, so too do their films' protagonists and outlook.[17] It is true that Linklater's "America" is as particular and exclusive an America as it has long been. If this selectivity might be excused in view of the director's own history and experience—by all accounts growing up in a white, middle-class family, in white, mostly middle-class communities and neighborhoods—it is nonetheless a sad indictment of the history of U.S. auteur and indie cinema more generally, a lack that only recently filmmakers and scholars have begun to address.

But to say that Linklater's "family" lives alongside other families—in this idiosyncratic but historically homogenous neighborhood somewhere on the outskirts of a middle-American town, presumably, Linklater ambling the same streets where Quentin Tarantino runs a shop with postmodern extravaganza and Dennis Hopper has parked his motor bike for a quick drink and brawl—is not the same as denying its distinct peculiarities. Linklater's films demonstrate a concern not just with an America but *for* an America. Films like *Last Flag Flying*, *Fast Food Nation*, and *Boyhood* not only look at the America that is, one defined more often than not by economic interests, the fast pace of modernity and alienation; nor do they solely look for the America that might be or have been, an America of community and ethical self-realization. They make a point also of *looking after* the gap between these two Americas, as well as the people who try to the best of their limited abilities to bridge it. If this sounds flag-waving patriotic, that's not what we mean. It's not about nationalism as much as embedded empathy. Linklater cares for the people around him, the people he shares his environment with, with whom he lives together in this ever-hopeful mess of a country.

SAME QUESTIONS, DIFFERENT ANSWERS: AUTEUR, GENRE, STYLE

The Films of Richard Linklater is divided into three parts covering three such conceptual resemblances to reflect this: "Auteur Cinema in Context," "Genre as Means," and "Style and Meaning." This seemingly conventional structure requires some explanation given Linklater's noted tendency to switch things up—which is, to be sure, precisely why we think it productive working out what this oeuvre might not be as well as working through what it might become instead. This is especially true for the first section, "Auteur Cinema in Context." This book argues that Linklater is recognizable and indeed widely recognized as an auteur—both critics and scholars speak of "Linklater films," after all (as opposed to categorizing them by industry, studio, genre, or universe)—even if neither his collaborative approach to filmmaking nor his generic itinerance align with that charged concept's historical demarcation. In other words, he is an auteur, just not an "auteur."

The essays in the first part consider Linklater's discrete and disparate directorial choices in the context of, and, importantly, as productive relations to, broader industrial, social, and cultural frameworks. These choices overlap as frequently as they contradict one another or their context. Indeed, in some instances, they do both at once. In the first chapter, for instance, Mary P. Erickson examines the independent creation of Linklater's breakthrough film *Slacker* in the context of its surprising corporate afterlife, through an analysis of the film's relationship to the place it was shot and set and with which it has been associated ever since, especially in city marketing: Austin. Jeroen Boom, too, looks at *Slacker* and space in Chapter 4, yet here the focus is less on the qualities of place, or, indeed, commerce, as it is precisely on the film's critical nomadism: an unwillingness to be bound by site or discourse, a "refusal to lay down roots." The other two chapters in the first part focus on similar tensions between authorial intent and contexts of industry, society, and culture. Claire Parkinson discusses Linklater's paradoxical pursuit of his political commitments (ranging from vegetarianism to worker's rights) not in spite of commercial interests but by way of them, suggesting an intersectional, embodied understanding of the world as opposed to a dialectical one. Rob Stone's chapter "The Little Space Between Hal Ashby and Richard Linklater" considers the continuities and discontinuities between Linklater's movies and Hal Ashby's oeuvre to argue that Linklater's political and aesthetic sensibilities are both in spirit with New Hollywood and stand in opposition to it, a split that Stone contends is the result of the changed context of production, especially the state of America at large. What these chapters demonstrate is that Linklater's authorial decisions are not essentialist but relational: they develop and form in relation to distinct affordances, concerns, or stories; and that these relations aren't antagonist but complicitous: they always already involve and implicate one another.

This is a sentiment that is discussed extensively in the book's second part, "Genre as Means", as well. In his chapter on Linklater's baseball movies—*Bad News Bears* and *Everybody Wants Some!*—Timotheus Vermeulen homes in on Linklater's explicit use of the "nation's favorite pastime" to contemplate the promise and problems of the American Dream and the players' attempts to negotiate them. One such promise, one that immediately announces its own problem, would appear to be that most of those players are white boys, which raises questions about the Dream's inclusivity and appeal. Mary Harrod's chapter also looks at a baseball film alongside war movie *Last Flag Flying* to discuss Linklater's representation of America. She argues that the director's choice of genre and use of intertextual references often fulfills a distinctly political motive: *Everybody Wants Some!* relies on the "fratboy" genre precisely so as to be able to reflect critically on American depictions of male coming-of-age, whilst *Last Flag Flying* infers the specter of Iraq to rethink U.S. discourses around masculinity. Genre is conventionally regarded in the first instance a contract between filmmaker or film and viewer: it stipulates the terms of exchange, the narrative affordances and limitations as much as the ontological circumscriptions, as well as, to a lesser extent, iconography and acting styles. What both these chapters stress is that for Linklater the relationship between genre and subject matters, or rather still, argument, is equally important: genre is not merely a means to reach out; it is also a means to reach deep, to grab hold of themes and sensibilities.

In their respective chapters Timothy Shary and Celestino Deleyto consider Linklater's employment of genre tropes to think through two separate yet related twenty-first-century phenomena: post-9/11 youth culture and transnationalism. Shary reads *Boyhood*'s original real-time take on the coming-of-age genre as what one might call process-archeologically: he pays attention to the ways in which Mason's encounters, experiences, and developments as he ages and the world changes allow the film to reflect on societal changes, including recession, instability, and the particular connectivity offered by the internet—which no other set-up would be able to do to the same degree. Deleyto's chapter "Stories So Far: Romantic Comedy and/as Space in *Before Midnight*" suggests that said film's generic tropes, especially those of the travelogue, afford a unique view of intimacy: as interval or passage generally speaking and as transnational specifically for our times. It is something of a truism that every plot requires a place, its own space. *Before Midnight*'s central narrative principle, however, is found precisely in-between places, a spatiality that inflects its possibilities and limitations for comedy, melodrama, and representation; one that allows for romance and comedy to take place in a realistic world without— since it passes through—being usurped by its many social concerns.

Partially because Linklater has continually moved between industrial modes and genres, partially because of his proclivity for collaboration, but also partially, one supposes, because of his character or at least public persona, his stylistic register is often thought to be unassuming. This might even be said to be the case for his films using Rotoshop, *Waking Life* and *A Scanner Darkly*, which match this new device to mostly conventional cinematographic choices. But unassuming of course does not equal uninventive, unoriginal, or powerful. The last part of the book, "Style and Meaning," offers close textual analyses of a number of Linklater's many stylistic interventions and the specific manners in which they afford communication and signification.

Unsurprisingly, two of the chapters in this section engage with Linklater's presentation of time. In the book's final chapter, Christopher Holliday considers how Rotoshop's modulating and sliding effects in the above-mentioned films are used to accentuate the cyclical or natural and linear or inorganic ritual forces that underwrite everyday life, at once emphasizing discordance (between the photographic and the painterly but also with regards to the end of one movement and the beginning of the next), doubling and repetition (of patterns of movement), and sensation (of feeling out what was and will be), amongst others, in the process expanding narrative film's temporal horizon. Bruce Isaacs's chapter "Keeping Time in *Dazed and Confused*, *Everybody Wants Some!!*, and *Boyhood*" offers a close reading of *Boyhood* to argue that the film's unique approach to historical duration does not only, as Shary shows, allow for a process-archeological reading, but affords a cinematic experience of what Henri Bergson dubbed lived time: of time not represented but presenting itself, as fleeting and slow, passing by and passing through.

Kim Wilkins and Wyatt Moss-Wellington, too, finally argue that Linklater is interested less in representation than in lived experience. Analyzing the use of conversation in *Bernie* and *Where'd You Go, Bernadette*, Wilkins finds that these films aren't interested in explaining or accounting for the baffling events and stupefying character decisions that they narrate, but in understanding them, empathizing with how they came to be. Moss-Wellington's chapter homes in on a similar sentiment, though through a different lens. He offers a close reading of *SubUrbia*'s spatial poetics to suggest that the film simultaneously exposes its characters' flaws, if that's the word, and encourages us to be forgiving and generous toward them—or in any case, to forego easy judgment.

Taken together, the twelve essays across the three sections offer detailed readings of a wide range of films to outline an image of a family whose members have different interests (and friends) and senses of style, varying ambitions and certainly degrees of success, but who share amongst them certain values and emotional intelligences, however they might be expressed: a sense that here and there, you and I are as much opposed as we are always already related; that the world is indifferent but we don't have to be; that stories can be found everywhere, they just need the right outlet to be told. As such, this book hopes to do justice to both Linklater's oeuvre as a whole and the individual films; that rare family portrait, you might say, that actually captures the tenor of the family relations as well as the distinct characters of each of its separate members. Whether it succeeds, we will leave up to the reader to decide.

NOTES

1. David T. Johnson, *Richard Linklater* (Urbana: University of Illinois Press, 2012), 2–3.
2. Rob Stone, *The Cinema of Richard Linklater: Walk, Don't Run* (New York: Columbia University Press, 2018), 3.
3. Ibid., 186.
4. Peter Hill et al., "90 Great Films of the 1990s," BFI (July 18, 2019): https://www.bfi.org.uk/lists/90-great-films-1990s; Peter Bradshaw et al., "The 100 Best Films of the 21st Century," *The Guardian* (September 13, 2019): https://www.theguardian.com/film/2019/sep/13/100-best-films-movies-of-the-21st-century; Manohla Dargis and A. O. Scott, "The 25 Best Films of the 21st Century, So Far," *The New York Times* (June 9, 2017): https://www.nytimes.com/interactive/2017/06/09/movies/the-25-best-films-of-the-21st-century.html
5. Jason Heid, "Richard Linklater, the Everyday Auteur," *Texas Monthly*, July 2020: https://www.texasmonthly.com/arts-entertainment/richard-linklater-film-texas-coronavirus/
6. Mary Harrod, "The Aesthetics of Pastiche in the Work of Richard Linklater," *Screen* 51:1 (2010): 21–37; Lesley Speed, "The Possibilities of Roads Not Taken: Intellect and Utopia in the Films of Richard Linklater," *Journal of Popular Film and Television*, 35:3 (2007): 98–106.
7. See, for example, Lilia Kilburn, "Ghost-Righting: The Spectral Ethics and Haunted Spouses of Richard Linklater's Before Trilogy," *Criticism (Detroit)* 60:1 (2018): 1–25; Peter Lurie, "Digital Déjà Vu: Cinephilia, Loss, and Medial Integrity in Linklater's Before Trilogy," *Film Quarterly* 68:3 (2015): 60–66; Robin Wood, *Sexual Politics and Narrative Film: Hollywood and Beyond* (New York: Columbia University Press, 1998), 318–335; Celestino Deleyto, *The Secret Life of Romantic Comedy* (Manchester: Manchester University Press, 2009), 148–176; James MacDowell, "To Be in the Moment: On (Almost) Not Noticing Time Passing in Before Sunrise (Richard Linklater 1995)," in *The Long Take*, edited by John Gibbs and Douglas Pye (London: Palgrave Macmillan U.K., 2017), 147–161, and James MacDowell "Comedy and Melodrama from to Sunrise Midnight Genre and Gender in Richard Linklater's Before Series," in *After "Happily Ever After": Romantic Comedy in the Post-Romantic Age*, edited by Maria San Filippo (Wayne State University Press, 2021), 47–63; Maria San Filippo, "Growing Old Together: Linklater's Before Trilogy in the Twilight Years of Art House Distribution," *Film Quarterly* 68:3 (2015): 53–59.
8. See for example, Katarzyna Malecka, "In Praise of Slacking: Richard Linklater's *Slacker* and Kevin Smith's *Clerks* as Hallmarks of 1990s American Independent Cinema Counterculture," *Text Matters (Łódź)* 5:1 (2015): 190–205; Maria Teresa Soldani, "The Performance of the Austin Indie Scene in *Slacker*: From the Body of a Scene to the Body of a Generation," *Imaginations (Edmonton, Alberta)* 7:2 (2016); Rob Stone, "About Time: Before Boyhood," *Film Quarterly* 68:3 (2015): 67–72; David Rudd, "'Life Doesn't Give You Bumpers: A Coming or Going of Age in *Juno* and *Boyhood*," *Quarterly Review of*

Film and Video 37:6 (2020): 582–597; Steven Shaviro, "Emotion Capture: Affect in Digital Film," *Projections* (New York) 1:2 (2007): 63–81; Paul Ward, "Independent Animation, Rotoshop and Communities of Practice: As Seen Through A Scanner Darkly," *Animation: An Interdisciplinary Journal* 7:1 (2012): 59–72; and Ellen Grabiner, "The Holy Moment: Waking Life and Linklater's Sublime Dream Time," *Film Quarterly* 68:3 (2015): 41–47.
9. Lynn Turner, "Wind Up: The Machine-Event of 'Tape,'" *Camera obscura (Durham, NC)* 22:1 (2007): 112–135; Katrina G. Boyd, "Grief Tragically Becoming Comedy: Time, Tasks, and Storytelling in Linklater's Bernie," *Film Quarterly* 68:3 (2015): 48–52; Wyatt Moss-Wellington, "Affecting Profundity: Cognitive and Moral Dissonance in Lynch, Loach, Linklater, and Sayles," *Projections* 11:1 (Summer, 2017): 38–62.
10. There are certainly exceptions, of course. As for instance Stone writes, even Linklater's most commercially successful, "crowd-pleasing" film, *School of Rock* (2003), evinces the slacker-ethos most keenly associated with Linklater's non-studio work. Indeed, Stone considers this Jack Black-led family comedy, which "inspires kids to ditch their studies, disobey their Republican parents, band together, and rock," one of the most subversive in recent American film history. Stone, *Cinema of Richard Linklater*, 47.
11. For an erudite account of traditional auteurism see Warren Buckland, "La Politique des Auteurs in British Film Studies: Traditional versus Structural Approaches," *Mise au point*, 8 (2016): n.p.
12. See Dan Hassler-Forest, "Richard Linklater's Post-nostalgia and the Temporal Logic of Neoliberalism," in *The Global Auteur: The Politics of Authorship in 21st Century Cinema*, edited by Seung-hoon Jeong and Jeremi Szaniawski (London: Bloomsbury Academic, 2016), 199–216.
13. Ludwig Wittgenstein, *Philosophical Investigations* (Oxford: Basil Blackwell, 1986), 32e.
14. Noel King, "'The Last Good Time We Ever Had': Remembering the New Hollywood Cinema," in *The Last Great American Picture Show: New Hollywood Cinema in the 1970s*, edited by Thomas Elsaesser, Noel King, and Alexander Horwath (Amsterdam: Amsterdam University Press, 2004), 32–33.
15. See essays in Linda Badley, Claire Perkins, and Michele Schreiber's excellent collection *Indie Reframed: Women's Filmmaking and Contemporary American Independent Cinema* (Edinburgh: Edinburgh University Press, 2016).
16. See Nicholas Godfrey, *The Limits of Auteurism: Case Studies in the Critically Constructed New Hollywood* (New Brunswick, NJ: Rutgers University Press, 2018); Yannis Tzioumakis and Peter Krämer's "Introduction" in their edited collection *The Hollywood Renaissance: Revisiting American Cinema's Most Celebrated Era* (London: Bloomsbury, 2018), xv–xvii; Charlene Regester, "A Matter of Race and Gender: Lady Sings the Blues (1972) and the Hollywood Renaissance Canon," in Tzioumakis and Krämer, *The Hollywood Renaissance*; and Molly Haskell, "The Mad Housewives of the Neo-Woman's Film: The Age of Ambivalence Revisited," in *When the Movies Mattered: The New Hollywood Revisited*, edited by Jonathan Kirschner and Jon Lewis (Ithaca, NY: Cornell University Press, 2019).
17. Kathleen A. McHugh, "Miranda July and the New Twenty-First-Century Indie," in Schreiber, *Indie Reframed*; Kim Wilkins, "Indie Courtship: Pursuing the American New Wave," in *New Wave, New Hollywood: Reassessment, Recovery, and Legacy*, edited by Nathan Abrams and Gregory Frame (New York: Bloomsbury Academic, 2021) 201–220.

PART I

Auteur Cinema in Context

CHAPTER 1

'I Think I Still Qualify as a Slacker . . . Just One that's Currently Lucky': The Myths of *Slacker*, Austin, and Richard Linklater

Mary P. Erickson

Richard Linklater's contribution to the Texas film community has been consistent over the length of his career, with continued involvement in Texas-based production and his stewardship of the Austin Film Society. Linklater's career is often held as an exemplar of the contributions made to build a thriving regional film community.[1]

Linklater's first feature film, *It's Impossible to Learn to Plow by Reading Books* (1988), is rather obscure unless one has closely tracked Linklater's career. His second feature, however, is heralded as one of the visionary standards of the 1990s American independent film movement and was recognized in 2012 by the U.S. Library of Congress's National Film Registry as a "work of enduring importance to American culture."[2] *Slacker* was released in 1990 to alternatively positive and negative critical attention. The film, shot during the hot summer months of 1989, roamed around Austin from character to character without much plot, and this observational piece became representational, in title, structure, and execution, of the independent film spirit that emerged in the early 1990s. As Linklater described, a slacker is "a Texas nickname for the type of non-student who clusters around the University of Texas campus eking out a marginal income while living a quasi-collegiate existence."[3] The term was soon applied to Gen Xers as a way to describe the disaffected generation in early adulthood at this time. As such, *Slacker* has since been used to represent a generation, a city, a mindset, and a way of life, and captured a fictional slice of life that, for many audiences looking back, emphasized the location just as much as the characters.[4]

Austin seems to spark a great deal of nostalgia for the city that once was, as it has undergone quite dramatic changes over the past three decades. The massive growth of the high-tech sector, in addition to its flourishing music, film, and video game industries, have changed the city from a somewhat sleepy, quirky town into a bustling metro area of two million people. Other results include high cost of living, traffic headaches, sprawling suburbs, urban gentrification, and displacement of some of Austin's (mostly marginalized) residents. The reality of Austin today does not mirror what Linklater captured in *Slacker*, and for many Austinites, this discrepancy is saddening. And yet, *Slacker* continues to be referenced as quintessential Austin. In the thirty years since its premiere, the film has been featured as an exemplar of independent filmmaking, and, ultimately, how living is done in Austin, the film's legacy imbued with cultural and economic subversion and a DIY ethos.

The myth of Austin is upheld by what is represented by the personification of *Slacker*'s qualities, Richard Linklater himself. He is no slacker, and never really has been, but his having been in Austin in the 1980s lends him a pedigree of authority and provides a link to the Austin That Was. It's strange to draw a line between an independent filmmaker's early career and a heavily corporatized city, and then to find the ways in which one is used to benefit the other. Plentiful myths are at play here, including nostalgia, independence, individualism, community, and creativity. These work within notions of the local alongside neoliberalism.

This chapter explores the ways in which *Slacker* the film has been utilized for over thirty years as a way to reaffirm Austin's reputation as a city operating outside the mainstream. Moreover, it explores how Richard Linklater is the link that allows for celebration of the slacker figure. The discursive purpose of the term "slacker" enables neoliberalism to flourish by appropriating subcultures and lifestyles in Austin without becoming threatening.

In this chapter, I will explore Richard Linklater's production and distribution of *Slacker*, as well as its impact on and relationship to Austin's development as a city and film community. Neoliberally tinged municipal policies of growing a "creative class" draw on *Slacker*'s slacker figure, in tandem with the city's "Keep Austin Weird" ethos and marketing push; these are embedded in racial and economic priorities that discount marginalized members of Austin's community. These points lead us to the ways in which Linklater himself is framed as the flashpoint to link the slacker with neoliberal economic development encased in myths of nostalgia and independence.

RICHARD LINKLATER AND THE PRODUCTION OF SLACKER

Richard Linklater arrived in Austin in 1983 from Houston and took some film classes at a local community college. He soon bought Super 8 film equipment to begin shooting his own work. He and another Austinite, Lee Daniel, started the Austin Film Society in 1985, screening arthouse films first in their living room and then at the Austin Museum of Art. After securing a grant from the Texas Commission on the Arts in 1988, the Austin Film Society opened up in its own dedicated space and featured ambitious and financially precarious programming.[5] Meanwhile, Linklater produced his first feature, *It's Impossible to Learn to Plow by Reading Books* (1988), and began to work on his next film, *Slacker*.

Prior to Linklater's emergence as a filmmaker, much of the regional film industry focused on drawing in Hollywood productions to the state. While film production companies existed even in the early days of cinema, much of the attraction of Texas for much of the twentieth century was based on its geographic specificity. Ever since *Wings* (William A. Wellman, 1927) was shot on location at Kelly Field in San Antonio, Hollywood studio attention turned toward the potential of Texas as a production location, utilizing natural landscapes or military bases along with cheap labor to bring down production costs. During the 1950s and 1960s, large-scale productions of *Giant* (George Stevens, 1956), *Hud* (Martin Ritt, 1962), and *Bonnie and Clyde* (Arthur Penn, 1967) were filmed in the state. The Texas Film Commission was founded in 1971; as Governor Preston Smith proclaimed, "Texas has a uniquely vast array of resources, natural, human, and economic, which lend themselves to the film and orderly development of a healthy film production industry."[6]

The regional arts scene, dominated by music and film, began flourishing in the 1970s. In 1976, the local PBS station launched *Austin City Limits*, a program showcasing live music (Willie Nelson was the pilot episode's guest); ACL would become syndicated and broadcast across the country, heralded as television's longest running music program. About a decade later, in 1987, the South by Southwest Conference and Festival (SXSW) premiered its first iteration with primary emphasis on music. According to the festival's history, "the local creative and music communities [in Austin] were as talented as anywhere else on the planet, but were severely limited by a lack of exposure outside of Austin . . . The solution being discussed was an event that would bring the outside world to Austin for a close-up view."[7]

Concurrently, many members of the nascent film community in Austin came out of the University of Texas at Austin's Radio-Television-Film (RTF) program, established in 1965; for example, much of the cast and crew of *The Texas Chainsaw Massacre* (Tobe Hooper, 1974) attended the RTF program, and, soon after, one of the Austin film scene's forebears, Eagle Pennell, enrolled in – and dropped out of – RTF.[8] Pennell's feature, *The Whole Shootin' Match* (1977), screened at the U.S.A. Film Festival in Dallas, and effectively launched Texas regional cinema into the national cinema spotlight. Primarily based in the state's major cities like Houston, San Antonio, and Dallas, film production work was present but the bulk of the consistent and visible work, particularly starting in the 1980s, came in the form of television production (mostly movies of the week and made-for-television movies).[9]

In the summer of 1989, Linklater pulled together a number of Austin locals, mostly non-professional actors, to put into motion his vision for a wandering narrative film. *Slacker* featured an eclectic mix of episodes as the camera meandered from character to character, an idea that Linklater had begun crafting during a late-night drive between Houston and Austin. He pulled together his US$23,000 budget mostly by borrowing from his parents and running up his credit card. He was also able to access networks within the community, including enlisting the technical expertise of local film professionals like Lee Daniel (his collaborator at the Austin Film Society); he borrowed or cheaply rented equipment that would otherwise be out of reach, including a Steadicam, a dolly, and a crane, and included a song by San Antonio band The Butthole Surfers, whose drummer Teresa Nervosa played the role of Pap Smear Pusher in the film.

Shooting finished within two months, and as the production moved into editing, Linklater and his team began to encounter some friction about what to include or omit. The nature of the story structure, which roamed from scene to scene, made it more difficult to simply cut one thing or another. Additionally, the editing process operated in part by committee, with multiple people vying for or against a particular edit.[10] A two-hour version was eventually cut down to 97 minutes, and Linklater shopped it around to festivals like Berlin and Sundance (both turned it down although *Slacker* played at Berlin's open market section in 1990). He then premiered the film at the 1990 U.S.A. Film Festival in Dallas which resulted in a contemptuous review from the *Dallas Times Herald*. But programmers at the Seattle International Film Festival invited the film, since the film seemed to capture a tenor familiar to Seattle audiences at the time.[11]

After viewing the film in Seattle, Robert Horton wrote a glowing piece about *Slacker* for *Film Comment*, and this article launched more critical lauding of the film as well as interest from an indie film producer's rep, John Pierson.[12] Linklater screened *Slacker* in Austin to much enthusiasm from the city's audiences. He had spearheaded a grassroots promotional campaign to spread word about the film; twenty-two consecutive screenings at the independent Dobie Theater sold out. Pierson coordinated a distribution deal with Orion Pictures, which paid for the film's transfer to 35 mm, and got the film into the 1991 Sundance Film Festival. The film experienced a good deal of critical success, building momentum in large part via word of mouth. Orion Pictures was disappointingly less than aggressive with its distribution plan, although the film played in several cities around the country and eventually grossed $1.2 million in box office revenue.[13] St. Martin's Press released a tie-in book as well. The film's home video circuit was not terribly successful, as Orion Pictures filed for bankruptcy in December 1991. The distributor shipped fewer than 10,000 units, fewer than the number shipped for many of *Slacker*'s contemporaries, such as Hal Hartley's *Trust*, and well under what HBO Home Video shipped for *Straight Out of Brooklyn* (Matty Rich, 1991).[14]

WEIRD AUSTIN, *SLACKER*, AND THE CREATIVE CLASS

One of the immediate interpretations of *Slacker*, and which became its primary legacy, was the conflation of subject matter with an entire generation. At the same time Linklater was screening his film about disaffected, rambling characters, Douglas Coupland was in Vancouver writing about the disaffection of the generation born after the Baby Boomers; he called them Generation X, after Fussell's nomenclature, "X people," or according to Coupland, "an 'X' category of people who wanted to hop off the merry-go-round of status, money, and social climbing that so often frames modern existence."[15] While Coupland's Generation X novel started off quietly, it very quickly became connected to both *Slacker* ("which was filled with overeducated and underoccupied oddballs," according to Coupland) and the Seattle grunge music scene, and very soon these rather disparate art endeavors became a hybrid spokespiece for all Americans born between the mid-1960s and the early 1980s.

Slacker is representative of Linklater's experience of Austin and of the slacker lifestyle; the film was shot around certain Austin neighborhoods familiar to Linklater; many of the "slackers" in the film were his friends. Much like college towns and other art-centered enclaves around the country, Austin has reveled in its offbeat and unusual character. This sensibility has been captured by the slogan, "Keep Austin Weird," allegedly first coined in 2000 by a resident donating money to a local community radio station, and adopted by city residents, city leaders, and local businesses alike as a badge of resistance.[16] The "Keep Austin Weird" campaign was intended "to alert fellow Austinites to the general commercialization, corporatization and over-development that was seen as dominating the city."[17] The campaign reinforced a strong and vital sense of place, "resonating strongly with individuals who feel that promotion of independent business, protection of nearby environments and support of local creative industries forges a sustainable sense of community solidarity and economic resilience."[18]

Community identity is discursively constructed; even when a community is geographically bound, individuals within that community are still responsible for defining the community itself and determining its values and members.[19] As globalization processes intensified in the 1980s and 1990s, threatening homogenization and standardization especially in non-Western contexts, scholars also examined the "local" within Western societies as a way to understand community and, partly, the preservation thereof. The ways in which globalization has impacted communities—and the idea of the local—are central concerns for community leaders seeking to strengthen their individuality as communities.

Neoliberalism has become more prominent as a concept to explore rather dramatic yet rather unnoticed societal shifts. While there are numerous definitions of the concept—enough that some scholars view it as deprived of meaning—neoliberalism in the American context is a valid and appropriate way of considering the changes that communities have experienced in the beginning of the twenty-first century. Hardin recounts Foucault's theorizations of neoliberalism: Foucault writes, "American neoliberalism uses 'market economy and the typical analyses of the market economy to decipher nonmarket relationships.'" In other words, "for Foucault, American neoliberalism is about the application of economic analysis to all phenomena."[20]

What has emerged, then, is a two-pronged concern for cities. First, cities feel under threat about losing their specificity in this cultural homogenization. Second, cities are struck with the perceived need to steadily compete for mobile capital in order to drive local economic development. These two prongs are interrelated, as a city that can differentiate itself in desirable ways will be more likely to attract investment and human capital.[21] As Miró argues, local governments become entrepreneurial agents, "producing the city based on competitive logics, in order to scale positions in the global urban hierarchy" and utilizing gentrification as a lucrative strategy to foster growth.[22] Furthermore, private entities are closely involved in decisions about urban development. Harvey observed these strategies in New York City in the 1980s as city leaders strove to address rampant crime and unrest. He observes, "The municipal government was no longer about benefiting the population, the municipal government had to address creating a good business climate. That was the goal, create a good business climate."[23] We can see this process in how many cities approached economic development in the 1990s and early 2000s, with the residual impact still seen today.

Throughout much of the twentieth century, as with the previous 100 years, Austin's Black and Latinx residents faced discrimination as they were residentially segregated from their white neighbors, particularly impacted as urban renewal plans called for the relocation of communities predominantly populated by minorities.[24] Meanwhile, city planning began to shift its growth focus to building a knowledge industry in the 1970s to differentiate its economy from other cities across the South and Midwest, which also served to segregate many of its residents of color. This early foray into a homegrown tech sector led to more investments in determining Austin as a suitable home for this industry.

Austin's municipal attention to growing its creative class is a strategy to bridge its "weird" character with economic drivers. Austin again prioritized building up its tech sector at the end of the twentieth century, attracting major companies to join Texas Instruments and Motorola, which already had a significant presence in the area. In the 1990s, over 300 companies moved to Austin, either basing their headquarters or locating offices in the metro area.[25] The tech sector, notoriously loaded with young, hip, entrepreneurial people, has exploded Austin into what Gibson and Butler label a "technopolis."[26] In the last thirty years, mobile capital has become a reality, no longer tied to specific locations, and Austin joined the fray as a community pitching offers to attract corporate offices, and it has worked. Silicon Hills is now home to offices for Facebook, eBay, Oracle, Cisco, IBM, and Apple, among others; in addition, the region boasts 5,500 startups and tech companies.[27] In 2010, *Forbes Magazine* named Austin's "Silicon Hills" as the second most innovative area in the U.S. after Silicon Valley, CA.[28] Additionally, Tesla began building Gigafactory Texas, a massive manufacturing facility complex near Austin, in 2020, signaling confidence in the region's capacity to provide a pipeline of employees with sought-after technical skills.

The influx of outsiders moving to Austin is in large part made up of what Richard Florida would term "the creative class," a segment of the labor force which specializes in knowledge work and which values vibrant creative amenities, progressive social policies, and active lifestyles.[29] Quite rapidly, this creative class became a golden goose for municipalities searching for an economic and cultural edge. While Austin did suffer quite drastically in the dotcom bust of 2001, losing over 22,000 jobs as companies shuttered their offices, the city recovered smoothly enough and continued to chase the creative class as a neoliberal project for economic growth.[30]

While it is still apparent that neoliberal policies have infused into nearly every facet of life, from economics to politics to culture, municipal governments want to view their communities with more humanization at play; however, many of the strategies to meet those very real human needs, whether it's about housing or environment or racial injustice, are still very much informed by neoliberalism. Indeed, as Hashimoto argues, the ways in which municipal governments implicitly distinguish between racially desirable and undesirable outcomes for a city are made explicit through policy that prioritizes "creative classes" (i.e., white, middle-class individuals).[31] Hashimoto writes that "understanding the creative class as an economic project . . . requires the construction of 'others' and inequality in order to succeed. The production of 'others' facilitates a bifurcation between the 'deserving' and 'undeserving' under the guise of a seemingly identity-neutral desire for creativity and consumption."[32]

The Austin metro area's population nearly quadrupled in the three decades since Linklater made *Slacker* in 1990 (from 569,000 in 1990 to 2,117,000 in 2021). Its racial make-up within city limits as of 2019 was 48.3% white only, 33.9% Hispanic only, 7.8% black, and 7.6% Asian; over 13% of Austin's residents live in poverty.[33] The rapid population growth signaled a cultural homogenization (and white cultural growth), and many city residents have been resistant to that homogenization that often marks a region's growth. Chain restaurants and stores proliferate while locally owned alternatives that are unable to compete close their doors; across the country, these changes signaled to many that the characters of individual American cities were flattening and homogenizing, and Austin has been no exception.[34] The "Keep Austin Weird" campaign presented itself as a way to respond to the city's rapid growth—and the attendant changes in community character. Some Austinites have clung to nostalgic impressions of the city, particularly what many recognize as distinctly Austin—oddball, unique, irreverent, *weird*.

Certainly, the city's creative community thrives, as Austin has long been a destination for musicians, artists, filmmakers, and other creatives. Clearly, the Austin sensibility, the *weirdness*, is attractive to these individuals, as demonstrated by the region's phenomenal population growth. The music scene in particular continues to be on the cutting edge, a legacy that flourishes thirty years after Austin's City Council formally declared the city "The Live Music Capital of the World" in 1991.

The city has not always been such a proactive champion of film production, nor of other sectors of the multimedia industry. Although the city expanded in the 1980s and 1990s primarily due to a blossoming tech sector, city leaders didn't address cultural policy quite yet. The Cultural Affairs Division (CAD) was established within the Parks and Recreation Department in 1986, but it did not play an overly active role in developing cultural initiatives in the city.[35] The CAD was relocated to the Economic Growth and Redevelopment Services Office in 2002, which signaled a shift in municipal understanding of what cultural initiatives could offer the city. It was around this time that Richard Florida published the widely popular *Rise of the Creative Classes*, which highlighted the concept of the "creative," the individual upon whom the contemporary knowledge economy would be built. The creative class, as proposed by Florida, would require a progressive community with a thriving art scene. The 2008 report, CreateAustin, proposed a ten-year cultural plan, funded by the National Endowment for the Arts (and not, incidentally, funded by the City of Austin), to map out how cultural and creative organizations and talent could drive economic growth.[36] The city's response was lukewarm, however, and instead of adopting the plan, the city initiated another task force in 2010 to explore some of the report's recommendations.[37] In part, CreateAustin was difficult to implement because of divisions within the creative/art community; coalitions did not readily happen.

More recently, Austin has emphasized filmmaking in its overall approach to cultural development, celebrating the area's history, legendary filmmakers, and up-and-coming talent. There is a close relationship between the Austin

Film Society and the city, with a 30-year lease on property at the former Robert Mueller Municipal Airport site to host a studio complex. Austin Studios is a twenty-acre multimedia facility with sound stages, production offices, and other production facilities. In addition, it hosts various small businesses, including the offices for Linklater's own production company, Detour Filmproduction. Also on the site is Troublemaker Studios, owned by Robert Rodriguez and producer Elizabeth Avellán. As of 2019, Texas's film and television industry generated US$172,542,000 in annual payroll, ranking fifth among the share of overall film and television industry payroll employment after California, New York, Georgia, and Florida.[38] In Travis County, home to Austin, annual payroll stood at US$48,004,000, the second largest in the state and about two-thirds the size of payroll in the Dallas-Fort Worth metro area. Austin consistently ranks in the top 10 "Best Places to Live and Work as a Moviemaker," a list compiled by *MovieMaker Magazine*, with the city securing third place in 2021, after Albuquerque and Atlanta.[39] Industry professionals cite the vast range of landscapes, the vibrant and friendly filmmaking community, and relatively easy navigation of government bureaucracy as some of Austin's most enticing features.

But while Austin may bill itself as a prime location for creatives to live and work, this promotion also comes with a downside, which many Austinites bemoan. Such a rapid population growth risks diluting the city's uniqueness; after all, how much weirdness can a city of two million possibly hold? Some residents are also cynical about actively calling themselves "weird"; after all, "you can't call yourself weird (that's like calling yourself a poet or genius – someone else has to do that for you)".[40] What does not enter the conversation is the racially and ethnically exclusionary ways in which this term operates within Austin's context, particularly when situated with the "slacker" label. This self-image is accessible and relevant to a certain population of Austin, while others are not readily associated therein.

The "weird" appellation has become rather empty since it has been rather regularly co-opted as a promotional tool for major corporations. Electronic Arts's (EA) revenue for FY2021 exceeded US$5.6 billion, ranking among the top 10 global gaming companies and producing massive video game franchises, including *FIFA*, *Madden NFL*, *The Sims*, and several *Star Wars* titles.[41] EA opened offices in Austin in 1992 and EA Austin has since grown to house hundreds of employees. In its recruitment efforts, EA Austin's website touts: "Austin's unofficial slogan is 'Keep Austin Weird,' which goes hand in hand with the fun and imaginative vibe of the studio."[42]

The use of this slogan taps into an outsider ethos that is attractive to many creatives, particularly those who work in the gaming industry. Gamers often view themselves as geeks, passionate about the art and craft of gaming, yet as social outcasts for precisely the same reason. The "fun and imaginative vibe" in this workplace, described as wholly compatible with "weird," is likely appealing. Yet this use reflects the ways in which neoliberal and corporate imperatives take over discursive identification for their own purposes, all the while rendering this assertion of resistance as superficial. Simply using the words "Keep Austin Weird" does not make a city weird; rather, the words seem to comfortably exist within a corporate framework because, in a neoliberal society, we are accustomed to recognizing certain types as outsiders, regardless of whether they work for a multinational corporation. Declaring EA Austin's vibe to be compatible with "weirdness" seems to make it unquestionably so.

Corporate adoption of "weird" is not dissimilar to the ways in which the concept of the "slacker" is used to discursively construct a collective understanding of what Austin is, regardless of the booming corporate presence, gentrification, heavy commercialization, and racial inequity that the city undergoes at a regular clip. It is a logical and typical strategy to promote economic urban development; after all, city leaders want to grow their hometowns. Yet with development also comes inevitable change, and this is precisely where many Austinites seem to get stuck in a nostalgia loop. Austin was already changing into a new version of itself with the burgeoning tech boom in the 1990s, increased national attention thanks to SXSW, and some residents could sense the old Austin slipping away.

WHO IS A SLACKER?

Some Austinites recognized themselves in *Slacker*, mostly those who participated in a very specific subculture that Linklater captured; these Austinites recognized the city they knew as home as well, and for them this visibility was vitally important. According to Stone, "This attention [in Linklater's film] paid to the everyday meant that ideas of what was local and regional (to Austin, for example) were important at a time when America's foreign policy and globalization were both driven by the alienating forces of capitalism."[43] *Slacker* provided reassurance that Austin could still exist as a unique locale despite corporate culture seeming to reproduce all over. *Slacker* offered a discursive template of wacky characters and recognizable locations representing a pre-existing community identity. With this template preserved in 16 mm celluloid, Austin could continue on, retaining its "original" character. As I will discuss later, this "original" character continues to be drawn on, thirty years post-*Slacker*.

The myth of the slacker is solidified by this film. The Linklater slacker figure resides within a particularly strong myth of alienation, ennui, and rejection from society. While the slacker may attempt to "[reject] most of society and the social hierarchy before it rejects them," this figure also enjoys the privilege of being able to situate themselves where they choose, and when to reject or accept social hierarchy.[44] Tretter contrasts this figure to one in African American literature, "the surly slacker," whose social marginalization by virtue of being non-white, is unchangeable. For Linklater, Tretter argues, "the Slacker is somebody made in his own image: a middle-class, college-educated White man"; "few of the characters in *Slacker* are socially or culturally marginalized."[45] It is important to revisit the Linklater slacker myth, as it is built upon a framework of privilege that enables certain individuals to move in and out of conventional society.

What also arises here is Linklater being painted as a slacker himself. As a young person directing a film billed as low budget, rambling, and non-studio in an era when American independent cinema was catalyzing, Linklater operated outside the mainstream. He rejected conventional filmmaking hierarchies by virtue of making a film in Austin; in Linklater's words, the production was "definitely down and dirty."[46] It is, however, important to acknowledge that he had access to resources and privilege that were not (and still are not) universally accessible to all filmmakers in the area, particularly filmmakers of color or women.

The Linklater slacker could dally in the arts, "piddling around for years," as he put it. Yet, the American ideal of productivity pokes through and collapses the distance between marginal and mainstream. "No one ever said slackers weren't productive," Linklater said. "It's just that their products often fall outside the market economy." Productivity, intimately linked to the production of capital, blends seamlessly into today's neoliberalism. Slackers operate outside the market economy, but still make *products*. Actually, a seemingly throw-away comment in Linklater's self-interview is perhaps the most insightful: "I think I still qualify as a slacker . . . just one that's currently lucky."[47] It is desirable to be *known and recognized* as a slacker, but you are so *lucky* if you can hit it big. The slacker can superficially upend the system but, ultimately, they are "non-threatening [and] pro-capitalist."[48]

It is precisely this sentiment that pinpoints the essence of the slacker—and Austin as a city, and, perhaps, Linklater himself. The slacker may momentarily be directionless yet with strong convictions, but the slacker is ephemeral. As Tretter notes, society ultimately welcomes these individuals back: "For Linklater, the Slacker's exit from society is always predicated on his ever-possible and, hopefully, profitable re-entry into the mainstream social order."[49] Similarly, Linklater was momentarily directionless, at least within the parameters of the mainstream film industry, when he made his first two features. But that Linklater was ephemeral. The success and acclaim of *Slacker* meant that an outsider "got lucky" and secured recognition for going about achieving success in a non-traditional way; Linklater further secured this success by next working with Universal Studios to direct *Dazed and Confused*, released in 1993.

Capitalism will extract value from the slacker figure, and neoliberal tenets will convince the slacker that they are achieving their goals. Individuals' false consciousness around their capacity to subvert capitalism obscures their ability to see that their goals of productivity and output are precisely within the bounds of capitalism. In order to demonstrate that one is an outsider subverting the system, one must produce some evidence. The very production thereof is within that system. And so, the slacker figure is a useful myth to feed the engine in which resistance against the mainstream can foment and yet be commodified for the mainstream.

In addition to, and arguably much more than, the slacker figure, the film is renowned for its Austin setting. When the film opened at Austin's Dobie Theater in 1990, audiences flocked to see their town—and themselves—onscreen. The griminess of *Slacker* reflected the atmosphere of the Austin experienced by *Slacker*'s fans. The Dobie Theater itself was "run down and seedy . . . and it was nasty. But everything on the Drag [the western side of UT-Austin's campus] was like that," according to one filmmaker. As audiences saw themselves and their friends in the film, "so much of that movie was my wonderland" mused this filmmaker.[50]

This connection, made immediately and persisting ever since for many viewers, conflates the film's setting with the city itself, as though the film were a documentary. Stylistically, Linklater aimed to adopt a documentary feel with fictional characters that one could potentially find in Austin. Yet the film remains that: fiction. The Austin in the film was not fully Austin in all its glory; rather, it captured a very specific slice of Austin life. "*Slacker*'s unique," says Linklater, "because it's not just Austin, it's West Campus, so it's kind of the university. So it made it a little less diverse-looking than Austin really is."[51] Linklater seems to be pointing more toward *Slacker*'s specific slice of a neighborhood, and not quite acknowledging the lack of racial and ethnic diversity that would actually reflect Austin's demographics.

As noted earlier, the Austin featured in *Slacker* reveals Linklater's experience of the city, by no means a universal experience: "all the unheralded individual activities, neighborhood anecdotes, spontaneous street theater and community art projects that made up the tolerant community of Austinites of which he was part."[52] This city "became a destination for the dispossessed: somewhere you ran to, not away from,"[53] and Austin started to grow rapidly, drawing people who felt like outcasts in their hometowns.

It's important to note that "non-white people are largely omitted from Linklater's portrait of Austin and its Slacker-scape," as Tretter observes.[54] This slice of Austin mainly focused on white characters, despite a metro population of a half million people in 1990, with 23% Latinx residents and 12% African American residents.[55] *Slacker*'s Austin held special significance for those involved in a specific neighborhood and corresponding white subculture of Austin; by no means did the film represent *Austin*. As *Slacker* became a map for what "cool" Austin looked like, it also contributed to the continued marginalization and growing displacement of Austin's non-white residents.

And since 1990, *Slacker*'s Austin has been used as shorthand to represent Austin, capturing elements that are utilized in economic development efforts that support neoliberal and racially imbalanced policies.

REVISITING THE MYTHS OF THE SLACKER AND AUSTIN: *SLACKER* AT 10, 20, AND 30

Slacker sits so familiarly in Austin lore that its anniversary is celebrated among the Austin film community at least every decade, if not more frequently. Local newspaper *The Austin Chronicle* spotlights the film at regular intervals, with various critics finding multitudinous ways to laud *Slacker*, even self-reflexively acknowledging its "20-year love affair with *Slacker*" in 2011.[56]

The Austin Chronicle honored the tenth anniversary of *Slacker*'s release by mapping out landmarks from the film and spotlighting which remained and which were gone.[57] Already, nostalgia for a bygone Austin was taking root; it seems to be the way of Austinites to chase "how Austin used to be," that idea of having just missed the city's halcyon era and pining to reclaim it. Film critic Marc Savlov wrote that *Slacker* is "a picture-perfect chronicle of an Austin era now long since faded . . . but like a good friend since passed, the memories of the fundamental locales linger in the minds of those who were present at this magical, formative time."[58] Already, the film had been situated into Austin citizenship: "Richard Linklater's film should be required viewing for the hordes of new arrivals that began inundating Austin some four years ago."[59]

At twenty years post-release, *The Chronicle* (again, through the loving words of Marc Savlov) celebrated *Slacker* as the last starlight before the dawn of a new Austin changed by a "positively tectonic shift in culture, commerce, art, and identity."[60] An even more acute bittersweetness emerged in this remembrance:

> It's human nature to enshrine the past and lament the loss of imagined innocence, especially when that sunny nostalgia for those salad days is intricately wound into your own artistic inclinations, your own private cultural DNA. And Austin itself is locked in a sweaty and seemingly ceaseless battle between remembering what it was and discovering what it is, and, most importantly, what it wants to be.[61]

At thirty, *The Chronicle* included more exposition about 1989 Austin, name-dropping but also painting scenes for Austin transplants to understand the legacy into which they have moved. "But," as critic Richard Whittaker wrote, "it wasn't that [*Slacker*] made Austin bigger or more mythic."[62] The subsequent nostalgia has done so. Over the years, these revisits to *Slacker* have repeatedly framed the Austin of summer 1989 as the place and time that Austinites are trying to get back to (or arrive at for the first time).

The Texas Film Commission has adopted a similar nostalgia approach to celebrate many of Linklater's films shot in Texas. But whereas the *Chronicle*'s approach appealed to "those who were present at this magical, formative time," and newer Austin residents, the TFC aims to transform some of Austin's cultural capital into economic benefit through tourism. The tourism and film industries both have long recognized their symbiotic relationship, and this partnership is actively promoted in conjunction with economic incentives to draw film productions to a locale.[63] The Texas Film Commission highlights the state's various filmmaking legacies by designing "Texas Film Trails," or self-guided tours in which film fans can visit locations featured in Texas-shot movies. The Richard Linklater Texas Film Trail inaugurated the program, "in recognition of Linklater's immense talent and commitment to the state."[64] Featuring eight locations from six of his films, the Film Trail encourages tourists to visit scenic and iconic locations in the southern half of the state, most of which are in and around Austin. Other Film Trails include Texas Westerns, Texas Classics, *Fear the Walking Dead*, and Texas Drive-ins. The film commission is deeply interested in drawing on Texas's cultural output to legitimize its role in producing economic value for the state.

CONCLUSION

At the time of *Slacker*'s release, Linklater served as inspiration for other filmmakers in Austin, and for independent filmmakers nationally as well. The American independent film scene at that time, with multiple instances of filmmakers working with comparably low budgets and original stories, opened up how people thought about filmmaking. Linklater's experience "demystified and democratized the creative process, made it all more reachable."[65] Yet, independent filmmaker after independent filmmaker experienced a more challenging environment, as the promises of institutions like the Sundance Film Festival—that showing a film here, for example, would lead to lucrative production deals with deep-pocketed and hands-off Hollywood studios—did not pan out as often as the Cinderella story would have one believe. Filmmakers from marginalized communities, such as Julie Dash, Matty Rich, Alison Anders, and Cheryl Dunye, didn't quite receive the same follow-up interest that the Kevin Smiths and Richard Linklaters did.

Linklater has retained his Austin pedigree, living in the area and staying intimately involved with the Austin Film Society. Contemporary framings of Linklater, the most fawning of which tend to be published by Austin and Texas based publications, at least briefly mention if not outright champion *Slacker*. As well, Linklater's continued stewardship of the film scene in Austin rather than Los Angeles, despite his professional reputation and accomplishments, positions him as the "face of the Texas film scene," a "maverick" who maintains his "authenticity."[66]

Some (mostly white) Austin residents who grew up in the city before the era of *Slacker* possess a certain nostalgia for the way the city "used to be." It's a consistent theme that *Slacker*, its misfits, and the Austin of 1989 are referenced as capturing that zeitgeist. Linklater's oeuvre is generally recognized thematically as a series of meditations on life's little moments, wherein he "find[s] meaning in the apparent meaningless of the everyday. Life is brief and time incessant, but Linklater teaches us to enjoy the pure joy of the frivolous moment."[67] And yet, his work on *Slacker* captured moments to which the City of Austin, along with some residents, wants to feverishly cling; these can't be ephemeral, because they are the very essence of Austin.

As the COVID-19 pandemic settled into its second year in 2021, many people were reconsidering their quality of life. For many, the environment in Los Angeles, hub of the American entertainment industry, has proven to compromise a healthy work-life balance. Austin experienced another massive surge in growth as corporations established offices in the region and remote workers searched for a calmer pace. Austin pops up as a possibility for escape, especially for those in the entertainment industry, where there are enough work opportunities and infrastructure, but with a friendly atmosphere and a relatively quick flight from Los Angeles.

This atmosphere, referenced by Texan actor Matthew McConaughey as "a secret" that might get leaked at any moment, continues to be linked closely to Linklater. In a profile of a Hollywood exodus to Austin in the summer of 2021, entertainment trade publication *The Hollywood Reporter* did not fail to mention *Slacker* and Linklater. Indeed, this is the most direct route to make the reader understand Austin's atmosphere: "The city's famously lackadaisical vibe—that indistinct word that you'll notice is used often by the city's fans—was epitomized in Richard Linklater's aptly titled 1990 feature *Slacker*, which also helped launch the city's indie film scene . . . Apparently, Austin's uniquely specific frequency is still tangible." McConaughey spoke of this vibe as "Austin's DNA."[68]

As Austin anticipates adding over a million more residents by 2040, signaling the "secret" of Austin's desirability reaching all corners of the U.S. and beyond, the economic and cultural sector align even more closely. And yet, it must happen carefully, surreptitiously, all the while reassuring Austinites that the Austin they saw in *Slacker* is being preserved and that the city isn't driven exclusively by corporate interests. Crass commercialism doesn't suit Austin's self-image, despite Austin's reality as a bustling economic epicenter. Many long-time residents lament the loss of a smaller Austin with quaint and quirky landmarks, oddball characters that everyone seems to know, and the "do what you want" sort of spirit. Some have relocated to other communities, fed up with Austin's current vibe. Others find Austin finally to be a place of interest, without such a parochial atmosphere.[69]

The Austin film industry is vibrant and is an important partner in the city's overall arts and culture scene. Robert Rodriguez, another forebear of the American independent cinema, continues his work in Austin, as do many other well-known and prolific filmmakers. Linklater too continues to make films—some are critically acclaimed and financially successful, and some are not. But it is primarily (and nearly singularly) Linklater who is a linchpin in preserving the Austin "vibe" as seen in *Slacker*. Discursively, Linklater's roots as the genesis for Austin's "slacker" figure signal a rejection of crass commercialism, even as he is used as a promotional tool for Austin's economic development of its film industry. There is something about Linklater that represents this "true" Austin, which itself is a myth that omits inconvenient, or rather, less commodifiable elements, according to corporate logic. The true Austin extends beyond West Campus, and it has been home to more than just middle-class, white people. But this is not the commodifiable, commercially successful Austin that draws economic investment.

It is strange to consider the tireless go-getter twenty-somethings migrating to Austin to work for major tech or media conglomerates as rebellious or slackers. Yet neoliberalism, in its valuing of the individual, seems to allow the ruse of retaining one's core outsider status while working within a commercial and corporate system. The myth of the *Slacker* Austin, which also draws on Austin as "weird," suits these goals quite nicely. In reference to his *Slacker* follow-up, *Dazed and Confused*, Linklater said, "There's something unproductive about nostalgia, about thinking backwards instead of forwards."[70] Yet this nostalgia seems quite productive for Austin indeed.

NOTES

1. See, for example, Rob Stone, *The Cinema of Richard Linklater: Walk, Don't Run* (London and New York: Wallflower Press, 2013); Alison Macor, *Chainsaws, Slackers, and Spy Kids: Thirty Years of Filmmaking in Austin, Texas* (Austin: University of Texas Press, 2010).
2. Susan King, "National Film Registry Selects 25 Films for Preservation," *The Los Angeles Times* (December 19, 2012): https://www.latimes.com/entertainment/la-xpm-2012-dec-19-la-et-mn-national-film-registry-20121217-story.html
3. Stephen Holden, "Life Without Gloss in the New Directors Series," *The New York Times* (March 15, 1991): C34: https://www.nytimes.com/1991/03/15/movies/life-without-the-gloss-in-new-directors-series.html
4. Richard Whittaker, "In 1990, Austin Audiences Watched Slacker . . . and Saw Themselves," *Austin Chronicle* (July 24, 2020): https://www.austinchronicle.com/screens/2020-07-24/in-1990-austin-audiences-watched-slacker-and-saw-themselves/
5. Macor, *Chainsaws, Slackers, and Spy Kids*.
6. Texas Film Commission, "History," State of Texas, Office of the Governor, Texas Film Commission, accessed August 9, 2021: https://gov.texas.gov/film/page/history

7. In 1994, the music festival added Film and Interactive, and now features conferences, trade shows, and spin-off festivals in other regional locations; the annual March event generates international visibility—and huge economic benefit—for Austin. Its current iterations are heavily corporatized, a stark difference from the early years of SXSW. Roland Swenson, "The History of SXSW," SXSW, accessed August 9, 2021: https://www.sxsw.com/about/history/
8. Macor, *Chainsaws, Slackers, and Spy Kids*, 19.
9. Ibid., 6.
10. Ibid.
11. Ibid.
12. John Pierson, *Spike, Mike, Slackers and Dykes: A Guided Tour Across a Decade of American Independent Cinema* (New York: Hyperion, 1995), 187.
13. Jason Heid, "Richard Linklater, the Everyday Auteur," *Texas Monthly* (July 2020): https://www.texasmonthly.com/arts-entertainment/richard-linklater-film-texas-coronavirus/
14. Pierson, *Spike, Mike, Slackers and Dykes*, 195.
15. Douglas Coupland, "Generation X'd," *Details Magazine* (June 1995): https://coupland.tripod.com/details1.html
16. Joshua Long, *Weird City: Sense of Place and Creative Resistance in Austin, Texas* (Austin: University of Texas Press, 2010), 15.
17. Joshua Long, "Sense of Place and Place-based Activism in the Neoliberal City," *City* 17:1 (2013): 58.
18. Ibid.: 65.
19. Monica Colombo and Azzurra Senatore, "The Discursive Construction of Community Identity," *Journal of Community & Applied Social Psychology* 15 (2005): 48–62.
20. Carolyn Hardin, "Finding the 'Neo' in Neoliberalism," *Cultural Studies* 28:2 (2014): 207.
21. Long, *Weird City*.
22. Sònia Vives Miró, "Producing a 'Successful City': Neoliberal Urbanism and Gentrification in the Tourist City—The Case of Palma (Majorca)," *Urban Studies Research* 2011: 1.
23. David Harvey, "Neoliberalism and the City," *Studies in Social Justice* 1:1 (2007): 9.
24. Texas is the site of long struggles among indigenous peoples and white settlers, and settler colonialism has shaped the state dramatically. As upwards of 30,000 Anglo-Americans arrived in the region in the early 1800s, viewing it as a "promised land" ready for the taking, indigenous populations began to decline rapidly. The region now known as Texas was home to about 40,000 indigenous peoples; among them were the Caddo and Tonkawa, along with Comanche and Kiowa. About a quarter of those individuals were refugees from neighboring regions. Austin was formally incorporated as a city in 1839, first under the name of Waterloo, as the capital of the Republic of Texas. The city, nestled on the Colorado River, remained the state capitol after Texas entered the United States in 1845. Texas continued to engage in bloody battles with various non-white groups between the 1830s and 1880s, as its government enacted policies of what amounted to ethnic cleansing to be executed by Texas Rangers. At the same time, the Austin area served as a haven of sorts for African Americans after the Civil War (over a third of Austin's population in 1870 was African American). Michael Barnes, "Texas History: What happened to the Native Americans in Texas?" *Austin American-Statesman* (March 23, 2021): https://www.statesman.com/story/news/history/2021/03/23/ethnic-cleansing-best-describes-what-happened-native-americans-texas/4750307001/; Andrew Graybill, "Rangers, Mounties, and the Subjugation of Indigenous Peoples, 1870–1885," *Great Plains Quarterly* 24:2 (Spring, 2004): 83–100; Campbell Gibson and Kay Jung, "Working Paper No. 76: Historical Census Statistics On Population Totals By Race, 1790 to 1990, and By

Hispanic Origin, 1970 to 1990, For Large Cities And Other Urban Places In The United States," Washington, DC: U.S. Census Bureau (2005); Andrew Busch, "Building 'a City of Upper-middle-class Citizens': Labor Markets, Segregation, and Growth in Austin, Texas, 1950–1973," *Journal of Urban History* 39:5 (2013): 975–996.
25. Long, *Weird City*, 39.
26. David Gibson and John Butler, "Sustaining the Technopolis: The Case of Austin, Texas," *World Technopolis Review* 2:2 (2013): 64–80.
27. Alyssa Schroer, "Silicon Hills: The Hottest Scene in Texas Tech," *Built in Austin* (February 15, 2020): https://www.builtinaustin.com/2018/04/24/silicon-hills-guide-austin-tech-scene
28. Gibson and Butler, "Sustaining the Technopolis," 74.
29. Richard Florida, *The Rise of the Creative Class and How It's Transforming Work, Leisure, Community, and Everyday Life* (New York: Basic Books, 2002).
30. Michael Hall, "The City of the Eternal Boom," *Texas Monthly Magazine* (March 2016): https://www.texasmonthly.com/the-culture/austin-and-the-city-of-the-eternal-boom
31. Yui Hashimoto, "Racing the Creative Class: Diversity, Racialized Discourses of Work, and Colorblind Redevelopment," *Urban Geography* 42:4 (2020): 528–550.
32. Hashimoto, "Racing the Creative Class," 536.
33. U.S. Census Bureau, "QuickFacts: Austin city, Texas": https://www.census.gov/quickfacts/fact/table/austincitytexas/LND110210
34. George Ritzer, *The McDonaldization of Society* (Thousand Oaks, CA: Pine Forge Press, 1993).
35. Carl Grodach, "Before and After the Creative City: The Politics of Urban Cultural Policy in Austin, Texas," *Journal of Urban Affairs* 34:1 (2011): 81–97.
36. Bill Bulick, *CreateAustin Cultural Master Plan* (Austin, TX: Cultural Arts Division, April 2008).
37. Grodach, "Before and After the Creative City," 81–97.
38. U.S. Census Bureau, "All Sectors: County Business Patterns, including ZIP Code Business Patterns, by Legal Form of Organization and Employment Size Class for the U.S., States, and Selected Geographies: 2019," U.S. Census Bureau Economic Surveys, Table CB1900CBP (2019): https://data.census.gov/cedsci/table?q=%20CB1900CBP&tid=CBP2019.CB1900CBP
39. "Best Places to Live and Work as a Moviemaker, 2021," *MovieMaker Magazine* (January 26, 2021): https://www.moviemaker.com/best-places-to-live-and-work-as-a-moviemaker-2021/
40. Hall, "The City of the Eternal Boom."
41. Electronic Arts Inc. Form 10-K 2021. Redwood City, CA: Electronic Arts Inc., 2021: 33.
42. Electronic Arts, "Inside the Studio: EA Austin," Electronic Arts website (2021): https://www.ea.com/news/tour-the-ea-austin-studio
43. Stone, *The Cinema of Richard Linklater*, 25.
44. Richard Linklater, "From the Archives: Linklater on Linklater: Our 1991 Self-Interview by the *Slacker* Filmmaker," *Austin Chronicle* (July 24, 2020): https://www.austinchronicle.com/screens/2020-07-24/from-the-archives-linklater-on-linklater/
45. Eliot Tretter, "The Slacker Colonialist and the Gentrification of Austin," *The End of Austin* (November 2020): https://wp.me/p2Q8kE-1bU
46. Heid, "Richard Linklater, the Everyday Auteur."
47. Linklater, "From the Archives."
48. Tretter, "The Slacker Colonialist and the Gentrification of Austin."
49. Ibid.
50. Whittaker, "In 1990, Austin Audiences Watched Slacker . . . and Saw Themselves."

51. Stone, *The Cinema of Richard Linklater*, 24.
52. Ibid.
53. Whittaker, "In 1990, Austin Audiences Watched Slacker . . . and Saw Themselves."
54. Tretter, "The Slacker Colonialist and the Gentrification of Austin."
55. Ryan Robinson, "City of Austin Demographic Profile," Department of Planning, City of Austin (July 2011): http://www.austintexas.gov/sites/default/files/files/Planning/Demographics/city_of_austin_profile_2010.pdf
56. Kimberley Jones, "More Slack: The Chronicle's 20-year Love Affair with Slacker," *The Austin Chronicle*, January 20, 2011: https://www.austinchronicle.com/daily/screens/2011-01-20/more-slack/
57. Marc Savlov, "Slacker, the Map," *Austin Chronicle*, January 26, 2001: https://www.austinchronicle.com/screens/2001-01-26/80370/
58. Ibid.
59. Ibid.
60. Marc Savlov, "Slack to the Future: Austin Gets Older; 'Slacker' Stays Forever Young," *The Austin Chronicle*, January 21, 2011: https://www.austinchronicle.com/screens/2011-01-21/slack-to-the-future/
61. Ibid.
62. Whittaker, "In 1990, Austin Audiences Watched Slacker . . . and Saw Themselves."
63. Roger Riley et al., "Movie-induced Tourism," *Annals of Tourism Research* 25:4 (1998): 919–935.
64. Texas Film Commission. "Richard Linklater Trail." Texas Film Commission Texas Film Trails (2021): https://gov.texas.gov/film/trail/richard-linklater-trail
65. Whittaker, "In 1990, Austin Audiences Watched Slacker . . . and Saw Themselves."
66. Jeff Salmon, "Cinema's Last True Maverick," *Authentic Texas Magazine* (Winter, 2017): 42–45.
67. Calum Russell, "The Beauty of Richard Linklater's Slacker Philosophy," *Far Out Magazine* (July 30, 2021): https://faroutmagazine.co.uk/the-beauty-of-richard-linklater-slacker-philosophy/
68. James Hibberd, "How Austin Has Undergone a Pandemic Influx From Hollywood: 'Growth on a Turbocharger,'" *The Hollywood Reporter*, August 6, 2021: https://www.hollywoodreporter.com/lifestyle/lifestyle-news/austin-texas-hollywood-pandemic-1234992037/
69. Hall, "The City of the Eternal Boom."
70. Emmanuel Levy, *Cinema of Outsiders: The Rise of American Independent Film* (New York: New York University Press, 1993), 177.

CHAPTER 2

On Being a Vegetarian in Texas: The Incongruities and Politics of Linklater's *Fast Food Nation*

Claire Parkinson

In the case of most directors, it is rare to have two films released in the same year. Not so for Richard Linklater when, in 2006 and for the second time, two of his films were released in a single year. In 2001, *Waking Life* and *Tape* had made their screen debuts and, five years later, 2006 saw the release of another Linklater duo, *Fast Food Nation* and *A Scanner Darkly*. Cannes in 2006 was a busy time for the director. *Fast Food Nation* competed for the Palme d'Or while *A Scanner Darkly* was screened as part of the Un Certain Regard competition, forcing Linklater to make multiple trips to the festival and juggle interviews and promotion. In addition to both films being in competition at Cannes, *Fast Food Nation* and *A Scanner Darkly* shared other similarities. Both were adaptations of well-known books; the former a 2001 non-fiction investigation and exposé of the fast-food industries by journalist Eric Schlosser, the latter a 1977 science fiction novel by Philip K. Dick. Both films harbored a dark tone, they both suggested a sense of disquiet with contemporary American culture and politics, and each treated its source material in innovative ways; *Fast Food Nation* was a non-fiction best-seller turned satirical drama for the screen and *A Scanner Darkly* used the interpolated rotoscope animation technique. The films' critical reception was however a different story and here the similarity ends. While *A Scanner Darkly* was reasonably well received, *Fast Food Nation* divided critics and was considered one of Linklater's less successful films. One reason given for the lackluster critical reception of *Fast Food Nation* was that it was an uncomfortable fit with the original source material which, it was proposed by a number of critics, surely leant itself better to documentary rather than drama.[1] Moreover, despite both films reflecting Linklater's political views–something that is arguably characteristic of much of this director's output–*Fast Food Nation* was branded as agitprop by reviewers.[2]

For many of the film's critics it was an odd decision to turn a piece of hard-hitting investigative journalism into a satirical drama. Yet, placed within the context of Richard Linklater's body of work, such incongruity can be understood as characteristic of this filmmaker's choices where his films and sensibility resist easy categorization. Moreover, thematically, the film chimes with Linklater's personal commitment to vegetarianism, animal rights, and workers' rights, political perspectives which are, by the director's own admission, at odds with his Texan identity. This chapter examines *Fast Food Nation* to explore what the film reveals about the complex relationship between Linklater's politics and his iconoclastic and commercial sensibilities. It considers Linklater as an activist filmmaker and examines the film from an animal studies perspective to propose that Linklater's narrative choices can be read productively through the lens of intersectionality. Indeed, this chapter argues that Linklater's politics are evident in his ensemble works which often engage with issues of intersectional oppression and social justice. To frame this critique, I draw from ecofeminist and critical animal studies scholarship on posthumanist intersectionality and the animal-industrial complex, an organizing concept that maps interconnections across the industries that institutionalize the exploitation of animals. The approach taken here is one that recognizes oppression across species and takes the position that there are interrelationships of human and non-human oppression which are apparent in the animal agriculture industries.[3] Using this critical framing, this chapter explores *Fast Food Nation* as a commercial activist film and proposes that it should be regarded as a successful exploration of transspecies intersectionality that, when considered alongside Linklater's wider political activities, reveals an iconoclastic sensibility.

INDEPENDENCE AND AUTONOMY

Linklater's career is one of contrasts and contradictions where his films sit within the categories of both "market-driven entertainment and contemplative art cinema"[4] while Linklater himself is "neither exclusively independent nor wholly dependent upon studios and distributors."[5] Indeed, Linklater's autonomy, even when working on a studio film, is well documented. From his first independent feature, *It's Impossible to Learn to Plow by Reading Books* (1988), which Linklater made alone, to films such as the commercial studio comedy *School of Rock* (2003) where Linklater, working as a director-for-hire, negotiated with Paramount for greater control over the filmmaking process, the director's career is characterized by differing degrees of independence. Linklater is one example of a wider trend of indie directors being brought onto studio films and then having careers which move between the independent and studio sectors.

Autonomy in the context of studio filmmaking is relative however and studio promotion of a film with an attached indie director will often emphasize their independence to build a marketing narrative pitched around the personal vision and style of the filmmaker. Linklater is no exception to this strategy, as reflected in a *Variety* article from 2003 on Paramount's decision to secure Linklater to direct *School of Rock*. The film is described as a product of the filmmaker's vision and quotes Linklater saying, "the studio stood behind all of the filmmaking team's decisions."[6] In such cases there are marketing advantages in highlighting the director's independence on a studio film which can be leveraged to emphasize an indie sensibility in terms of tone or style. As Michael Z. Newman points out, Linklater is one of a small cadre of directors who "are admired for retaining their indie sensibility even when making movies with wider appeal"[7] and Tom Esther asserts that Linklater blurs "the distinction between the filmmaking styles, apparatuses and esthetics of independent and commercial filmmaking."[8] According to Rob Stone,

> Linklater's career must be plotted with an entire arsenal of sliding scales that includes the one that major studios use to calibrate film budgets ranging from those that are appropriate to the absolute autonomy of filmmakers whose talents suit a narrow marketing strategy to those that factor in the servitude of those whole skills can be applied to industrial franchises.[9]

In the case of *Fast Food Nation*, financing for the film was intrinsically bound up with Schlosser's and Linklater's concerns about independence of style, personal vision, and voice. As the author of the book, Eric Schlosser asserted, "It's a Richard Linklater film so it has his particular voice and sensibility" and emphasizing the authorial differences between the book and the film Schlosser explained, "So they're very very different things. What they share is a title, some themes and hopefully a spirit; a spirit that is iconoclastic and trying to look below the surface of American society."[10]

Prior to writing the *Fast Food Nation*, Schlosser had been commissioned by *Rolling Stone* to write a series of articles about fast food. The articles "Fast Food Nation Part One: The True Cost of America's Diet" and "Fast-Food Nation Part Two: Meat and Potatoes: From Slaughterhouse to Styrofoam, the Dark Side of the American Diet" were originally published in September and November 1998. The articles became the basis of the book which took Schlosser a further two years to write. Published in 2001, *Fast Food Nation* was adapted for children as *Chew On This; Everything You Don't Want to Know About Fast Food* which was published in 2006, the same year Linklater's *Fast Food Nation* was released. Following the publication of *Fast Food Nation*, Schlosser wanted to use the book as source material and the basis of a feature documentary film.

Discussions between Schlosser and various documentary filmmakers including Michael Moore took place in the eighteen months following the book's publication and despite coming close to a deal on a number of occasions, Schlosser did not sign over the rights; the author's reservations being due to the limited funding and distribution opportunities for documentaries at the time.

To maintain the spirit of the book and the autonomy of the filmmaker, the deal for *Fast Food Nation* was reliant on the film's funding having no connection to the fast-food industries. The obvious choice was to make *Fast Food Nation* as a television documentary; however, such a route was complicated by the links between network television and fast food through advertising and sponsorship. This was not the case for a fiction film that was aiming for a theatrical release. It is therefore important to acknowledge how the wider industrial context and notions of independence impacted the eventual decision to make *Fast Food Nation* a satirical drama rather than a documentary and how this guaranteed Linklater's creative autonomy.

Although by 2004 there were signs of an emergent market for documentaries that came from the festival circuit and were screened in art house cinemas,[11] at the end of the 1990s and in the early 2000s there were very few cinema-release documentaries. At the same time, television remained the primary distribution option for documentary filmmakers and, by 2004, revenues from the worldwide business in television documentary were estimated at US$4.5 billion.[12] With limited options for a theatrical release, the deals with documentary filmmakers that were presented to Schlosser necessarily involved television networks, organizations that had links to the fast-food industries through advertising or corporate sponsorship deals. As Schlosser explained in an interview, "I was very eager for there to be a documentary based on the book [. . .] I liked the filmmakers but each of them was backed by a different network of some kind," and referring to Disney's corporate sponsorship of the children's program *Sesame Street*, "[. . .] even PBS has this tie with the fast food industry."[13] Wary that such arrangements would present conflicts of interest, Schlosser was concerned that this would result in unacceptable compromises to the original intent of the book:

> I was really clear [. . .] that there was a need for really strong director to be empowered and I wasn't going to sign over [. . .] the rights of the book until it was clear that Rick really wanted to do this, that it was clear he would have full creative control, and that the money would be raised entirely outside of the Hollywood system.[14]

The film was eventually funded in 2005 by BBC Films, the film arm of the public service broadcaster the British Broadcasting Corporation (BBC) and Participant Productions (now Participant), a film company founded by Jeffrey Skoll, the first president of eBay, which had been established to make social issue films. As well as *Fast Food Nation*, 2006 releases for Participant Productions included *The World According to Sesame Street*, a documentary that examined the cultural impact of the children's program, and *An Inconvenient Truth*, a documentary about Al Gore's global warming campaign that won the Academy Award for Best Documentary Feature and is widely regarded as being a watershed moment for the environmental movement. A relatively new player in the film industry having been established in 2004, only two years before the release of *Fast Food Nation*, Participant Productions' President Ricky Strauss claimed in a 2005 article in *The New York Times* that the film advanced Participant's mission "in the sense of encouraging corporate responsibility."[15] However, the *New York Times* article questioned the company's social issue credentials and pointed out that the Skoll Foundation (also established by Jeffrey Skoll who remained as the foundation's chairperson) had invested in fast-food companies and held US$1.3 million of shares that included Yum! Brands, the parent company of chains such as Pizza Hut, KFC and Taco Bell, Kraft Foods, Cadbury Schweppes, Pepsi Bottling Group and Coca-Cola. Participant Productions defended its integrity, noting that there were no direct ties between it and the Skoll Foundation. Despite this defense, the *New York Times* article highlighted an important issue about the complexities of feature film financing, the difficulties of finding funding that aligns with a particular ethical position—in other words the "ethically clean dollar"—and the inescapable links, however remote, between corporate interests.

WORKERS ON SCREEN

The idea to make *Fast Food Nation* as a fiction film came from the film's producer Jeremy Thomas following a conversation with Malcolm McLaren (also credited as a producer) who said that he believed the book "would make a wonderful dramatic film."[16] Thomas approached Schlosser with the idea of adapting *Fast Food Nation* as a drama and, despite initial reservations, the author arranged to meet with Linklater in Austin, Texas during a book tour to discuss the project. Linklater was intrigued by the idea of making a fiction film based on the book but admitted in interviews that when he read *Fast Food Nation* it had never occurred to him that it would be the basis for a drama. Using Sherwood Anderson's novel *Winesburg, Ohio* (1919)—a series of short stories set in a fictional small town in Ohio—as inspiration, the development of the idea for *Fast Food Nation* took a further two years before Linklater and Schlosser agreed that the project was viable. Linklater was particularly driven to make a story about small-town workers, a concept that had interested him for some years, but it had proved difficult to find the right project that would attract funding. For Linklater, a filmmaker who openly acknowledges that his films contain autobiographical elements, his previous experiences of working in restaurants and on an oil rig shaped his views and interest in workers' rights. Linklater explained: "I kind of know what it's like to be at the very bottom, the very expendable labor at the bottom of an industry. That viewpoint, that becomes your worldview."[17]

Fast Food Nation follows the interconnected stories of workers at different levels within the fast-food industries, but this was not the first time Linklater had attempted to tell the stories of exploited workers. Linklater had previously tried to make a film which adapted Ben Hamper's 1992 memoir *Rivethead: Tales From the Assembly Line*, parts of which had been commissioned by Michael Moore in his capacity as editor of *The Michigan Voice* and, later, *Mother Jones*. Unable to get the project financed, Linklater reasoned that the film industry did not consider workers' stories to be suitable material for movies, but that television might prove a potential alternative. In 2004, Linklater made *$5.15/Hr.*, a comedy pilot for HBO about the underpaid employees of a diner chain called Grammaw's. Set in Linklater's hometown of Austin, Texas, the opening scene of *$5.15/Hr.* is set at the headquarters of Grammaw's parent company, Hoak Industries. The CEO Jim Hoak sits behind a large wooden desk while two suited men, only seen from behind, explain that a drop-off in "per guest profits" can be addressed through the introduction of a new dessert treat. In the next shot a group of scientists surrounded by cakes and various containers of brightly colored fluids are hard at work perfecting the treat. Cut to a boardroom and a presentation about the success of the apple treats in consumer testing followed by shots of factory workers standing in front of a huge vat of a beige mixture and pushing large-wheeled containers of beige-colored apple filling. The camera follows a conveyor belt which transports row after row of the burrito-style dessert treats to a freezing machine then cuts to the product being packed by more factory workers. Another conveyor belt takes the boxes of product to be taped shut and loaded onto a forklift truck. The bluish cast to the lighting throughout the factory scene enhances the sense that the product is processed and artificial. The sequence cuts to a shot of a food photographer preparing the product shot in a studio. Behind the plated apple treat are bottles of chemicals used to enhance the product's visual appeal. The picture is taken, and the sequence ends with a diner worker pinning up a banner advertising the new fandango apple treat. In the next scene, one of the diner cooks opens a plastic bag of frozen treats which fall clunking onto the metal kitchen surface and says, "They looked like something that dropped out of an Eskimo's ass." Driving home the joke that fast food is abject, the pilot episode ends back in the CEO's office where the marketing executives explain that the newly developed range of treats will be edible within six weeks and that the name of the new product is very similar to the Navaho word for excrement.

There are some important and interesting parallels between *$5.15/Hr.* and *Fast Food Nation*. In dealing with the issue of workers' rights, Linklater uses the narrative structure of *$5.15/Hr.* to make the viewer aware that there is a corporate hierarchy and that decisions made at the top level have implications for workers lower down the organizational ladder. The viewer is taken on a journey with the product from idea development through production, promotion, and finally to the sales destination. Along the way, each shot is populated by the workers from the corporate level to the laboratory, the factory, through promotion, and finally to the diner. In *Fast Food Nation*, Linklater uses some similar narrative strategies to emphasize the interconnectedness and the difference between the corporate world, the restaurant staff, and the slaughterhouse workers, and the abject nature of fast food. The opening sequence of *Fast Food Nation* is set in a fast-food chain restaurant, Mickey's. Upbeat music accompanies close-up shots of The Big One burger, smooth tracking shots show happy, smiling families eating burgers and fries and carefully controlled lens flare from the sunlight gives the whole scene a warm glow; all these elements converge to suggest the aesthetics of a slick television advert. As the burger box opens in the final brand and product shot, the music changes and becomes ominous as the camera moves in slowly to an extreme close-up of the burger which looks increasingly less appetizing until the shot fades to black. The next scene opens at night in a Mexican town at the U.S. border. Two young women are part of a group which plans to cross the border illegally. Money exchanges hands and an older man cautions that the group must look after one another. There is a visual jolt from night to bright daylight in the next scene where two flags flap in the breeze outside Mickey's Californian corporate headquarters. A sales and marketing team comprised of white, middle-aged men in suits discuss the success of The Big One, the increase in profits, and the next product for promotion. An executive says that plans for a corporate tie-in with Disney have been unsuccessful and another explains that a deal with PBS has fallen through because Burger King and McDonald's "have Teletubbies all locked up"; a reference to Schlosser's concerns about the links between the television and fast-food industries. The setting moves to the laboratory which creates the chemical aromas that are used to make the burgers smell and taste more appealing to consumers. One of the executives from the boardroom, Don Anderson (Greg Kinnear), discusses the aromas with a scientist before meeting with the company CEO to talk about a recent study by some grad students that has found that the company's best-selling product, The Big One, contains large quantities of fecal matter. "There's shit in the meat" the CEO explains to Anderson who is then sent to find out how such high levels of feces are ending up in the burgers. As Anderson's investigation unfolds, the narrative introduces each of the other groups that make up the movie's ensemble: the Mexican immigrants who end up as slaughterhouse workers working for Uni-Globe which supplies the meat to Mickey's and the college students who work at a Mickey's outlet and end up as animal activists, attempting to free the cattle on the slaughterhouse lot.

The message that fast food is "shit" runs through both *Fast Food Nation* and the *$5.15/Hr.* pilot. The abject nature of the food is visually referenced by the development of the product by scientists in laboratory settings and reinforced through the dialogue and narratives which, in the case of *Fast Food Nation*, make it clear that the burger is actually tainted with fecal matter. Against the criticism of the products produced by the fast-food industries, the narrative in both the film and the television pilot moves from one group of workers to another, emphasizing the relationality of their stories and existence, contrasting their viewpoints and experiences. Linklater is well known for ensemble films with loosely connected characters, beginning with his second feature and breakout movie *Slacker* (1991). While *Fast Food Nation* is also an ensemble film with loosely connected characters, the difference between this and *Slacker*, for example, is that in the former, the interconnectedness of the characters is used to emphasize the industrial hierarchy and by extension the differences between workers and executives, while *Slacker*'s structure uses the narrative hand-off from character to character to emphasize their equivalence. The issues of worker exploitation are discussed by the characters in *Slacker* and explored through the dialogue and narrative structures of *$5.15/Hr.* and *Fast Food Nation*, all of which harbor an anticorporate message that is characteristic of Linklater's work. However, *Fast Food Nation* stands apart from Linklater's other films which critique corporate capitalism in a less obvious manner. As Mary Harrod argues, the anticorporate message in *A Scanner Darkly* becomes more apparent when watched alongside *Fast Food Nation*.[18] Linklater's radicalism is present in his films, but it is often discreet and easily overlooked if his films are taken individually. As a body of work with *Fast Food Nation* at its metaphorical center, Linklater's nods to an anticorporate position are amplified elsewhere.

INTERSECTIONALITY

The funding dilemma that surrounded *Fast Food Nation* is mirrored in Linklater's handling of the issue of corporate influence and control in the film where the narrative provides no easy answers and instead offers a bleak envisioning of everyone's inability—human and non-human animal—to escape the grip and exploitation of corporate capitalism. The narrative structure highlights the transspecies intersectional oppression of human workers and cows, all of whom are connected in Linklater's depiction of the animal-industrial complex. In a scene where Don speaks with a rancher, Rudy (Kris Kristofferson), the executive is told,

> This isn't about good people versus bad people, it's about the machine that's taking over this country. It's like something from science fiction. The land, the cattle, human beings, this machine don't give a shit. Pennies a pound, pennies a pound, that's all it cares about. A few more pennies a pound.

Moments such as this make apparent how the material exploitation of animals within the food production system intersects with the oppression of human workers under the rubric of corporate capitalism. In *Fast Food Nation*, speciesism, sexism, and racism are shown to be clearly intertwined and the interlocking system of oppressions is amplified at the slaughterhouse setting where the lives of animals are measured in cents per pound, Mexican workers are cheap labor forced into dangerous working conditions, and female slaughterhouse workers are subjected to sexual abuse. And, while the film's ensemble cast exposes the relationality of human-animal entanglements and the inability of anyone to escape corporate control, white patriarchy structures this web of relations to ensure that, in this system of exploitation, some fare better than others.

Partway through the film, the executive, Don Anderson, finds evidence that the meat processing plant is running its lines too fast. As a result, the workers are being injured and fecal matter is getting into the meat. He lays out his concerns to Harry Rydell (Bruce Willis), the meat supplier, who tells Don "We all gotta eat a little shit sometimes" and implies that Don's job will be at risk if he reveals the problems to anyone. Faced with the choice to expose the practices at the meat processing plant and risk losing his job or to stay quiet and keep his position, Don opts for the latter. Up to this point the narrative has foregrounded Don's investigation as a major plotline. Following his decision to say nothing, Don disappears from the film and the narrative shifts to explore the experiences of a group of college students. The abrupt end to Don's story is a narrative reminder that everyone is expendable and, despite Don's position in the company, he is unable to influence any change and his concerns about the meat and the workers are never communicated upwards.

During the conversation between Don and Harry, the Mexican workers' choices are laid out through the logic and language of neoliberal capitalism. Harry explains that, in Mexico, the workers are poor and earn only $3 or $4 per day. In the meat packing plant they earn $10 per hour. "That's more money that he makes in one day than he makes back home in a whole month. So frankly I don't see the problem. Nobody's making these people come up here, right? Nobody's telling them to work for UMP." In the world that Linklater creates, there is no hero of the piece, and the Mexican workers are trapped into extreme poverty or the exploitative and dangerous working conditions of the plant. Pitched as a problem of choice for the individual rather than an endemic structural issue of oppression and injustice, there is no escape and there is no disruption to the business, which continues as usual. Linklater presents the stark realities of corporate capitalism; even though it is cruel and exploitative, it is too big for one person to challenge alone and the choices available are only those that continue to benefit the corporate machine and its capitalistic drive for profit. Don does return briefly at the end of the film in a mid-credits scene, still in his executive position, clearly troubled by what he has discovered but trapped by the threat of losing his well-paid job. In this short scene, the board of executives is told that the company is in a strong position to introduce a new product, the development of which has been headed up by Don. He presents the new "BBQ Big One" to the executive board telling them "we couldn't be more ready to go" as he casts his eyes downward, evidently uncomfortable with his part in the process but unable to escape. The end credits then resume over the image of a seemingly endless conveyor belt of burger patties, the electronica techno music track by Nortec Collective serving to emphasize the relentlessness of production.

An inability to escape, even when given an alternative choice, is explored again in the film when a group of animal activists cut a hole in the fence of the slaughterhouse lot in an attempt to free the cattle. Under cover of darkness, the group cut through the fence, enter the pen, and try to usher the cows out through the gap. Against a soundscape of loud mooing, the cows back away from the activists and the broken fence. "They're not doing anything," "Why won't they go?", "What the fuck is wrong with them?", "How stupid are they?" the activists exclaim in frustration and disbelief. "Don't you want to be free?" one activist, Amber (Ashley Johnson), shouts as the sequence cuts to a shot of a cow mooing hard, her neck straining. "Don't you know they're going to kill every single one of you?" The lights of an approaching vehicle prompt the activists to abandon their plans and they run away. In the next scene they are in a college dorm room discussing the failure of their mission. Questioning again why the cows stayed in the pen, Andrew (Aaron Himelstein) muses "Who knows, maybe it's easier in there. They get all the food they want. I bet that genetically engineered shit tastes a lot better than grass." Amber replies "I think they're just scared." The scene ends with Alice (Avril Lavigne) saying "I don't know. How come in real life the bad guys always win." "Well, you know," Andrew responds off camera, "they do until they don't." Throughout the film, Linklater draws attention to the impossibility of escape and the fear of alternatives to a system that is damaging to everyone.

There is however a clear hierarchy of oppression, and while the white college students' activist efforts are unsuccessful and their options for work are limited to low-paid serving jobs in fast-food outlets, their situation is markedly different to that of the young Mexican immigrants who work in the slaughterhouse. Having already risked their lives to get across the border, the Mexican workers are subjected to the harsh conditions of the slaughterhouse, which pushes many of the workers to turn to drugs. After confronting her sister, Coco (Ana Claudia Talancón), over her drug use and sexual relationship with one of the supervisors, Sylvia (Catalina Sandino Moreno) is told by her boyfriend Raul (Wilmer Valderrama) "Look, she's not alone. A lot of people at work are taking drugs. It's hard, the drugs make it easier." Following an accident at the plant which results in Raul's leg being amputated, Sylvia, who has a job at a hotel, is forced to seek work at the slaughterhouse. She visits Coco and explains that the hotel has refused to give her any more hours and that, with Raul unable to work, their situation is desperate. Coco agrees to ask Mike (Bobby Cannavale), the supervisor she has been having an affair with, if he will get Sylvia some work at the plant. Sylvia meets Mike at dark in a car park where he manipulates her into having sex in return for a job. In a later scene, the camera follows Sylvia as she dresses for work at the slaughterhouse and is taken through the white corridors of the building to the kill floor. Her journey to the kills floor is cross-cut with the movement of the cattle to the same destination. The parallel editing cuts from Sylvia walking past the gutting line to cattle being forced along the chute and into the crush where a captive bolt gun is fired into the back of one cow's head and she falls to the floor. The scene cuts back to a close-up of Sylvia's face and then cuts again to the blood-soaked crush. The camera zooms in to a close-up of the head of another cow who has been stunned, her eyes still open, her head slowly falling away from the camera. The scene cuts back again to a close-up of Sylvia's face, only her eyes are visible, the rest of her face is covered by a white mask. Workers sharpening their blades and shots of cows hanging upside down, having their throats slit, the blood gushing out and on to the floor are followed by shots of the cows' bodies being butchered, their lower legs being sliced off, their torsos hanging from hooks, their skins being peeled away and horns being sawn from their heads. These are intercut with shots of Sylvia's face as she looks at the bodies and the blood and continues to walk further into the plant. A wide shot shows Sylvia at a chute, the floor around her is covered in blood and she is told "breathe through your mouth" as she is shown how to "pull kidneys." As the cows' internal organs slide down the metal sluice, blood spatters onto Sylvia's face and she begins to cry. The scene changes to a wide shot of Mexican immigrants being taken across the border; some of the group are young boys. As they approach the truck that will take them over the border, the man responsible for smuggling them—known colloquially as the coyote—gets out of the truck and hands the two boys "itty bitty meals" from Mickey's fast-food restaurant. The film ends with a freeze frame of the Mickey's "itty bitty" bags emblazoned with the cartoon smiling faces of children before the shot fades to black and the credits begin. The final scenes reinforce the bleak and relentless cycle, the cows and the workers are treated as exploitable commodities, and they are all caught up in the animal-industrial complex which has no care or concern for anyone or anything other than the drive for profit.

Reading these final scenes through a transspecies intersectional lens, Linklater lays bare the realities of interconnected forms of oppression within the animal-industrial complex. As Malecki et al. discuss "it is precisely because people from underprivileged groups are considered less worthy of moral consideration by dominating groups that today's societies typically assign to the former the most dangerous and poorly paid jobs related to animal exploitation."[19] In the Global North, the meat industries have poor safety records with a high likelihood of injury, and they rely heavily on poorly paid immigrant workforces.[20] Moreover, slaughterhouse work is stigmatized and has been characterized as "dirty work"; occupations "which have explicit connotations of social disapproval" and work which is considered "tainted."[21] This stigmatization of slaughterhouse as "dirty work" coupled with low wages reinforce the social and economic oppression experienced by immigrant workers. As *Fast Food Nation* makes clear, intersectional oppressions within the animal-industrial complex are structurally maintained by corporate capitalism, a point that is driven home by Rudy the rancher when he refers to the industry as a machine, only concerned with "pennies a pound." In his discussion of feminisms and intersectionality that takes account of species, Richard Twine argues "corporate capital accumulation has been a significant factor in the emergence of globalized industrialized animal production" and, he notes "corporate interests have had a direct interest through marketing, advertising and flavor manipulation in constructing the consumption of animal products as a sensual material pleasure."[22] *Fast Food Nation* challenges the pleasures of meat consumption envisioning the abject nature of fast-food meat products as literal "shit" while also engaging with what Anat Pick refers to as "the politics of visibility." Noting that, worldwide, more than 50 billion land animals are slaughtered annually, Pick argues that "the stakes of making killing visible are high in a climate that aggressively targets animal and environmental activists as 'extremists' and 'domestic terrorists.'"[23] The politics of visibility play out in an interesting way through the slaughterhouse scenes in *Fast Food Nation* which makes what is usually invisible, visible.

In the film, the footage of slaughter, more often associated with undercover animal rights films, blurs the line between fiction and non-fiction filmmaking. The scenes were filmed in a real slaughterhouse in Mexico and, as Linklater has attested, Catalina Sandino Moreno's tears were real and a response to what she was actually seeing as the filming moved through the slaughterhouse. Linklater waits until the end of the film to finally reveal what Don, the executive, was unable to see. In an earlier scene, Rudy asks Don if he has seen the kill floor. Unsure, Don explains that he was taken on a tour of the facility and he "saw a lot of things." "You'd remember," says Rudy. "You see any cattle gettin' their heads cut off? Were you walkin' ankle-deep in blood?" "No" Don responds. "So they didn't show you a damn thing." Instead of the seeing the realities of the slaughterhouse from Don's point of view, Linklater reveals the practices of slaughter and dismemberment from Sylvia's point of view. The scene begins by cross-cutting between Sylvia's and the cows' journeys to the kill floor until the moment of death, then the shots describe Sylvia's field of vision and her experience of the slaughterhouse. As she moves deeper into the slaughterhouse, the cows' bodies are reduced, at each stage, into smaller parts until, when Sylvia arrives at her workstation, all that is visible of the cow's body is the viscera—her digestive system, intestines, and reproductive organs. It is thus Sylvia who sees the whole truth of the slaughterhouse, a visual truth which is denied to everyone else, even the company executives.

ACTIVIST-FILMMAKER

The "politics of visibility" refer to the truths of the slaughterhouse which are routinely denied to the public. In efforts to keep the realities of animal agriculture from the public view, "ag-gag" laws were introduced in some American states after 2011. These laws criminalized filming or photography at an animal facility, a response to undercover filming by animal activists. Linklater stopped eating meat in the early 1980s and became vegetarian in 1985. In an interview for the animal advocacy group PETA, Linklater cited Peter Singer's book *Animal Liberation* (1975) as an important turning point in his thinking about human animal relationships.[24] *Animal Liberation* is widely regarded as the seminal text for the animal rights movement of the late twentieth century. In it, Singer used the concept of speciesism to argue for a basic principle of equality grounded in equal consideration for other animals. "Equal consideration" Singer asserted "may lead to different treatment and different rights."[25] Linklater considered Schlosser's book *Fast Food Nation* to be an animal rights text for a new generation. In adapting the book for the screen, Linklater was clear in his intentions. Positioning himself as an idealist who believes that people will want to change but lack the information to do so, *Fast Food Nation* was intended to be a film that would give audiences the opportunity to gain insights into the fast-food and meat production industries that are otherwise denied to them. There was no doubt that Linklater saw the film as a call to action and wanted *Fast Food Nation* to challenge audiences: "If it makes people feel uncomfortable or have to confront that in themselves, then good."[26]

Although filmed in 2005 and prior to the introduction of ag-gag laws, *Fast Food Nation* was shrouded in secrecy during production, primarily because Linklater and Schlosser anticipated hostility toward the film from meat packing and fast-food companies, a situation that would hinder shooting on location, particularly in fast-food franchise restaurants and slaughterhouses. Few details about the film were released initially and during production the film was referred to as *Coyote*, a pseudonym that referenced the role of a character in the film who brings Mexican immigrants across the American border for profit. Linklater was unsuccessful in finding a U.S. meat processing plant to film in. With no North American slaughterhouses willing to allow Linklater to shoot in their plants, filming for the meat processing plant scenes took place at a slaughterhouse in Mexico.[27] It is not too much of a stretch to suppose that the *Coyote* pseudonym riffed on the colloquial term, to allude to Linklater bringing illicit footage of slaughterhouse operations back over the border for the purposes of making a commercial film.

Because the book that preceded the film had been perceived as an attack at the very heart of the fast-food industry and specifically at the McDonald's Corporation it was widely accepted and expected that the film would follow suit with an overt anticorporate message. Moreover, with backing from Participant Productions, a company which developed campaigns to sit alongside their social issue films, expectations were high that *Fast Food Nation* would be Linklater's "activist" movie. However, the social action campaign attached to *Fast Food Nation* was confused. A 150-second flash animation, *The Meatrix II1/2*, spoofed *The Matrix* to show the realities of the meat packing industry but the campaign encouraged consumers to use an online directory of "sustainably raised" animal products. In this way, the consumer action was related to how animals are reared rather than the practices involved in their slaughter. And, despite concerns about the financing being free from links with fast food, *Fast Food Nation* was eventually distributed in the U.S. by Fox Searchlight, the parent company of which had promotional deals and strong ties with Burger King. Moreover, the marketing plan for the film was based on the expectation that McDonald's would mount a public campaign against the film. However, Linklater's and Thomas's plan to capitalize on the free publicity from the anticipated backlash by the fast-food industry did not materialize and the film's limited release garnered a little over US$1 million at the domestic box office and only slightly more through international releases.[28]

Failure to provoke the fast-food industries' ire suggests that the film was seen as little or no threat to their business and, in this sense, *Fast Food Nation* arguably fails as an activist film. By electing to make the film a drama rather than a documentary, *Fast Food Nation* was, arguably, less threatening to the reputational capital of the meat packing and fast-food industries. Yet, Linklater's activism is better understood through the iconoclasm that is evident across his wider body of work. Despite many of his films reflecting Linklater's anticorporate position and personal views regarding American politics and culture, the director is not known as an activist filmmaker. In part, this is because Linklater's politics tend to be quietly present in his fiction films. Compared with the overt political engagement that is more usually associated with documentary filmmakers, Linklater's style of politicized critique is nuanced and restrained. Linklater has said "So many of my films are very personal explorations of ideas, things I'm trying to learn more about or make peace with."[29] A vegetarian socialist living in Texas, Linklater's involvement in political and animal rights activism outside of his feature film career is more overt. For example, in 2015, Linklater, playing himself over a period of thirty years, spoofed his universally acclaimed 2014 drama, *Boyhood*, for the animal rights organization People for the Ethical Treatment of Animals (PETA). In 2018, Linklater directed a thirty-second anti-Ted Cruz television advertisement that featured the actor Sonny Carl Davis and parodied a scene from his 2011 film, *Bernie*. In 2020 Linklater executive produced a ten-episode documentary series for CBS, *That Animal Rescue Show*, to "shine a light on the folks I've met who are making a difference every day in the lives of unwanted, abused and disabled animals."[30] It is useful to consider Linklater's *Fast Food Nation*, with his anti-Cruz advertisement and his PETA video, to better understand another dimension of this director's iconoclasm. In Linklater's case, it is pertinent it makes a distinction between an activist filmmaker and filmmaker-activist where the former is directly engaged in making visible the fundamental conditions and mechanisms of oppression in their works and the latter is a hyphenate whose discrete activities include both filmmaking and activism. However, even in making this distinction, it is apparent that, much as he does in his career between the studio and indie sectors and between commercial and arthouse filmmaking, Linklater slips across the boundaries between each.

NOTES

1. See for example: Ruthe Stein, "A Plentiful Serving of Diet Don'ts," *San Francisco Chronicle*, November 17, 2006: https://www.sfgate.com/movies/article/A-plentiful-serving-of-diet-don-ts-2466570.php; Peter Bradshaw, "Fast Food Nation," *The Guardian*, May 4, 2007: https://www.theguardian.com/film/2007/may/04/thriller.drama
2. For example, in a 2014 review and ranking of Linklater's body of work, two *Variety* critics had *Fast Food Nation* languishing at either number twelve or thirteen out of seventeen films claiming "The result doesn't entirely work, but it's a flavorsome concoction nonetheless, and there's no doubt that, as a piece of anti-McDonald's agitprop, it comes straight from the heart" and "infused with obvious passion, just not much of a movie"; Justin Chang "The films of Richard Linklater: Ranked from best to worst," *Boston Herald*, July 11, 2014: https://www.bostonherald.com/2014/07/11/the-films-of-richard-linklater-ranked-from-best-to-worst/
3. Richard Twine, "Revealing the 'Animal-Industrial Complex' – A concept and method for Critical Animal Studies?" *Journal for Critical Animal Studies* 10:1 (2012): 12–39.
4. Lesley Speed, "Possibilities of Roads Not Taken: Intellect and Utopia in the Films of Richard Linklater," *Journal of Popular Film and Television* 35:3 (2007): 99.
5. Rob Stone, *The Cinema of Richard Linklater* (London and New York: Wallflower Press, 2013), 64.
6. Dana Harris, "New Film Legends of the Fall," *Variety*, October 12, 2003: https://variety.com/2003/film/news/new-film-legends-of-the-fall-1117893767/
7. Michael Z. Newman, "Indie Culture: In Pursuit of the Authentic Autonomous Alternative," *Cinema Journal* 48:3 (2009): 48.
8. John Esther, "The Transparency of Things: An interview with Richard Linklater," *Cineaste*, (Fall, 2006): 64.
9. Stone, *The Cinema of Richard Linklater*, 63.

10. BBC, "Fast Food Nation: Eric Schlosser Interview," August 8, 2007: https://www.youtube.com/watch?v=sIlknPHnScY
11. Keith Beattie, *Documentary Screens: Non-fiction Film and Television* (Basingstoke and New York: Palgrave Macmillan, 2004), 207.
12. Patrcia Aufderheide, *Documentary Film* (Oxford and New York: Oxford University Press, 2007), 4.
13. Syd Field, "Interviewing Richard Linklater and Eric Schlosser, writers of '*Fast Food Nation*,'" February 7, 2017: https://www.youtube.com/watch?v=lK7Prrenqms
14. Field, "Interviewing Richard Linklater."
15. Michael Joseph Gross, "Want Stealth With That? The 'Fast Food Nation' Film Goes Undercover," *The New York Times*, October 30, 2005: https://www.nytimes.com/2005/10/30/movies/want-stealth-with-that-the-fast-food-nation-film-goes-undercover.html
16. Jennie Kermode, "Fast Food and Fierce Film," *Eye for Film*, February 19, 2007: https://www.eyeforfilm.co.uk/feature/2007-02-19-qa-with-jeremy-thomas-about-film-fast-food-nation-feature-story-by-jennie-kermode
17. Field, "Interviewing Richard Linklater."
18. Mary Harrod, "The Aesthetics of Pastiche in the Work of Richard Linklater," *Screen* 51:1 (2010): 37.
19. W. P. Malecki et al., "Narrating Human and Animal Oppression: Strategic Empathy and Intersectionalism in Alice Walker's 'Am I Blue?'" *Interdisciplinary Studies in Literature and Environment* 0.0 (2020): 2.
20. Harvey Neo and Jody Emel, *Geographies of Meat: Politics, Economy and Culture* (London and New York: Routledge, 2017), 71–75; Eric Schlosser, *Fast Food Nation: What the all-American Meal is Doing to the World* (London: Penguin Books, 2001), 169–190.
21. Darren McCabe and Lindsay Hamilton, "The Kill Programme: An Ethnographic Study of 'Dirty Work' in a Slaughterhouse," *New Technology, Work and Employment* 30:2 (2015): 97.
22. Twine, "Revealing the 'Animal-Industrial Complex,'" 15.
23. Pick, Anat, "Animal Rights Films, Organized Violence, and the Politics of Sight," in *The Routledge Companion to Cinema and Politics*, edited by Yannis Tzioumakis and Claire Molloy (London and New York: Routledge, 2016), 93.
24. PETA, "Director Richard Linklater's Exclusive Interview with PETA," November 12, 2012: https://www.peta.org/videos/fast-food-nation-director-richard-linklaters-exclusive-interview-with-peta/
25. Peter Singer, *Animal Liberation* (London: Pimlico, 1995 [1975]), 2.
26. PETA, "Director Richard Linklater's Exclusive Interview with PETA."
27. Gross, "Want Stealth With That?"
28. Source: Box Office Mojo.
29. Simon Hattenstone, "Richard Linklater: 'Someone's Living Back There, and he Murdered Somebody,'" *The Guardian*, April 30, 2016: https://www.theguardian.com/film/2016/apr/30/richard-linklater-film-director-murderer-lodger-simon-hattenstone
30. Elaine Low, "Richard Linklater Animal Rescue Docuseries Ordered to Series at CBS All Access," *Variety*, January 12, 2020: https://variety.com/2020/tv/news/richard-linklater-animal-rescue-ordered-series-cbs-all-access-1203464403/

CHAPTER 3

The Little Space Between Hal Ashby and Richard Linklater

Rob Stone

INTRODUCTION

The Last Detail (Hal Ashby, 1973) and *Before Sunrise* (Linklater, 1995) make an unlikely double bill, which nevertheless serves to frame Linklater in relation to the history of American independent filmmaking and to consider the evolution of a prominent trope in its history, one that links his cinema to that of Hal Ashby. Both films follow characters that have just met, choosing

Figure 3.1 Intervals of flânerie in *The Last Detail* (Hal Ashby, 1973) . . .

to disembark a train and killing time overnight in a city, while making tentative connections as they move toward inexorable separation. In *The Last Detail* Buddusky (Jack Nicholson) and Mule (Otis Young) interrupt their mission to take Meadows (Randy Quaid) to prison, while Jesse (Ethan Hawke) persuades Céline (Julie Delpy) to pause her journey home. They each play out as interludes of flânerie between trains and narrative resolution—in Washington, New York and Boston, and in Vienna, respectively. Both disembarkations create, as Gilles Deleuze would have it, intervals "between the action and the reaction" which are occupied, instead, by affection: affection-images.[1] For Deleuze:

> The interval is not merely defined by the specialisation of the two limit-facets, perceptive and active. There is an in-between. Affection is what occupies the interval, what occupies it without filling it or filling it up. It surges in the centre of indetermination, that is to say in the subject, between a perception which is troubling in certain aspects and a hesitant action.[2]

In discussions of Ashby, this interval has been likened to "spiritual drift."[3] In the films of Linklater, meanwhile, I have argued it assumes the "form and content of slack."[4] The interval is, as Céline expresses in her soliloquy in *Before Sunrise*, a "little space in-between":

> If there's any kind of god it wouldn't be in any of us, not you or me but just this *little space in-between*. If there's any kind of magic in this world

Figure 3.2 . . . and *Before Sunrise* (Linklater, 1995)

it must be in the attempt of understanding someone sharing something.
I know, it's almost impossible to succeed but who cares really? The
answer must be in the attempt.

Importantly, however, 1970s spiritual drift and 1990s slacking are not the same, which results in their respective trains heading, one might say, in opposite directions: Ashby's toward defeat and Linklater's away from it. Thus, in *The Last Detail* and *Before Sunrise* these intervals are occupied by affection in disparate ways that suggest the changing nature of the affection-image between and across these filmmakers' outputs. As this chapter will consider, Ashby and Linklater have much in common, but the way they occupy the little space between them differently is precisely what sets them apart.

BETWEEN MEETING AND SEPARATING AND MEETING AGAIN

Both *The Last Detail* and *Before Sunrise* are centered on intervals between trains but they respond to the defeat of pending separation differently. In *The Last Detail* this response amounts to a downward spiral of inchoate nocturnal incidents in diners, bars, and brothels, while in *Before Sunrise* it plays out in the opposite direction as ephemeral encounters with actors, poets, and stargazers. In both films these intervals spent wandering cities resemble metaphysical experiences that surrender to the resurgence of real time in their final moments; but whereas Buddusky discards his burgeoning paternal relationship with Meadows, Jesse and Céline suture their connection with a gesture of deferral that does not presuppose the end of their romantic one. Buddusky is done in by Vietnam, but Jesse and Céline first meet in June of 1995, twenty years after the end of "the Vietnam war's defining experience."[5] They are too young to remember "the onset of trauma resulting from a realisation of powerlessness in the face of a world whose systems of organisation – both moral and political – have broken down."[6] Unlike Buddusky and Meadows, they might exist beyond that trauma and be capable of sustaining their potential. Thus, in promising to reunite six months later, they are able to defer resolution until December. Of course, this little space between them that is this deferral of their romance would actually extend for nine years until *Before Sunset* (Linklater, 2004). This revealed that they had failed to keep their appointment, but that their potential was still valid and would be realized in Paris because by then they had reflected enough to act differently.

At least until pairing *The Last Detail* with its "spiritual sequel" *Last Flag Flying*,[7] curating double bills of films by Ashby and Linklater may seem random; but doing so by dint of character and narrative coincidences forces comparative analyses that highlight formal similarities and illuminate philosophical differences. Holding that further comparative analyses may explain the little space in between the films of Ashby and Linklater, this chapter also attempts to close the little space between the 1970s and the 1990s and between the perception-image and the action-image. It does this by seeking trace elements of the political commitment born out of defeat in the 1970s that would be sidelined in the 1980s and deferred to a different ideation by Linklater in the 1990s and 2000s. This is not intended as a postmodern consideration of a modernist impulse and neither does it presuppose a loss of value due to the prolongation of that 1970s defeat in the films of Linklater, but it does suggest that whereas the cinema of Ashby essays "moral ambivalence and political rage"[8] and traffics in disillusionment, that of Linklater tends to emphasize the potential for change in dialogue rather than pressing for any substantive change in action. That said, the nature of change in the little space between Ashby and Linklater is not predicated upon further distancing from centers of authority such as the government, mainstream media, and Hollywood. Instead, the change is a minor modification, an inflection visible in the directionality provoked by their respective affection-images or, moreover, by their deferral and difference. By these means, while the films of Linklater sustain a critique of the stalled revolutionary movements of the 1960s that remains relevant in the 1990s and, indeed, in the present, they can also sometimes reconcile with the loss of potential in ways that resolve that defeat and even absolve the defeated.

BETWEEN THE ACTION-IMAGE AND THE PERCEPTION-IMAGE

Much like Linklater, Ashby was an innately anti-studio filmmaker, who nevertheless made profitable, even Oscar-winning films that now seem like bystanders to the battles that wrought modern American spectacular cinema from the wreckage of Classic Hollywood. Linklater's observational humanism aligns with the "amble to [Ashby's] work, unhurried but unambiguous"[9] and their films concur on warnings against authoritarianism and the unconsidered life. Dropping out and leaning in, both their careers waver on the imaginary line separating the big studios from independent filmmaking, while their characters tend to perform lawlessness as a means of shoring up their oppositional politics or philosophy. On the one hand, therefore, this kinship suggests a lack of evolution between New Hollywood of the 1970s and the Indies of the 1990s, with their films sharing a fondness for hanging out with dialecticians that loiter similarly at the border between conformity and rebellion. Ashby and his characters, for instance, appear emblematic of those Americans who suffered late-Vietnam frustration and post-war malaise. Reeling from Nixon, they sought to purge their emptiness and sense of being played by connecting with other loners who turned away from recent history and neoliberalism. By pretending their idleness was on purpose, they occasionally made a grab for substance by means of opportune protest, which typifies too the second generation of slackers, who came of age in the 1990s and populate the films of Linklater by engaging in familiar, secular, spiritual drifts that oppose capitalist rhetoric by the deliberate inaction of slacking. Yet all this turning away and drifting, this inaction and slacking, is precisely that which defers what Deleuze theorized as affection-images, which is why they tend to be different in the films of Ashby and Linklater and why their films resemble passing trains, which carry similar passengers and comparable baggage, but travel in opposite directions.

Deleuze links the affection-image to the close-up and defines it as a vehicle for the absorption of a tendency to expression prior to movement that "replaces the action which has become momentarily or locally impossible."[10] The affection-image occurs between perception and action and usually acts as prelude to movement or taking responsibility for an action. It is an interval in which potential is considered but can also be contained or deferred and therefore frustrated, meaning the affection-image can exhibit "an internal frigidity"[11] that is not separate from self-awareness, especially when this carries expectation of defeat. The addled close-up therefore tends to be the primary platform in practice of what Thomas Elsaesser describes as the "realism of sentiment that tries to be faithful to the negative experiences" of many Americans, with actors in New Hollywood films of the 1970s performing "the moral and emotional gestures of a defeated generation."[12] The description is apt because the close-up on the face of America during the 1970s was otherwise often knowingly performative, resembling a collage of subscriptions to ideas and consequent poses. Tom Wolfe called it "the Me decade"[13] and Norman Mailer wrote that it was "the decade in which image became preeminent because nothing deeper was going on", such as political commitment, post-Vietnam revolution, or responsibility for defeat.[14] Such narcissism was allied to and enabled a feint of indifference, but some films barely hid the fear, depression, and exhaustion that came with the traumatic end to U.S. involvement in the war in Vietnam. Ashby's six films during the 1970s, for example, commemorate America being outpaced by the lies it told itself about itself and they correspond to Christian Keathley's diagnosis of a "post-traumatic cycle"[15] of American cinema in the 1970s that, I contend, duly returns as cycles do in the Indies of the 1990s.

The 1970s wave explored how "systems of organisation – both moral and political – have broken down" in response to the war in Vietnam, revealing "what Gilles Deleuze has described as 'a crisis of the action-image.'"[16] In mainstream cinema dominated by linear narrative and movement-images on their way to a resolution, the affection-image as Deleuze defined it could be elided in favor of a cause and effect in the editing that resembles a simple "I see, therefore I do" without any interval. This interval—the affection-image—is where the emotional experience of being in the space between seeing (the perception-image) and doing (the action-image) is felt as (and is at the same time subject to) a "delay between action and reaction [that] thereby expresses the subject's experience of itself from the inside."[17] In Ashby's *Shampoo* (1975) and other films of New Hollywood such as *Five Easy Pieces* (Bob Rafelson, 1970) and *Night Moves* (Arthur Penn, 1975), however, Keathley identifies "the possibilities inherent in the interval between perception and image [which] privileges, expands, and explores the affection-image."[18] Given the post-Vietnam moral and political breakdown that underscores these films, moreover, Keathley contends that the affection-image serves as a platform for cynicism, disillusionment, and alienation and he argues that these isolating sentiments block the shift from perception-image to action-image and divert time and attention to the affection-image's representation of trauma. Consequently, the action-image is postponed as an affection-image is deferred or withheld in elliptical, uncertain narratives prone to avoid conclusions.

BETWEEN THE 1970S AND THE 1990S

The box-office and cultural triumph of spectacular cinema in the late 1970s would exile cynicism about Reaganism to the edges of the mainstream in the space between Ashby and Linklater that is the 1980s. These were the years of the yuppies, who favored the privileges that came with economic stability and yet mistook consumerism for the security promised by the neoliberalism of the Reagan-Bush years with its booming Wall Street and buzzing Silicon Valley. Protesting voices on film were uncertain and muted, while those that sought to represent the contemporary radicalization of emancipatory movements in civil rights were pushed to the sideline of American independent cinema, where, for example, films such as *Smithereens* (Susan Seidelman, 1982), *Variety* (Bette Gordon, 1983), *Smooth Talk* (Joyce Chopra, 1985), and *Desert Hearts* (Donna Deitch, 1986) sustained an investigation into the language of feminist cinema. This movement to the margins, where more radical creativity was possible, also inspired many filmmakers to move to places such as Austin, Texas, and Portland, Oregon during the economic downturn of the late 1980s, thereby seeding regional, independent film hubs that would go on to submit their films to new American film festivals like Sundance in the 1990s. Portland in the 1980s "was developing a reputation as an ideal haven for authors"[19] and this breakout literary, music, and cultural scene in the place where Ashby spent his childhood and adolescence would nurture and attract independent filmmakers such as Gus Van Sant, Miranda July, Aaron Katz, and Kelly Reichardt. Linklater, meanwhile, seeking to revive a nostalgic idea of counterculture that his generation assumed had been deferred to them by a "tight group of bohemian friends" that was Ashby's experience of the 1970s,[20] moved to Austin as the result of "a very specific decision based on, 'Where can I live cheap, watch a lot of movies and be around cool people?'" and founded the Austin Film Society.[21] Consequently, the cycles of oppositional creativity in which Ashby collaborated in the late 1960s and 1970s, and Linklater would foster in the late 1980s and 1990s, suggest that their filmmaking responded to the post-traumatic cycle identified by Keathley as originating in:

> the counter-culture films of the late 1960s [that] first foreground the apparent necessity of choice or feature protagonists who believe in the existential responsibility an individual has to make choices (especially moral choices); but they then undercut this notion, showing instead that the privileging of choice implies the opportunity of the individual to gain power and self-determination – something these films reveal to be an impossibility.[22]

Indeed, this foregrounding of defeat as a consequence of both ineffectual choice and a lack of choice is the subject of the affection-image in the films of Ashby, where affection-images tend to be deferred, and in those of Linklater, where affection-images appear and tend to defer those choices. In other words, whereas Buddusky abandons Meadows because they know themselves to be powerless (so whatever they "choose" will have the same consequence regardless: their parting), Jesse and Céline make a big emotional scene out of postponing their romance till six months later. So is the affection-image, which Keathley uses to identify characters that "do not directly challenge the established system as the figures of the counter-culture cycle did [but] are at least partly alienated from it,"[23] what opens or closes the little space between Ashby and Linklater?

BETWEEN CRISES

Until its final freeze frame, *Harold and Maude* resembles a collage of life and death impulses juxtaposing the fake suicides of Harold (Bud Cort) with the vivacity of Maude (Ruth Gordon). This informs the film's concertina-like structure, which alternates claustrophobic scenes of Harold with his family with those of him carefree with Maude, until Maude takes an overdose on her eightieth birthday. Then, however, the close-up of Harold that might signify the effect of Maude's death on him and be identified as an affection-image is elided. Instead, Ashby shows Harold in a long shot in the hospital with his back toward the camera and a consequently unreadable expression, followed by a medium shot of him driving fast with such intense concentration that his long stare acts as a kind of placeholder for the deferred affection-image, keeping multiple, virtual, possible action-images simultaneously in play and at bay. Even when Ashby cuts to a long shot of Harold's car hurtling off a cliff and smashing onto rocks, duality is maintained by a shot of crashing waves that illustrates both a death wish and the film's Buddhist themes of human impermanence and natural cycles. The concluding cut or fade to black does not transpire, however. Rather, the camera tilts up to pick out Harold atop the cliff, banjo in hand, plucking out the inspirational song Maude taught him: "If You Want to Sing Out, Sing Out." Because Ashby has pulled the exact same trick earlier in the film when Harold self-immolates (that is, eliding a shot that reveals his safe exit from one of many performances of suicide), another of Harold's staged deaths should not surprise, but it does so because unlike in previous "suicides" where the audience is "in on" the gag, the absence of an affection-image here withholds any definitive indication of Harold's reaction to Maude's death. The little space between her real death and his fake one, which is followed by Harold's minstrel-like capering away from the cliff's edge, is therefore both predictable and surprising, rendered ironic too by the capturing of Harold clicking his heels in a final freeze frame that extends the duality by leaving Harold both fully alive and embalmed in the stilled shot: Schrödinger's counterculture, whose box will not be opened until the 1990s.

Freeze frames as final shots form a barrage in several other non-conformist American films of the early 1970s, including *Joe* (John G. Avildsen, 1970), *Wanda* (Barbara Loden, 1970), *WUSA* (Stuart Rosenberg, 1970), *Two-Lane Blacktop* (Monte Hellman, 1971), and *Electra Glide in Blue* (James Wiliam Guercio, 1973). Since they are frozen, the characters in these frames cannot move forwards, thereby denying the apparent form and purpose of the film that contains them and suggesting consensus about what Keathley identifies as Deleuze's "crisis of the action-image" in American cinema during this decade.[24] During the 1980s, however, the final freeze frame in American cinema was largely repurposed so as to enshrine individualistic victories associated with resurgent Republicanism in popular mainstream films such as *An Officer and a Gentleman* (Taylor Hackford, 1982), *Flashdance* (Adrian Lyne, 1983), *Beverly Hills Cop* (Martin Brest, 1984), and *The Karate Kid* (John G. Avildsen, 1984). Not until the early 1990s would these final freeze-framed snapshots of success be subject to parody in sitcoms such as *Seinfeld* (1989–1998) and numerous skits on *Saturday Night Live* (1975–).

The little space between Ashby and Linklater consequently prompts a different final shot in *Slacker* (Linklater, 1991), which ends the same as *Harold and Maude*, by pretending to throw itself off a cliff. In *Slacker*, a group of young people filming themselves for fun, jump from their car, race up a cliff, and fling their camera off it. *Slacker* thus differs from *Harold and Maude* by revealing from within how the apparatus (car there, camera here) was released from human hands before it plummeted. Indeed, because the final shot by the unmanned camera in *Slacker* is subject to the throw, it does not communicate the act of throwing, which might be read as an action-image, but a visualization of the condition of being thrown, which is a perception-image. Consequently, as for Ashby, the action-image is postponed in *Slacker*. Falling to the bottom of their cliffs, the camera and the car are both unmanned "elements in motion"[25] illustrating Lyotard's notion that "something has come undone: all of a sudden [. . .] cliff edges appear, lurching forth before your startled eyes."[26] Yet, although the final shots appear to coincide, they are like the aforementioned passing trains, moving in opposite directions; for Ashby's shot is outside the car's crash and moves up, while Linklater's shot is inside the camera's crash and, being subject to gravity, moves down. Both shots exhibit momentum that coincides with what Deleuze terms "the historical crisis of psychology [which] coincided with the moment at which it was no longer possible to hold a certain position,"[27] and both shots express the crises of the action-image because they result in deluded gestures toward the illusion of flight and freedom in *Slacker* and the pretense of positivity in Harold's grief and isolation. Correlatively, Ashby and Linklater may be described as "laid-back, doobie-inclined, scruffy [,] gentle [and] bittersweet,"[28] but this is only a performance of nonchalance that is symptomatic of the "post-traumatic cycle," being one that prompts deferral of the affection-image when confronted with inevitable defeat. What is yet to appear in the cinema of Linklater as a differential factor is the notion of deferral conveyed in an affection-image, one that postpones the action-image of the crashing defeat and inserts instead the possibility of an alternative, such as Jesse and Céline accomplish on that train station in Vienna. This finding duly focuses our attention on comparative analysis of the deferral of affection-images in the films of Ashby and the attempts at affection-images aimed at further deferral of defeat in the films of Linklater.

BETWEEN DEFEAT AND ITS DEFERRAL

The notion that double bills of films by Ashby and Linklater can support comparative analyses finds traction in pairing *Bound for Glory* (Ashby, 1976) with *The Newton Boys* (Linklater, 1998), which both examine the media-savvy fashioning of stubborn American folk heroes, and *Coming Home* (Ashby, 1978) with *Tape* (Linklater, 2001), which both observe men trapped in the past competing for a woman who has learnt to love herself in the present. In addition, *Being There* (Ashby, 1979) and *School of Rock* (Linklater, 2003) combine to consider the interval between Nixon and Trump as one in which solipsistic males can triumph, while *Harold and Maude* (Ashby, 1971) also goes well with *Bernie* (Linklater, 2011) because they are both eccentric, borderline grotesque black comedies that track the relationship of a peculiar young man with a much older woman and how his self-esteem is, albeit ironically, edified by her death. In Ashby's film, Harold plots against his family and their middle-class conventions and finds romance with the 79-year-old Maude. But Maude, having decided that eighty is the right age to die, takes an overdose on her birthday and, as described, seemingly gifts Harold fresh resolve. In Linklater's film, however, the dynamic is flipped, with the 80-year-old Marjorie (Shirley MacLaine) a malevolent crone who flattens the effervescent Bernie (Jack Black) until he cracks and kills her, whereupon the cheerful townsfolk of Carthage, Texas rally to his defense. In essence, Ashby's film transfuses the vibrant life of its octogenarian into its somber youth, while Linklater has an aging community inoculated by the zest of a young man and thus able to withstand the enervating spite of one old lady. Although similar, therefore, even when at their closest points, when all is sweetest between Harold and Maude and between Bernie and Marjorie, there is still a little space between them like that between passing trains that are moving in opposite directions, which resembles a motif in all our double features.

Bernie is closest to Harold when in the trauma-induced deferral of definitive action and defeat. Like Harold, Bernie first asserts his identity through exaggerated performative gestures, such as by leading the local amateur dramatics club and performing good deeds that reveal his unrequited need for love and willingness to be indentured to the widow Marjorie. Such performativity is a ruse that postpones reflection that might lead to self-awareness, however, for unlike Harold, who blooms in Maude's company, Bernie pauses his own true self-affirmation in order to serve Marjorie's demands. Unlike Harold thriving in the company of Maude, therefore, Bernie defers his potential until killing Marjorie perverts this and leads to a trial that is a theatrical celebration of her murder featuring a chorus of townsfolk justifying the killing and demanding Bernie's release, thereby denying any responsibility for their harboring a murderer. The performativity of the townsfolk in Linklater's film is structured to resemble the chorus in classical Greek drama and it evokes the sense of celebrity that can accompany serial killers and murderers. Yet the chorus of cheerful townsfolk at the micro level of Carthage also suggests a self-deluding deferral of defeat representing the wider population's disregard for the plethora of gun violence in America. Thus, between Harold, who loves Maude in 1971, and Bernie, who hates Marjorie in 2011, there is a difference between them that is deferred, still pending acknowledgment of defeat that is nevertheless ironized when, again like passing trains, Harold looks ahead, chooses solitude and is seemingly free, while Bernie looks back, chooses a community and goes to prison. The difference in the little space between Ashby and Linklater is that deferral of defeat is enacted by an individual in *Harold and Maude* and forty years later in *Bernie* is performed by an entire town that gets over the loss of Bernie, the widow, and this dramatic episode by patting itself on the back about the community spirit that arose from it in time of need. Thus, despite the plight of Bernie, the townspeople make their protest a performative celebration of themselves, one that lauds the kind of small-town spirit that, though irresponsible and immoral, will indeed warrant a film to be made about it. Both endings posit that Americans can turn a blind eye to defeat (including death and murder) but the move from an individual to a whole town suggests that America's logjam of postponed responsibilities (and potential trauma) caused by its deferral of acknowledgment of defeat is growing.

BETWEEN DEFERRAL OF THE AFFECTION-IMAGE AND THE AFFECTION-IMAGE THAT DEFERS DEFEAT

Like Harold in his cliff-top freeze frame, George (Warren Beatty) ends *Shampoo* abandoned on a hilltop, imprisoned in his libertarian lifestyle, as Jackie (Julie Christie) speeds away. The final shot has him blurred with his back to the camera, thereby deferring the affection-image that might bridge the gap between his perception of loving her and acting upon it with at least some sense of responsibility. It is a deferred defeat that Jackie foretold:

> GEORGE: Hey, I know I'm a fuck-up, but I'll take care of you. I'll make you happy. I swear to God I will. What do you think?
> JACKIE: It's too late.

What the missing close-up withholds is any sense of responsibility or awareness that George is actually "in the domain of the perception of affection, the most terrifying, that when all the others have been destroyed: it is the perception of self by self, the affection-image."[29] Complacent in his apolitical womanizing and lacking courage, George fails to manifest any movement that might result in an affection-image that risks ruining the preened perfection of his multiple reflections in his salon mirrors, one that that is distinct "from everything that they have not yet become."[30] But the deferral of an affection-image at the end of *Shampoo* is also a ruse by which George, with his back to the camera, abrogates responsibility for an affection-image that might acknowledge his defeat. His withheld affection-image is not quite the embodiment of Elsaesser's fidelity "to the negative experiences [of] being defeated,"[31] but comparing him with Wooderson (Matthew McConaughey) in *Dazed and Confused* (Linklater, 1993) does reveal how this postponement of defeat enables a self-deluding recycling of the past that supposedly occurred before trauma, thereby precluding Keathley's "post-traumatic cycle,"[32] with vague hopes of achieving a different present.

Accordingly, pairing *Shampoo* with *Dazed and Confused* works well because they both have single-day time spans that aggregate and aggravate male cravings. Like George, Wooderson is self-deluding in supposing himself capable of recycling the non-traumatic past by loving a succession of young female students because "I get older, they stay the same age" and as such he illustrates Keathley's assertion that "post-traumatic films can be said to be a replaying or recollection of the process lead-ing to the traumatic event."³³ But whereas Ashby's George never attempts an affection-image that might risk him suffering defeat by Jackie's rejection or, worse, self-awareness of his own aging, Linklater's Wooderson does at least enter the "terrifying" domain of the affection-image that requires him to participate in "the perception of self by self,"³⁴ albeit (like Jesse and Céline) by attempting an affection-image aimed at further deferral of defeat and (like the townsfolk of Carthage) further abrogation of responsibility for postponed action. He does this, if only ironically, when he sends *Dazed and Confused* in the opposite direction from *Shampoo* by being unlike George in being quite "all right" doing what he is not doing: "Let me tell you this, the older you do get the more rules they're gonna try to get you to follow. You just gotta keep livin' man, L-I-V-I-N." Unlike George, whose pose is a vacant veneer, Wooderson does factor some self-awareness born of experience into his philosophy, which justifies his stunted pose and which he uses to offset his own deferred defeat by (unlike George) factoring his aging into his attractiveness. Thus Wooderson still gets to go to an Aerosmith concert, unlike George, who suffers the crushingly sarcastic critique of Ashby imposing "Wouldn't It Be Nice" by The Beach Boys, which expresses an adolescent fantasy about love between grown-ups, on the film's final image of the blurry back of his deflated pompadour.

BETWEEN *THE LAST DETAIL* AND *LAST FLAG FLYING*

The longer the interval between perception-image and action-image, the greater perhaps is the abrogation of responsibility for an affection-image that might acknowledge and even resolve this. Yet, as for Wooderson, the lengthening interval must also factor in aging, which has become a dominant theme in the recent films of Linklater. *Boyhood* (Linklater, 2014) is about growing older in form as well as content, Jesse and Céline are cracking as a middle-aged couple in *Before Midnight* (Linklater, 2013), and *Where'd You Go, Bernadette* (Linklater, 2019) essays a mid-life crisis. Thus, with the little space between Ashby's films of the 1970s and Linklater's recent films also growing and the twenty-two years between *The Last Detail* and *Before Sunrise* doubled by that between *The Last Detail* and *Last Flag Flying*, consideration is now due the notion of the latter as "spiritual sequel" to the former and how this explicit connection might close the little space between the filmmakers.

The films are based on 1970 and 2005 novels by Darryl Ponicsan, who co-wrote the screenplay for the latter with Linklater; but the films have an uneasy kinship, displaying differences of character, tone, and directionality. Both feature mediated images of American interventionism in far-off wars and both are resentful of triumphalism. They also both acknowledge casualties as well as collateral damage on grieving families that are erased by subscription to a brand of patriotism that needs more heroes. The three main characters in Linklater's film are ill-fitting palimpsests of those in Ashby's, however, with different names, ranks and war records. Sal (Bryan Cranston) suggests the bullish Buddusky by blowing smoke rings and lobbing empty beer cans across hotel rooms into the trash, but lacks Nicholson's fine details of impotence. Doc (Steve Carrell) is too smart to be Meadows, although both went to military jail at the same age, and Mueller the Mauler (Laurence Fishburne) does not resemble Mulhall the Mule apart from being black. The films take place in similarly framed diners, bars, waiting rooms and train carriages but are moving in different directions all along. Whereas in Ashby's film the mission is to deliver a young man to the military, in Linklater's it is to reclaim one from it: Doc's son, killed in Iraq and due to be buried in full dress uniform in Arlington National Cemetery against his father's wishes: "I am not going to bury a marine. I'm just going to bury my son." Both films are mostly "hang-outs" with three guys killing time, but whereas Ashby's film reflects on the Second World War and the Korean War and finds no subsequent moral apprentice in the years leading up to Vietnam, Linklater searches for something similar in what came after Vietnam and finds facets of veterans' pride and patriotism leaking into nostalgia for war. Both groups of men appear angry but only *The Last Detail* matches this in its form, being austere, naturalist, and abrasive, featuring outsiders who make transactional connections. *Last Flag Flying* is mannered and contained in comparison, observing the redundancy and compromise of three veterans who can barely make sense of the contracts offered to "civilians" by car hire and cellphone companies. Buddusky picks fights to keep his adrenaline up—"I *am* the motherfucking shore patrol, motherfucker!"— while Sal eats candy to stay awake.

Last Flag Flying has nothing of the spit and vinegar of *The Last Detail*, whose cold and barren urban vistas are often replaced by boxed-in domestic settings in Linklater's film, which may also be compared to the contemporary *Da 5 Bloods* (Spike Lee, 2020), wherein four black Vietnam veterans try and fail to overcome their collective trauma. Paul (Delroy Lindo) in *Da 5 Bloods* is a monument to pained ferocity and therefore much closer to Buddusky than to Sal, which suggests, in comparison with *Last Flag Flying*, a stalling of forty years and more in black America's coming to terms with the trauma of Vietnam. Indeed, this distinction underlines how the traumas of *Last Flag Flying* are settled in racially problematic ways. Firstly, because Mueller's experiences of racism are elided in a gag involving pompous Homeland Security officers, who confront him after hearing Sal jokingly mispronounce his name as Mullah. Scenes of Mueller being taken into custody and having to prove his innocence are omitted, however, as the scene of his arrest is curtailed by a cut to Sal roaring with laughter at the event's retelling. Thus, the notion that the definition of war has changed since Ashby's time from combat in a foreign land against an anonymous army to one waged against suspect Americans by Homeland Security, where even black ministers reading bibles suffer the abuse of their rights, is thus neglected. Later, black people's suffering is again neglected when Doc aims to do penance by admitting to a frail old black woman (Cicely Tyson), the mother of a fallen, fellow soldier in Vietnam, that her son's agonizing death was exacerbated by their drug-fueled negligence. Except, when confronted by her pride in her son's supposed self-sacrifice, Doc balks at hollowing her sustaining belief in her son's bravery, even though it is based on the same jingoistic fabulation of heroism that the military imposes on Doc's son. Instead, Doc defers his admission, thereby dismissing the pain of the dying soldier and postponing indefinitely the trauma of his mother, by pretending that they were indeed rescued by her son's final act of valor. Thus, the affection-image he offers her in response to his perception of her pride is both false and a genuine deferral of the defeat that his admission would provoke. Indeed, the absolution Doc seeks and defers in close-up is also granted because his symbolic act of surrender to the military fable that sustains her is transmogrified into a selfless deed for her well-being that carries a suggestion of his own redemption. Doc's redemptive arc is then completed in the scene where his sense of guilt is absolved by their black chaperone, Lance Corporal Washington (J. Quinton Johnson), who, after explaining that he lost his own father to gun violence, assures Doc that his dead son was different from him and all his fellow soldiers because his son had a happy childhood, which implies that this was due to him not being black. And the film then cuts away from the stolid Washington to show the catharsis of a close-up of Doc's teary relief. Crucially, therefore, while all three scenes approach greater traumas affecting black Americans, they defer to affection-images that deal with the concerns of white characters. *The Last Detail*, *Da 5 Bloods*, and *Last Flag Flying* all grieve, but only *Last Flag Flying* bestows relief and absolution: "We can't redo the choices we made back then."

Rescuing the coffin of Doc's son from its regimented line-up in the pristine hangar at Dover Air Force Base (as an identical coffin is wheeled into its place), Sal, Doc and Mueller turn the corpse's journey home into their final mission together and the film inverts the directionality of the odyssey traversed by Buddusky, Mule and Meadows. *The Last Detail* takes place in the interval of powerlessness between the perception of injustice and the deferral of any counteraction, where nobody is watching or waiting for an affection-image because, as Mule declares: "When you're in the Navy, shitbird, and you're in transit, nobody knows where the fuck ya are!" However, *Last Flag Flying* does fill this interval with close-ups that are the long-deferred affection-images, albeit self-pitying and mawkish: "I lost one [son]; he lost two" nods Doc to a news image of the captured Saddam Hussein, for example. Thus, whereas *The Last Detail* realizes and conveys ineffectuality, resentful compliance, defeat, and the irrelevance of an affection-image to the men's fate, *Last Flag Flying* makes an awkward pitch for consequentiality, which results in a scrambled sermon on the muddled motives of those who choose to wear a military uniform. Doc has insisted that his son be buried in civilian clothes, but the military commander Colonel Wilits (Yul Vázquez) demands the corpse be dressed in full uniform. Doc is ultimately persuaded to comply because of the likelihood that his son's old clothes will no longer fit him by Lance Corporal Washington, who is acting on orders to ensure this posthumous dress code from Colonel Wilits. Sal and Mueller then wear their old uniforms (which somehow do still fit) and turn the hometown burial into a miniature military pageant, methodically folding the American flag before passing it to Doc: "You put this somewhere and you let it remind you what was in your son's heart." Facets of patriotism are glimpsed in this scene but any overt questioning—can one serve proudly in shameful wars?—is dismissed by the final revelation that Doc's son, who Doc has already asserted "was only twenty-one; he wasn't thinking about dying," had entrusted Washington with a letter home in the event of his death in which he asks to be buried in his uniform. That this letter is only handed to Doc by Washington after the funeral denotes a needlessly belated act that, if it had happened earlier, would have annulled the film's gestures toward nonconformism from the start.

CONCLUSION

Comparison of *Last Flag Flying* with *The Last Detail* demonstrates that the little space between Ashby and Linklater that might be expected to close in this particular double bill actually gets wider in comparison of the deferral of the affection-image in Ashby's film with the affection-image that defers defeat in that of Linklater. Bear in mind, however, that Ashby was under forty when he made *The Last Detail* and Linklater was almost sixty when he made *Last Flag Flying* and that between these films are four decades and several wars. Note too that at the age of sixteen, the unruly Ashby was sent to Puget Sound Naval Academy on Bainbridge Island and "took his role as a cadet officer very seriously and was as tough on the other cadets as a staff member might have been,"[35] while Linklater went to his hometown Houston University on a football scholarship and thereafter joined what he ultimately coined as the slacker community in Austin. Also consider, therefore, that *The Last Detail* was filmed in 1972 at a time when Ashby was actively campaigning against the Nixon government that won a landslide victory buoyed by its commitment to the war in Vietnam,[36] while *Last Flag Flying* was made at the start of the Trump presidency, which suggests that Keathley's "post-traumatic cycle"[37] might indeed have been ending its second iteration in response to the attack on the World Trade Center and the protracted war in Iraq (2003–2011). In this context, *Last Flag Flying* is one of the first American films about America of the Trump era and its attempt to move past the trauma of the Vietnam War by means of reconciliation with that in Iraq is perhaps less cynical than it is weary and weighed down by Sal's recognition that "every generation has their war. Men make the wars and wars make the men. It never ends!" Indeed and in sum, while Ashby's films tended to defer defeat, postpone aging, and elide the affection-images that might have prompted an explicit reckoning with the abrogation of responsibility for either, *Last Flag Flying* deploys affection-images to reconcile with getting older and accept some responsibility for defeat. Ultimately, therefore, some semblance of closure is created, one that narrows the little space between Buddusky and Sal and between Ashby and Linklater because, as Sal states in an affection-image: "Guys like us, we take all that shit till it's a disaster. And then we're cool. The worst has happened, like we knew it would."

NOTES

1. Gilles Deleuze, *Cinema 1: The Movement-Image*, trans. Hugh Tomlinson and Barbara Habberjam (Minneapolis: University of Minnesota Press, 1997 [1983]), 61.
2. Ibid., 65.
3. Ian Mantgani, "Where to Begin with Hal Ashby," *BFI* (September 2, 2019): https://www2.bfi.org.uk/news-opinion/news-bfi/features/where-begin-hal-ashby
4. Rob Stone, *Walk, Don't Run: The Cinema of Richard Linklater* (2nd ed.) (New York: Columbia University Press, 2018), 74.
5. Christian Keathley, "Trapped in the Affection Image: Hollywood's Post-traumatic Cycle (1970–1976)," in *The Last Great American Picture Show: New Hollywood Cinema in the 1970s*, edited by Thomas Elsaesser, Alexander Horwath, and Noel King (Amsterdam: Amsterdam University Press, 2004), 293.
6. Ibid.
7. Owen Gleiberman, "Review: Richard Linklater's 'Last Flag Flying,'" *Variety* (September 28, 2017): https://variety.com/2017/film/reviews/last-flag-flying-review-richard-linklater-bryan-cranston-1202574087/
8. Darren Hughes, "Ashby, Hal," *Senses of Cinema* (February 30, 2004): https://www.sensesofcinema.com/2004/great-directors/ashby/
9. Sean Fennessey, "The Realistic Magic of Hal Ashby, the Greatest Director of the 1970s," *The Ringer* (September 6, 2018): https://www.theringer.com/movies/2018/9/6/17826818/hal-ashby-documentary-haroldmaude-last-detail-hollywood-shampoo-being-there-coming-home
10. Gilles Deleuze, *Cinema 2: The Time-Image*, trans. Hugh Tomlinson and Robert Galeta (London: Continuum, 2007 [1985]), 68.
11. Ibid., 92.
12. Thomas Elsaesser, "The Pathos of Failure: American Films in the 1970s," *Monogram* 6 (1975): 17.
13. Tom Wolfe, "The Me Decade and the Third Great Awakening," *Group and Information Studies* 1.4 (1976): 27–48.
14. Norman Mailer, "Mailer on the '70s – Decade of 'Image, Skin Flicks, and Porn,'" *U.S. News & World Report*, December 10, 1979, in Sam Wasson, *Fosse* (Boston and New York: Houghton Mifflin Harcourt, 2013).

15. Keathley, "Trapped in the Affection Image," 293.
16. Ibid.
17. Louis Schwartz, "Deleuze, Rodowick, and the Philosophy of Film," *Film-Philosophy*, 4.16 (2000): http://www.film-philosophy.com/vol4-2000/n16schwartz
18. Keathley, "Trapped in the Affection Image," 293.
19. Douglas Perry, "1980s Oregon: 17 Key Events that Defined the State During Reagan Years, From Scandals to Nu Shooz," *The Oregonian* (August 29, 2019): https://www.oregonlive.com/news/erry-2018/10/81c8bdb1174142/1980s-oregon-17-key-events-tha.html
20. Nick Dawson, *Being Hal Ashby: Life of a Hollywood Rebel* (Lexington: University Press of Kentucky, 2011), 34.
21. Stone, *Walk, Don't Run*, 17–18.
22. Keathley, "Trapped in the Affection Image," 297–98.
23. Ibid., 299.
24. Ibid., 293.
25. Jean-François Lyotard, "Acinema," in *Acinemas: Lyotard's Philosophy of Film*, edited by Graham Jones and Ashley Woodward (Edinburgh: Edinburgh University Press, 2017), 33.
26. Ibid.
27. Deleuze, *Cinema 1*, 56.
28. Oliver Lyttelton, "The Films of Hal Ashby: A Retrospective," *Indiewire* (May 6, 2011): https://www.indiewire.com/2011/05/the-films-of-hal-ashby-a-retrospective-118773/
29. Deleuze, *Cinema 1*, 67–68.
30. Ibid., 60.
31. Elsaesser, "The Pathos of Failure," 17.
32. Keathley, "Trapped in the Affection Image," 293.
33. Ibid., 304.
34. Deleuze, *Cinema 1*, 68.
35. Dawson, *Being Hal Ashby*, 19.
36. Ibid., 140.
37. Keathley, "Trapped in the Affection Image," 293.

CHAPTER 4

On Drifts and Swerves: Linklater's Love for Lacunae

Jeroen Boom

Many of Richard Linklater's films unfold like roadmaps, traveling through different landscapes and drawing assiduous attention to empty streets, apartment rooms, and urban architecture. Therefore, it comes as no surprise that we encounter the filmmaker himself in the first minutes of his cult film *Slacker* (1991) on the back seat of a bus, on the road and half asleep. After a few seconds, we see him slowly waking up, while a landscape of flickering neon billboards rushes up outside the large windows. The speed of the bus generates a feeling of fleetingness, fostering a scenery of blurry facades and urban textures. Linklater, whose character is later credited as "should have stayed at bus station," gazes at the motels and fast-food advertisements that are flashing by, his backpack laid down next to his seat, on his way to a yet unknown destination. After exchanging a bus for a cab, he starts a semi-philosophical monologue on how taking a possible "route" or "direction" always precludes taking others, how we always miss out on other "places" that conjure up entire alternative realities. This verbalized stream of thought foreshadows the structure of the film, which offers one such a route across Austin, Texas from dawn to dawn, in which the viewer hovers over its streets and parking lots in a nomadic fashion. *Slacker* maps out many of the interlaced and molecular lives that compose this college town, presenting a collection of tiny little universes, yet associates them with one another via the unpredictable movements of an itinerant and swerving camera.

Linklater's persona in *Slacker* could be taken as a metonym for a larger population of "drifting" youngsters, whose walks of life have turned into directionless wanderings. The film has often been discussed as mapping a morally bankrupt MTV generation of disconnection and moral relativism, whose members were young in the 1990s and whose attitude was one of sarcastic consumerism and ironic distance. These twentysomethings, or slackers, as many critics wrote at the time, had lost their belief in conservative middle-class values, in those master narratives and capitalist promises that did not bring them the same economic affordances as their parents benefitted from, and therefore exchanged political commitment for sarcastic disengagement.[1] At the zenith of this new cultural formation, Linklater's filmic travelogue plunges viewers into a splintered mosaic of some of these eccentric youngsters and their idiosyncratic worlds. Jeffrey Sconce, among others, firmly frames this cinematic habitat within the larger contours of a postmodern cultural dominant that was "fixat[ed]" on "quotation," "distance," and "ironic cultural consumption."[2] He situates the film within a wide range of works that all share a similar ethos against the "dumbness" of mainstream cinema and opt for "fatalis[t], relativis[t] and, yes, even nihilis[t]" tonal registers. The slackers in the film indeed evoke the postmodern prose of Kurt Vonnegut, Bret Easton Ellis, and Douglas Coupland, being part of a disaffected post-baby-boom generation, bored stiff and immunized against the allure of idealism.

Yet, as someone born in the early 1990s, growing up in the internet age and writing amid pandemic lockdowns, I find a sense of energetic optimism in Linklater portrayal of Austin. There is a sense of communal belonging, an enthusiasm for daily public life, in which human contact happens on the streets, where one might bump into strangers and have a nice chat.[3] It is this particular creation of a vibrant shared space, formed within and through the swerves of the camera, that demonstrates the intimate geographical bond between the filmmaker and the area, in which drifting does not connote a sense of indifference but an urge to let go of known terrain and discover new grounds. I suggest in this chapter that Linklater engages in a cartographic practice that is based on nomadic movement, drawing a map that has no margins or directions, in which the fabric of the urban landscape appears to be "stronger" than the stories of its individual inhabitants. It is for this reason that this chapter considers Linklater as a *topophilic* and *cartophilic* filmmaker, motivated and impelled by a strong passion for, or rather, love of, mapping place.

Anchoring the film in the theoretical climate of its time, this chapter—staying close to the swerving camera it describes—meanders through a myriad of voices and situates *Slacker*, and Linklater's cartographic topophilia, in the context of broader postmodern discourses, zooming in on, among other things, Gilles Deleuze and Félix Guattari's nomadic thinking, Giuliana Bruno's voyageuristic cartographies, and Jean-François Lyotard's discursive archipelago.[4] Although vastly different in their critical purposes, I take these postmodern theories as indications of a cartographic shift, in which places are reconsidered as open and dynamic events rather than enclosed territories, in which mapping is rethought as an experiential and subjective practice rather than an objective and scientific instrument. The map that Linklater sketches out, as the upcoming pages will demonstrate, dovetails with these postmodern tendencies, as it favors movement over stasis, multiple directions over linear progress, nomads over dwellers, erratic swerves over straight lines. Postmodernism here functions as a discursive framework to situate *Slacker*'s wandering spirit against its usual indictment of apathetic disengagement and to relocate it within a more amorous discourse of nomadic liberation. In a humble but impossible effort to map the wide range of Linklater's work, I will conclude by putting extra emphasis on the figure of the nomadic swerve as a metaphor for his oeuvre: an endless deviation from singular generic frameworks or pre-existing categorizations, a refusal to lay down roots or to stay in one place.

CINEMATIC NOMADISM—LINKLATER AS PASSENGER-DIRECTOR

While Linklater's work has often been discussed in terms of time, both as a thematic and formal concern, his memorable urban geographies have received less critical attention.[5] Besides the depiction of Austin in *Slacker*, and in *Waking Life* (2001), other examples may include the focus on the infinite facades of suburban America, as traversed in the opening moments of *SubUrbia* (1996) and *Boyhood* (2014), or the romanticization of Vienna in *Before Sunrise* (1995) and Paris in *Before Sunset* (2004), in which two lovers wander through the urban landscapes while their conversations take similar unpredictable swerves, ending with a series of returns at night to the then desolated squares and streets we have visited before together with them. Although Linklater's later films are far more conventional in their narrative structure than his first independent ones, what these depictions have in common is that they stem from a fascination with the fabric of open roads and infinite streets. Because we, as spectators, always travel through them without staying long, these urban spaces seem to be borderless, endless even. Their frontiers seem to move along with us as we voyage onwards.

Linklater's breakthrough film *Slacker* can be seen as an early manifestation of this cinematic nomadism. The film is organized according to a vagabond camera that drifts in an almost continuous motion through the urban fabric of Austin, eagerly traversing from one site to another. In his distinctive documentation of a directionless generation of youths, he crosses a great number of bored students, armchair intellectuals, and anticorporate non-believers. The nomadic camera takes a random route and draws a chaotic map while recording the conversations and interactions between these personas who happen to meet each other along its random paths. Rather than granting one person or a couple of people most of its narrative time, the film revolves around a continuous chain of events whose interrelation is defined by short encounters with and between a multitude of characters. In a continuous and restless vein, the film keeps shifting its focus from stringing along with one (group of) individual(s) to pursue other figures who have just sauntered into the scene, thwarting the possibility for linear narrative progress, against the conventions of causality in mainstream narrative cinema in the Classical Hollywood tradition. It is because of this lack of dramatic tension or coherent action that it is space and rhythm, rather than a plot-based arc, that propel the film forward.[6] The nickname of the film's script, "the roadmap," further stresses this cartographic interest in places, roads, and landscapes.

Linklater indulged his nomadic passion for the first time in his *It's Impossible To Learn To Plow By Reading Books* (1988), a student film which can be seen as a prequel to *Slacker*, in which the filmmaker travels across the United States, waiting on bus stops and sleeping in trains. It is a particular cartographic travelogue, one that is reminiscent of some of the road movies of Wim Wenders and the travel diaries of Jean Baudrillard, mapping the nondescript spaces in-between Montana, San Francisco, Houston, and Austin.[7] In a series of long takes, trains, buses, and automobiles move him in his desire to travel, voyaging through a wasteland of neon-lit roadsides and gas stations. The film is not eager to arrive at a destination, but finds its solace in transitions and movement, in the infinite possibilities and endless encounters on the road. It is for this reason that Rob Stone describes Linklater as "a nomadic subject," since his first film is "less concerned with departures and arrivals than it is with the in-between times and spaces."[8] Captivated by the in-betweenness of these non-places, *It's Impossible To Learn To Plow By Reading Books* shows us Linklater as a travelling passenger-director, with a bag on his back and a camera in his hand, mapping his itineraries and embracing a notion of nomadism that will continue to affect his next film.

In the words of Stone, within the span of the filmmaker's career, Austin has proven "to be not just a location," as it also serves as "a representation of an alternative state of mind and lifestyle."[9] The college town of Austin is presented in *Slacker* as a patchwork of free spirits, college drop-offs, and anticonformist bohemians, who are stuck in a limbo where anything comes and goes, hanging around on the streets and spending their last money on drinking beers in bars. Stone asserts that "[o]ther film locations such as Vienna and Paris are partly metaphors for what Linklater found and founded in Austin, albeit with a dressing of old European cinephilia."[10] The filmmaker's characters find themselves in environments that, as in Céline's (Julie Delpy) description of a Seurat painting in *Before Sunrise*, "are stronger than the people," often in moments when the camera takes off to go from one scene to the next, or one conversation to the other, when his (sub)urban landscapes are freed from diegetic weight, rendered autonomous and independent from eventhood. His work abides in the in-between and the passage, always roaming and straying off the beaten path, crafted with a meticulous attention to exterior space. It is instructive, therefore, that Linklater has taken on the role of passenger or traveler in many of his other films, sometimes in a literal sense, as in *Waking Life* or *It's Impossible To Learn To Plow By Reading Books*, but more often in a more metaphorical manner, as someone whose cinema emerges from traveling, drifting, and swerving.

For Gilles Deleuze and Félix Guattari, swerving figures as a feature of nomadic thought, preferring erratic vectors over axioms and straight lines. Like the continuous movement of the camera in *Slacker*, the nomad travels from destination to destination, but privileges the spaces and routes between these positions. This interstitial space is "rhizomatic," because it:

> does not designate a localizable relation going from one thing to the other and back again, but a perpendicular direction, a transversal movement that sweeps one and the other away, a stream without beginning or end that undermines its banks and picks up speed in the middle.[11]

Against travel as a form of territorialization or mapping as a stratifying practice, the cartographic endeavors of nomads resist closure and fixation, focusing on the affective and swerving itineraries between topological points. Linklater, as a nomadic director, goes astray to drag us into the movement and flow of the in-between, creating relational routes among a series of micro events. It is in these transitional "intermezzos,"[12] when the camera swerves from one encounter to the next, that landscapes present themselves outside the constrains of narrative signification. The nomadic swerve thus initiates topophilic contemplation and liberates landscape from its subordination to action. It initiates a horizontalization of space that makes every element in the frame of equal importance, robbing the viewer of a stable ground to hold on to and encouraging them to diverge their focus over the screen.[13] This shift obscures the thin line between fore- and background and attunes our vision to a more mundane and democratized perspective, one that embraces a loss of clear divisions and directions. The filmmaker's nomadic drive even guides us, at the end of the film, into an abstract space of color patches and circular shapes without horizon, when a group of slackers start messing around with a Super 8 mm camera, which swerves, tilts, and overturns, and is eventually thrown off a cliff. During this point-of-view footage, in this moment of disorientation, our eyes are in constant motion in order to get hold of the continuous amorphous transformations on screen.[14] The film thus ends in an open space without limits, a diagram of pure abstraction and nomadic movement, a teeming void in-between axiomatic matrixes of meaning.

CARTOGRAPHIC TOPOPHILIA—LINKLATER'S LOVE FOR LACUNAE

Slacker feels like a tour that never ends, in a college town that has as many faces as it has buildings. Linklater's film is not about *being in* Austin, but rather about *moving through* its many changing landscapes. The nomadic camera swerves across squares and streets in a series of unhinged encounters, forcing viewers to let go of linear narrative cohesion and voyage with its unpredictable zigzagging movements as it surveys their spatial textures. *Slacker* features numerous locations, such as gritty nightclubs, busy lunchrooms, messy apartments, a ruined police station, an empty parking lot, and a stuffy bookshop, but for most of its duration interactions take place on the streets between them, among graffiti-covered walls, and along semi-overgrown driveways. These streets accommodate urban dwellers who are always walking from one place to another, sometimes leading us inside their homes, sometimes directing us to some other souls chattering in a bar. At one time the camera captures a bunch of kids kicking a soda machine, while at another it follows an old man wandering and recording some of his most precious life lessons on a tape recorder. The film seems to draw a never-to-be-finished map, postponing sketching out its contours, always driven by a curiosity about what comes next. Linklater's cinema is motivated by a cartographic interest: his moving images are maps in motion, explorations of shifting environments, careful inspections of moving landscapes. The filmmaker's wandering cartographies acknowledge and define cinema as a form of swerving and affective navigation, which points to a cine-cartographic continuum that film theorists such as Giuliana Bruno and Tom Conley propose in their work. In contrast to the assumption that the modus operandi of these types of representation are too far apart, Bruno and Conley argue that, like cartographers, filmmakers construct particular territories and topographies, mapping clusters of signs and bringing them in relation to one another through motions and movements.[15]

If the real has become deceiving in postmodern times, the map as a passive and objective instrument to extricate hidden universal meanings has lost its unrivaled reputation and given way to a more mobile and somatic practice of mapping.[16] As an elaborate response to this, in her book *Atlas of Emotions* Bruno reads cinema as moving and affective cartographies: "its haptic way of site-seeing turns pictures into an architecture, transforming them into a geography of lived, and living, space."[17] Bruno theorizes spectatorial emotional investment in defiance of a Lacanian tradition in film theory, in which a fixation on the disembodied gaze makes the viewer a motionless voyeur.[18] In her account of the filmic image as an affective and visceral experience, she proposes instead the figure of the *voyageur*, who maps and wanders, while they, in the words of film theorist Eugenie Brinkema, are "moving and being emotionally moved."[19] Immersed in affective movement, the voyageur problematizes cartographic distinctions between the panoptic strategies of "maps" and the embodied tactics of "tours," between the fixedness of "seeing" and the stirring motions of "going."[20] Within the cartographic-filmic connection, as Bruno argues, the opposition between map and tour fades: "both are a form of architectural narration[, as] seeing is going."[21] Following this figure of the voyageur, Linklater does not resign himself to a form of cold clinical observation, but maps out a cosmos of affects and sensibilities on an ever-receding horizon. The voyageur critiques orthodox descriptions of topophilia, such as the original definition by geographer Yi-Fu Tuan, whose definition was based on static matrixes and fixated categories, founded on a conception of place as bounded and inert.[22] The voyageur, however, suggests a postmodern mode of cartographic topophilia that assumes a definition of place that is more mobile and indeterminate, not cast in stone nor held together by borders. Linklater's love of mapping place, in that sense, is structured around the yet unknown and always to come. It is, following Bruno's more nomadic definition, "driven by a passion for mapping that is itself [. . .] routed not on wholeness but on the fabric of lacunae."[23] Austin exists in his film as a prism of evanescent social and spatial configurations, as a site whose many faces can only be glimpsed at while being on the move. The voyageur-filmmaker does not take time to linger or dwell on characters or conversations but is always moving onwards in a never-to-be-satisfied urge to fill in the ever-emerging blank gaps on the map.

From this cartographic and topophilic perspective, *Slacker* produces a map without coordinates and inscriptions, a map whose street names are erased and whose edges are forever expanding. When reading this map, it is impossible to situate oneself in it, or imagine oneself within a larger terrain. There are no recognizable landmarks, nor identifiable locations that the film returns to.[24] Navigation here is a form of topological intuition.[25] Jay Watson has compared *Slacker*'s landscape to what Fredric Jameson terms a hyperspace, a confusing and dizzying space symptomatic of postmodern urbanism, which induces a sense of fragmentation and an experience of schizophrenia.[26] When watching the film, as Jon Radwan agrees, it is impossible for viewers to grasp their position on a static map, as this "slacker space" can only be represented in constant movement: "their space is not on a map with clear relationships and distances between landmarks."[27] Linklater never lingers long enough to provide a wider perspective of the film's urban landscapes or the characters within them, but immerses one in a drift without overview or closure. In one of the first minutes of the film, for example, the camera runs into an unknown woman stretched out in the middle of a crossroad with her eyes closed and her groceries scattered on the street. It remains unclear if she is still alive or what had happened to her a few moments before our encounter. In contrast to Classical Hollywood's rules and methods of holding the viewer in suspense, as opposed to lingering long on the drama, the camera pulls back from the scene and starts to track a young man on his way home. It never returns to the woman on the crossroad again, denying any form of closure. Another instance of a swerve shirking dramatic momentum occurs when the camera enters the apartment of someone who has just gone missing and left a collection of postcards, hinting that he went to Europe and after some time will return to commit an act of nuclear terrorism.

Whereas in a Classical Hollywood narrative structure the film would be prone to dwell on these strange happenings, his housemates do not seem to be impressed after this discovery and the camera soon wanders off to follow one of them, leaving the suspicious case for what it is. In this manner, *Slacker* constitutes a chain of unpredictable swerves and unforeseen deviations, constantly taking on new directions and following a different course in moments when the viewer least expects it.

The swerving camera in *Slacker* causes an experience of disorientation at every turn, but also retains a strong democratic distribution of space that creates a feeling of freedom and a sense of openness. As Radwan notes, characters are never cooped up or pushed into cramped frames, they are at any time free to exit or enter, always positioned as equal elements within their compositions.[28] The film's sporadic cutting, numerous long shots, and countless instances of deep focus create the sense of a continuous space,[29] while the permanent presence of off-screen background noise and chatter makes us aware of the restless and invisible flow of life that lies outside our view. These stylistic and narrative choices make the spaces traversed in *Slacker* contribute to the creation of a more mobile and transitive map, one that never creates borders and whose ink is never dried up, one that never gives in to stratification or settles for the tendencies of territorialization. The film is a cartographic endeavor that attests to a more flowing and nomadic form of topophilia. This form of spatial desire is different from nostalgic yearnings for a return to a static, physical, or unattainable home—especially, as Bruno writes, "when [nostalgia] is used to advocate univocal attachment to one's land of origin"[30]—but resides in crossings and passages, in being on the move. In the words of Radwan, this "[f]reedom of movement can be read as a central metaphor for slacker culture as a whole,"[31] resonating with Stone's observation that "the key to understanding how meaning is constructed in the cinema of Linklater is found by going slacker-like with the flow."[32] It is thus a certain floating aimlessness or wandering spirit that defines Linklater's topophilic writing of place. This slacker-like drifting here does not connote or metaphorize an apathetic disengagement from *any* political or moral investment, but, as Sconce contends, "it is a retreat from the moral map of [a dominant] social formation" in order to look for "a new terrain."[33] As the slackers in the film refuse to resign to the social order of their parents and always look for other ways of living, embracing the possibilities for unlikely interactions, there is also a sense of optimism in the film's construction of the swerve as an act of resistance against marked out routes, opening up to the hidden multiplicities of urban space.

ARCHIPELAGO—ISLANDS OF MEANING

In tension with the fleeting landscapes described in the previous section, Linklater's cartographic topophilia also grounds his characters in their environments, in their own milieus, their own apartments or favorite spots, which serve as metonymic manifestations of their quirky inner worlds. Many of the youngsters in *Slacker* are obsessed with collections and conspiracies, surrounding themselves with maps, books, or television screens. For example, when one of these characters, named "Conspiracy A-Go-Go Author," sneaks into the scene and starts bothering a girl with his JFK assassination conspiracies, he finds himself in a local bookshop immersed with books and theories on the controversial topic, ultimately leaving the store after scoring a magazine that almost completes his collection. Or, some moments later, when the camera encounters a video junkie in his apartment, showing how he has been living in simulation by surrounding himself with television screens, bombarding him with an abundance of euphoric affects—images of violence, sex, suffering, and death that demonstrate how, in a Baudrillardian fashion, an "immanent surface" of "obscenity" and "ecstasy" has substituted more traditional notions such as "seduction" and "passion."[34] In this vein, Linklater maps the interior worlds of his characters onto the architectural interiors they inhabit, mediating between brain and bricks, soul and setting.[35] But these architectonic hints are clues to nowhere: characters are hard to pin down because their inner worlds are made up of incredulous conspiracies and simulacra surface effects. By tracing the conversations of its characters, only getting bits and pieces, *Slacker* rather spans a dense web of pop cultural references and allusions to media-driven spectacles, ranging from sitcoms and celebrities to the moon landing and the JFK assassination.

Many slackers in the film are surrounded by their own obsessions and taxonomies, creating their own little islands of meaning. It is as if, in the words of film critic Chris Walters, these youngsters have been "atomized [. . .] into subcultures of which they are the only member, free radicals randomly seeking an absent center as the clock beats out its senseless song."[36] These individual subcultures are among other things materialized into the obscure merchandise that they wear, often with an ironic or cynical attitude, such as anti-establishment slogans or cartoonish jokes printed on T-shirts.[37] This sense of cultural and political fragmentation also translates into the ways in which characters speak, always delivering passionate monologues in which nobody really interferes.[38] They are stuck in the echo chambers of their own self-righteousness, bound to repetition, like the traumatized woman at one of the coffee bars, "Traumatized Yacht Owner," who keeps repeating the same maxim about the sin of harassing women, or like the video tape that keeps looping the same childhood memory in the apartment of a man credited as "Roadkill."[39] This splintering of a cohesive master narrative into a tombola of little fragments, this sense of ever moving without knowing where to go, this removal of the epistemological ground beneath our feet, can feel as a loss of meaning (as in the pessimistic prose of Baudrillard) or as a liberation of the subject (in the affirmative spirit of Deleuze).

This loss of a single, all-encompassing narrative does not mean however that these slackers surrender themselves to live but nihilistic isolated lives and therefore do not long for connection. Although their collections and monologues suggest a sense of fragmentation and intellectual imprisonment, they are at the same time free to leave their own built milieus, their homes and their interiors, to visit other places. The "Conspiracy A-Go-Go Author" character, for instance, leaves his beloved bookshop after his friendly interlocutor has left the conversation and walks into someone else who is tinkering with his car to again start talking about JFK-related conspiracy theories. Even though he seems not be interested in his blather, having his gaze fixed at the engine, the young man remains friendly and answers him politely. These short moments of encounter create a patchwork of loose connections between figures. Even the video junkie is not limited by his cramped self-created milieu, as, in the words of Radwan, he is able to "guide his own journey across the myriad potential tracks of life, [. . .] hold[ing] the remote in his hand."[40] Against the disaffection and anomie that has often been ascribed to the film, its cartographic writing seems to embrace the paradoxical nature of postmodern life and the unbridgeable epistemological differences that come with it. Austin seems to be carved up into a collection of tiny little universes, inhabited by fanatics caught in the trenches of their own truths, but these worlds coexist and can be traversed. Together with the continuous flow and openness that the long takes create, always pointing or turning to off-screen space, the willingness of characters to meet with others and strangers produces a sense of enthusiasm and freedom which makes possible those encounters that form the dramatic foundation of the film and constitutes the public arena that it traverses.

This paradoxical double bind of freedom and isolation is formalized in the film's open frames vis-à-vis its boxed aspect ratio. The film's visual compositions never feel cramped or tight, always suggesting open continuous space, but these are at the same time always boxed in an encapsulating rectangular square. The film could have been shot in a wider scope to emphasize open and empty spaces, allowing the urban environment to be liberated from compositional constraints, but is instead shot in the more classic 1.37:1 or 4:3 ratio to focus on characters who fill in the frame in medium shots. People flow in and out of the screen, but always balance the composition in the end, always filling in the hollow space left behind during the transition from one character to another.[41] At the end of the film, for example, when night has turned into dawn, a young girl is about to leave on-screen space, walking closer to the edges of the frame; an old man mumbling in a tape recorder passes her and takes in her previous position, after which the camera pans away again to start following a truck driving past, moving from the margins of the screen to its center. It is an endeavor to halt and enclose, indeed to taxonomize, that which is always open and forever flowing. In this effort, the boxed frame also duplicates the TV screen, sometimes also made explicit when the film shows the pixelated images of a switched-on television set, filling in and doubling the frame, reflecting on what Guattari has termed "the fix of television"[42] or what Baudrillard called the "dissolution of TV in life [and the] dissolution of life in TV,"[43] in which the televisual stream is confused with the flow of life, reducing the real to a simulacrum of free-floating signifiers.

The camera paves its way across different boxed-in islands of meaning, never staying long enough to ground or find its rest, never preferring one broken narrative over the other, always swerving to the next. On both a formal and thematic level, therefore, the film is a literalization of Jean-François Lyotard's description of the discursive archipelago, a cartographic image of a group of isolated islands that a captain sails between without setting foot on land. Lyotard uses this metaphor to illustrate how with the repudiation and dethroning of grand narratives, with the waning status of self-evident and collectively assumed foundations of universal truths, the postmodern subject is torn between a diverse surfeit of different and incomplete micro narratives and epistemological standpoints. "Each genre of discourse would be like an island," he writes:

> the faculty of judgement would be at least in part, like an admiral or like a provisioner of ships who would launch expeditions from one island to the next, intended to present to one island what was found (or invented . . .) in the other, and which might serve the former as an 'as-if intuition' with which to validate it.[44]

To navigate the heterogenous raffle of narratives and language games in the postmodern moment, the ship in Lyotard's metaphor tries to bridge the oceanic separation between these islands and to chart their differences, but is always caught in the middle of them, unable to extrapolate or assume a wider panoptic perspective. The camera in *Slacker*, in other words, takes on the role of a captain moving between positions without choosing to stay or throw out an anchor.

Transposing this Lyotardian metaphor of islands and a ship to television channels and a remote control, Linklater's macrocosmic mosaic mirrors the infrastructure of a multi-channel televisual stream. In the paratext of his later published "roadmap" and transcript screenplay, the filmmaker defines a "slacker" as someone who is "floating from school to street to bookstore to movie theatre with a certain uncertainty," which is "like TV channel-cruising": there is "no plot, no tragic flaws, no resolution, just mastering the moment, pushing forward, full of sound and fury, full of life signifying everything on any given day."[45] In an interview with Marc Savlov, in a similar vein, Linklater notes that "*Slacker* was that kind of film from the generation that was probably the first to have the TV remote," one that started to "[create their] own narratives by watching five minutes of this and then one minute of that and then seven minutes of this."[46] This mode of restless "channel surfing," this postmodern practice of sailing and zapping, assumes a form of mapping and cartographic production which rejects coherent or overarching geographies, but offers itineraries defined by sudden swerves and unexpected deviations. In the formulation of Lawrence Grossberg, echoing Deleuze and Guattari's writings on nomadism, television points to a kind of subjectivity that "functions as, and is articulated out of, a nomadic wandering through ever-changing positions and apparatuses," one that "is constantly remade, reshaped as a mobilely situated set of vectors in a fluid context."[47] This form of televisual nomadism, which structures and drives the film, stirs up an urge for the yet-to-come and the not-yet-been, mapping and zapping between enclaves of meaning without taking the time or lingering too long.

CONCLUSION—A CINEMA THAT SWERVES

Against a definition of *topos* in topophilia as an inanimate and pre-established spatial constellation, like in its lower-budget prequel, *Slacker* favors moving through landscapes and therefore refuses to define place as such an enclosed essence. Within the context of the film, place is revalorized and rethought as unsettled, versatile, and processual, resisting stability or dwelling, escaping determinate conceptions, and therefore destabilizing its traditional definition as a locus of meaning.[48] In other words, as opposed to considering maps as static and definite rationalities, *Slacker* is made of errant and non-hierarchical cartographies, founded on the unpredictable nature of swerving wanderings and sudden deviations. Linklater's cartographic endeavor does not constitute a rigid and resolute map, whose grids and lines are perpetuated for good, but engages itself in a constant process of sketching out routes, which become and suspend, but never to the point of completion. I have argued that, structured like a rhizome à la Deleuze and Guattari, as an indication of a postmodern interest in more fluid and flowing cartographies, this fuzzy map has no limits and may unfold in every possible direction. What holds this cartographic film together, is a slacker "atmosphere" or "vibe," an assemblage of resonating sensibilities and transient affects that defines a day and night in the college town of Austin, a prevalent mood distributed among characters and their filmic milieus, irreducible to individual articulations, but made visceral through the many relations that these swerves constitute.

True to the splintered epistemologies of postmodernism, many characters cling to their own islands of meaning and truth, but when the camera leaves them in medias res to invest in other figures walking around, its swerve associates them with one another, stressing that their sharing of the same public space accommodates but also goes beyond individual experiences. Although the encounters between these characters are brief and ephemeral, there is a co-presence that is felt both by the viewer and the slackers, who wander and wonder who is about to cross the street this time. The swerve creates relational vectors that are loose but nonetheless affective ties that create a common ground between characters, as it draws attention to small moments of spatial nearness or with-ness. The camera does not dwell on individual lives, always disrupting a narrative or divesting a conversation of its context, but it rather weaves a plethora of voices into an open and equalizing assemblage. I took the swerve in this chapter as an archetypal postmodern figure that resists striation and territorialization, but also as a democratizing force that creates the conditions for a shared public arena in which slackers can express their answers to the postmodern loss of meaning. In swerving from one position to the other, the film skims a multitude of possible realities and truths without granting a privilege to one of them.

The topophilic metaphors that I used in this chapter—swerving, mapping, cruising, sailing, and zapping—all indicate a sense of spatial curiosity, a nomadic impulse to hop and wander from place to place. In my view, these swerving metaphors prove to be apt descriptions of Linklater's individual films within the larger context of his entire filmic landscape and the clear cinematic course that he resists to follow. His inclination to escape from the pigeonhole of stylistic auteurism makes his work swerve and roam, never truly belonging to a coherent cluster or generic framework, always somewhat out of place. While zigzagging between Indie and mainstream cinema, his work covers a wide range of different projects, including among others a low-budget travelogue, a three-part romance in different cities, a philosophical hybrid between motion picture and animation, a studio comedy about an unorthodox school teacher, and a coming-of-age drama following a child becoming a teenager, and drawing inspiration from directors as diverse as Chantal Akerman, James Benning, Robert Bresson, and Martin Scorsese.[49] Except for some recurrent cast members (such as Ethan Hawke and Jack Black) or motifs (like characters taking long walks and playing pinball), it is difficult to discern patterns and connections between these works. Also, within the contours of one single film, in this case *Slacker*, which has been considered an important voice to a pessimistic postmodern generation, the filmmaker strolls around the boxes that have been ascribed to him. The film at once captures the lives of wandering slackers and their ironic attitudes, sometimes fitting the frame through which this "disillusioned" and "nihilistic" generation has often been described, while also portraying their anarchic spirit, their energetic willingness to share ideas, and drift to establish meaningful contact. I argue therefore that it is the swerve itself that defines Linklater's cinema, a continuous deviation from expectations and anticipated directions, a cartographic urge to always move away from taken-for-granted positions and take novel routes.

NOTES

1. For an overview of some of these voices, such as Douglas Coupland and David Foster Wallace, see, among others, Jeffrey Sconce, "Irony, Nihilism and the New American 'Smart' Film," *Screen* 43:4 (2002).
2. Sconce, "Irony, Nihilism and the New American 'Smart' Film," 368, 356.
3. Rob Stone makes a similar observation in his book on Linklater, in which he writes that the streets in his cinema accommodate potential spiritual encounters, also his discussions of Guy Debord's dérive and James Joyce's *Ulysses* in connection to *Slacker* are important here, see: Rob Stone, *The Cinema of Richard Linklater: Walk, Don't Run* (New York: Columbia University Press, 2013), 29.
4. In that sense, this chapter functions as a map in and of itself, offering different trajectories and possible entryways with every endnote.
5. Theorists and critics that have discussed Linklater's work in relation to time include, but are not limited to, Aaron Cutler, Ellen Grabiner, David T. Johnson, James MacDowell, Hans Maes, Adrian Martin, Erick Neher, Rob Stone, Katrien Schaubroeck, and Marya Schechtman.
6. This contrasts with Linklater's later multi-character narratives, which all tend to be more linear and conventional in their organizational form.
7. Apart from Wenders, Stone also mentions Rainer Werner Fassbinder and Jim Jarmusch as the forerunners of "the bleak aesthetics of displacement and dislocation" that Linklater tries to capture in his nomadic film; see *The Cinema of Richard Linklater*, 20.
8. Stone, *The Cinema of Richard Linklater*, 20.
9. Ibid., 4.
10. Ibid., 5.
11. Gilles Deleuze and Félix Guattari, *Thousand Plateaus: Capitalism and Schizophrenia*, trans by Brian Massumi (Minneapolis: University of Minnesota Press, 1987), 25.
12. Ibid.
13. For more on the distinction between setting "as the location for some unfolding action" and landscape "as a space of aesthetic contemplation," see Martin Lefebvre, "Introduction," in *Landscape and Film*, edited by Martin Lefebvre (New York and London: Routledge, 2006), xviii.
14. For more on nomadic art, haptic vision, and the "scanning" gaze, see Jay Hetrick, "What is Nomad Art? A Benjaminian Reading of Deleuze's Riegl," *Deleuze Studies* 6:1 (2012): 35; or Laura U. Marks, *The Skin of the Film: Intercultural Cinema, Embodiment, and the Senses* (Durham, NC and London: Duke University Press, 2000).
15. Tom Conley, *Cartographic Cinema* (Minneapolis and London: University of Minnesota Press, 2007).
16. For a more in-depth philosophical and historical contextualization of this postmodern cartographic shift, see Peta Mitchell, *Cartographic Strategies of Postmodernity: The Figure of the Map in Contemporary Theory and Fiction* (New York and London: Routledge, 2008).
17. Giuliana Bruno, *Atlas of Emotions: Journeys in Art, Architecture, and Film* (London and New York: Verso, 2002), 9.
18. Eugenie Brinkema describes this figure as an important conceptualization of embodied spectatorship in her genealogy of affect theories vis-à-vis close reading within film studies; see Eugenie Brinkema, *The Forms of the Affects* (Durham, NC and London: Duke University Press, 2014), 29. In an interview with Jiří Anger and Tomáš Jirsa, however, she attempts to release Jacques Lacan's legacy from its connotations with the "cold analytic structures of perversity and desire" and redirect attention to the prominent place of affect

in his psychoanalytic work, see: Eugenie Brinkema, "We Never Took Deconstruction Seriously Enough (On Affects, Formalism, and Film Theory): An Interview with Eugenie Brinkema," interviewed by Jiří Anger and Tomáš Jirsa, *Illuminace* 31:1 (2019): 70.
19. Ibid.: 29.
20. Ibid.: 245.
21. Bruno, *Atlas of Emotions*, 245.
22. Yi-Fu Tuan, *Topophilia: A Study of Environmental Perception, Attitudes, and Values* (New York: Columbia University Press, 1990 [1974]), 4; in Bruno, *Atlas of Emotions*, 354.
23. Bruno, *Atlas of Emotions*, 354.
24. Jay Watson, "Mapping Out a Postsouthern Cinema: Three Contemporary Films," in *American Cinema and the Southern Imaginary*, edited by Deborah E. Barker and Kathryn McKee (Athens and London: The University of Georgia Press, 2011), 226.
25. More on intuition in relation to time see Stone's discussions of Linklater and the philosophies of Henri Bergson.
26. Watson, "Mapping Out a Postsouthern Cinema," 224, 231.
27. Jon Radwan, "Generation X and Postmodern Cinema: Slacker," *Post-Script: Essays in Film and the Humanities* 19:2 (2000): 39.
28. Radwan, "Generation X and Postmodern Cinema: Slacker," 39.
29. For more on "open style," see: Radwan, "Generation X and Postmodern Cinema: Slacker," 40.
30. Bruno, *Atlas of Emotions*, 355.
31. Radwan, "Generation X and Postmodern Cinema: Slacker," 38.
32. Stone, *The Cinema of Richard Linklater*, 249.
33. Sconce, "Irony, Nihilism and the New American 'Smart' Film," 367–369.
34. Jean Baudrillard, *The Ecstasy of Communication*, trans by Bernard Schütze and Caroline Schütze (Los Angeles, CA: Semiotext(e), 2012 [1987]).
35. Giuliana Bruno writes about a similar kind of connection between "the architectonics of character" and "[the] architecture or landscape" in relation to the cinema of Michelangelo Antonioni, see Bruno, *Atlas of Emotions*, 97.
36. Chris Walters, "*Slacker*: Freedom's Just Another Word for Nothing to Do," *The Criterion Collection*, September 13, 2004: https://www.criterion.com/current/posts/1059-slacker-freedom-s-just-another-word-for-nothing-to-do
37. Douglas Kellner writes that these clothes "produce meaning, pleasure, and identity in [the] lives [of these slackers]," see: Douglas Kellner, *Media Culture Cultural Studies, Identity and Politics between the Modern and the Postmodern* (London and New York: Routledge, 1995), 140.
38. For David T. Johnson, rather than indications of self-absorption, these "unbroken monologues" point to the "ephemeral orality of arguments, reflections, rants, and other hypotheses" which can be seen as "a celebration of the present moment" because "these monologues are lost the second they are spoken," see: David T. Johnson, *Richard Linklater* (Urbana, Chicago, and Springfield: University of Illinois Press, 2012), 23.
39. Lesley Speed uses these examples to demonstrate how in *Slacker* mobility is "an ironic metaphor for existence as stasis," in "The Possibilities of Roads Not Taken: Intellect and Utopia in the Films of Richard Linklater," *Journal of Popular Film and Television* 35:3 (2007): 103. More on these monologues as a form of postmodern "relativism and egalitarianism," see Radwan, "Generation X and Postmodern Cinema: Slacker," 37.
40. Radwan, "Generation X and Postmodern Cinema: Slacker," 46.
41. Jon Radwan attributes this "choice [to] maintain character presence in the center of the screen" to a "non-judgmental camera attitude" in which "the viewer [is left] to decide in what manner to evaluate the given character", in "Generation X and Postmodern Cinema: Slacker," 39.

42. Félix Guattari, *The Three Ecologies*, trans. Ian Pinder and Paul Sutton (London and New Brunswick, NJ: The Athlone Press, 2000 [1989]), 42.
43. Jean Baudrillard, *Simulacra and Simulation*, trans. Sheila Faria Glaser (Ann Arbor: The University of Michigan Press, 1994 [1981]), 30.
44. Jean-François Lyotard, *The Differend: Phrases in Dispute*, trans. Georges Van Den Abbeele (Minneapolis: University of Minnesota Press, 1988 [1983]), 130–131.
45. Richard Linklater, *Slacker* (New York: St. Martin's Press, 1992).
46. Marc Savlov, "Slack to the Future: Austin Gets Older, *Slacker* Stays Forever Young," *The Austin Chronicle*, January 21, 2011: https://www.austinchronicle.com/screens/2011-01-21/slack-to-the-future/
47. Lawrence Grossberg, "The In-Difference of Television," *Screen* 28:2 (1987): 38–39.
48. For a more substantiated history of the notion of place, in particular in relation to terms such as "topos," "locus," and "cosmos," see: Edward S. Casey, *The Fate of Place: A Philosophical History* (Berkeley and Los Angeles, CA: University of California Press, 1997).
49. For a full list of intertexts, allusions, and inspirations see Johnson, *Richard Linklater*, 6–7.

PART 2

Genre as Means

CHAPTER 5

Richard Linklater and the Field of American Dreams[1]

Timotheus Vermeulen

This chapter considers the use of baseball in the oeuvre of Linklater. It is concerned specifically with the function of the game, its players, and its culture in the director's two sports genre movies *Bad News Bears* (2005) and *Everybody Wants Some!!* (2016); but it also takes into account its presentation in other films. Drawing on close textual analysis, cultural history, and critical theory, the chapter argues that baseball—which Linklater himself played at college level before a heart problem ended his chances of going pro (if that was really ever an option at all)—is used to contemplate both the joys and the traumas of youthful, male, and mostly white comradery in U.S. culture; and, conversely, to reflect on an American culture historically dominated by white old "boys." Indeed, if baseball is frequently said to be a symbol of the American Dream,[2] Linklater suggests it is a rather distinct and exclusive one.

"A METAPHOR FOR EVERYTHING"

Few contemporary directors are associated with baseball as much as Richard Linklater, the exceptions being, perhaps, his compatriots Ken Burns and James Benning. Strictly speaking, however, only one or two of Linklater's movies could be argued to be "baseball movies," movies whose focus lies with the athletic pursuits of a player or team (often against all odds).[3] The first of these is the adaptation *Bad News Bears*, an account of a misfit little league baseball team and their disillusioned, alcoholic coach Morris Buttermaker (Billy-Bob Thornton). The second is college flick *Everybody Wants Some!!*, which tracks scholarship ball player's Jake's (Blake Jenner's) first few days on campus in 1980s Texas, but spends little time on the field. Yet the sport recurs in one form or another across the filmmaker's oeuvre. Linklater's one-off ESPN documentary called *Inning by Inning* (2008) is a portrait of college coach Augie Garrido as much as it is a paean to the game. Baseball is one of the central chronotropes in the high school drama *Dazed and Confused* (1993), while it makes a short but memorable appearance in the coming-of-age document *Boyhood* (2014). Though there is no baseball being played in any of the *Before* trilogy, it is topic of an emotional and existential conversation between the two leads in the last installment, *Before Midnight* (2013). Indeed, so important is baseball to Jesse (Ethan Hawke) that he calls it, in his typically exaggerated but self-unaware fashion, "a metaphor for everything."

Of course, for Linklater as for Jesse, "everything" does not mean "everything." (Does it ever?) Neither at any point suggests baseball covers the entirety of life's possibilities, just as the *World* Series has little to do with anywhere but America. What "everything" would appear to mean are two things, specifically—and though they aren't everything, they aren't exactly insignificant either. The first is that across Linklater's films baseball represents a defining feature of coming-of-age, at least for American boys. It is the context in which one can—but of course does not necessarily have to—become a "man." The second thing is that baseball negotiates values that have, justifiably or mistakenly, historically been associated with America and the American dream: competition, fair play, diversity, equal opportunity, *community*.[4] Baseball, thus, is what produces America's future by reproducing its past—a textbook case of what Louis Althusser called "apparatus," interpellating subjects to become what they were already (supposed to be).[5] It is worth citing Jesse's speech to Céline (Julie Delpy) in full here. He talks about baseball to discuss his alienation from his son Hank, who lives with his mother in Chicago.

> JESSE: Look, he doesn't even know how to throw a baseball.
> CÉLINE: Who cares?
> JESSE: He just . . . he leads with his elbow. He throws like a girl.
> CÉLINE: That's not your fault.
> JESSE: No, it is my fault. A father is supposed to teach you that.
> CÉLINE: Okay, he just doesn't like baseball does he? Who can blame him?
> JESSE: No, it's an example, okay? It's a metaphor for everything. He's turning fourteen and he needs his father.

Jesse suggests that Hank's inability to play baseball at once stands in the way of his coming-of-age ("he doesn't *even* know," "he is turning fourteen"), makes him effeminate ("throws like a girl"), and is an expression of their alienation ("a father is *supposed* to teach you that," "he needs his father"). Baseball, in other words, is a rite of passage essential to becoming a man amongst other men; it's the apparatus turning boys into Americans. (Maybe this is all that the lonesome, disoriented characters in many of Linklater's other movies—the slackers, murderers, thieves, drug addicts, disenfranchised and suburbanite loiterers—need in order to become swell, law-abiding American consumers: a neat game of baseball).

Implicit in these surprisingly conservative notions of masculinity, family, and belonging is the context of America. If baseball is associated with any of these frameworks of signification at all, it is exclusively in the U.S. It's called the "national pastime," after all. Commentators often joke: "what are the last two words of the national anthem? Play ball!" As the political theorist Robert Elias has noted: baseball's quest is "quintessentially national" to the point of representing the entirety of "the pursuit of the American Dream."[6] Indeed, writes the cultural critic Lawrence Samuel, "baseball is the American dream incarnate."[7] And here is what the official MLB historian John Thorn has to say about it:

> the national pastime became the great repository of national ideals, the symbol of all that was good in American life: fair play (sportsmanship); the rule of law (objective arbitration of disputes); equal opportunity (each side has its innings); the brotherhood of man (bleacher harmony); and more.[8]

It is no surprise, as media scholar Aaron Baker observes, that the baseball field's green pasture "symbolizes pastoral landscape" and its architecture the "ultimate goal of returning home."[9] Certainly, Jesse's lamentation concerns not just Hank's absence from his life, but his incomplete American upbringing. What Jesse means when he suggests Hank isn't a man, is that he isn't an American man.

INNING BY INNING

Linklater draws on baseball to negotiate coming-of-age, masculinity, and the American dream differently in each of the films that includes the sport, even though there are some commonalities to which I will return later. In *Bad News Bears*, the emphasis lies with baseball's ability to socialize even the least popular kids, the loveable misfits that will grow up—one imagines—to be slackers. The film achieves this socialization in two ways. First, through their dialectical interaction with misanthropic coach Buttermaker, in the process of which they learn that they deserve to be cared for and he to take the responsibility to care for others. Second, by banding together in the face of adversity, stepping up to the plate to take on the outside world. In *Everybody Wants Some!!*, on the contrary, the focus is with team dynamics (or "brotherhood," to use Thorn's words cited above) and self-realization in virtual isolation from the outside world. Coaches and other teams are not participants in the process but mere figurants, facts of life. The players make up their own rules, continuously enacted in seemingly congenial but surprisingly cutthroat games—table tennis, "bloody knuckles," drinking; protagonist Jake determines his own path, conceives of a future that includes but is not limited to baseball. *Dazed and Confused* plays out only one scene on the baseball field, but it is one of the defining moments for young Mitch (Wiley Wiggins). Pitching out the game, he sees from the corner of his eye the seniors that will give the freshman an ass-whooping after the match—a yearly ritual to mark a rite of passage from middle or junior high school to senior high school. Though visibly shaken, he nonetheless manages to control his arm to strike out the batter. As his friends flee, he faces his fate head-on, walking over to the sidelines to accept his beating—like, it appears is the message, "a man." It's a decision that is rewarded, in any case, with entry into a seniors' party, alcohol, and a kiss from a girl.

In *Boyhood* and *Before Midnight* none of the characters is seen playing baseball (they play soccer instead). However, in the former, divorced father Mason (Ethan Hawke) watches a game of the MLB outfit The Astros together with his kids Mason Jr. (Ellar Coltrane) and Samantha (Lorelei Linklater), whilst in the latter, as established above, Jesse laments having had the opportunity to enjoy such experiences with the son he shares with his ex-partner. Both films draw on baseball for all of the reasons mentioned earlier (coming-of-age, masculinity, America), but specifically in the context of father-son relationships. The apparatus's machinery is in full view, in other words, with one generation greasing the wheels—or the mitt—for the next. This is awkwardly obvious during Mason's visit with his children to the Astros stadium. Seated next to his son, his daughter one chair removed, he explains the game to the male heir more than his eldest child. Indeed, when the Astros hit a homerun, he high-fives and hugs Mason Jr. but not his daughter, at whom he stares uncomfortably. This, the implication is, is a boys' game. Girls are tolerated but not the main demographic.

Linklater certainly does not always work this apparatus sincerely, nor is it necessarily entirely sympathetic. Across the movies, the pursuits of baseball go hand in hand with alcohol. I don't think it is an exaggeration to say that at least half of the sports' imagery shows characters swinging a bat in one hand whilst holding a beer in the other. Indeed, alcoholic consumption often bookends, or, to use the proper cinematographic language, frames, the athletic achievements. Buttermaker drinks a can of beer mixed with hard liquor before he heads out on the pitch to coach his team, whilst his little leaguers are rewarded for their effort all season with alcohol-free lagers. In *Everybody Wants Some!!*, college ball newcomer Jake spends over an hour and sixteen minutes of the film partying with his teammates before ever stepping on a baseball field. He continues the party right after training.

The game does not bring out the best in all of those involved. In *Bad News Bears*, opposing coach Ray Bullock (Greg Kinnear) is able to behave like a narcissist bully because of his team's success. He talks down to parents, emotionally abuses the kids on his team (including his own son), and openly disrespects his opponents. The manner in which the players in *Everybody Wants Some!!* treat women is sexist at best and misogynist at worst. Women are consistently seen as sexual objects to be conquered, prizes to be won. Indeed, at various instances, they are discussed through reference to baseball, as scores, strikes, or balls to be caught. Other nomenclature is even less respectful. Women are alternately labelled "bitches," "groupies," "buns," "poon," "chick," "snatch," and "pussy." Yet Linklater rarely uses baseball to explicitly critique either contemporary notions of masculinity or the American dream; such commentary is reserved, interestingly, for the movies where the sport does not play a role. Certainly, if Linklater shows anything, it is that baseball penalizes the bad behavior it might facilitate; it shows these excesses precisely to evidence the game's appreciation of fair play, rule of law, and equal opportunity. Coach Bullock receives scorn from his own family, embarrassment in front of the fans, and ridicule from his opponents—and, by extension, us. The machoism of the college players is suggested to be not merely a reference to the period setting, to the discourse of the time, or even the "frathouse" or "gross-out comedy" genre, but also a sign of their age, immaturity, and insecurity. They are boys, the film implies, that behave in the manner they mistakenly imagine men do (whether that excuse is sufficient to render them as sympathetic to the audiences as they would appear to be to the filmmaker, is another question; as is the ambiguity it raises about where they might have retrieved this image of masculinity).[10] Baseball is an apparatus, but not a repressive one. It is an ideological state apparatus in every sense of the word: it does not threaten but persuade—by way of misdirection—its subjects to understand its relations to itself and the world in one sense rather than another.

"BLEACHER HARMONY"

Community is a central trope across Linklater's baseball films. Whether it is the "stepping onto the plate" in the face of adversity that characterizes *Bad News Bears* or the brotherly competitiveness of *Everybody Wants Some!!*, or even the attempt at connection in *Boyhood*, one of the emancipatory qualities that baseball demands from and develops in its players is team spirit, an understanding that whatever each's personal beliefs and interests, you rely on and support others. In *Bad News Bears* team spirit is conceived of both as an end and a means. In the beginning the team is portrayed as a rag tag bunch of outsiders, with as little in common with one another as they have talent for the game. Among them are a hapless, rich kid and the two Spanish-speaking sons of his mom's gardener, a constantly eating obese boy, a small kid with anger management issues, a math geek, an effeminate dreamer, and a boy in a wheelchair (part of the film's exceptionally poor critical reception, it would seem, is a result of these). The kids appear unable to interact with each other in any manner except for mockery, conflict, or abuse; and with us exclusively as two-dimensional stereotypes, laughable on the one side and redeeming on the other.

What Linklater suggests baseball offers these lonesome outsiders is the context, purpose, and empathetic register to bond and belong. It offers them a context in that it puts them together regardless of their otherwise obviously diverse characters, socio-cultural backgrounds, and interests. This is all the more obvious the moment Buttermaker's talented stepdaughter from a previous relationship and the town rebel join the team, clearly traumatized but determined, self-sufficient kids who would otherwise never hang out with their fellow players—and who indeed initially inspire disbelief and awe, respectively. Baseball provides a common ground that does not so much require the players to disavow their sensibilities, values, or interests as that it affords a space where they can meet without dwelling on them: the practice of playing the game, of walking out onto the field together and sitting in the bleachers, of batting one after the other and looking for balls to catch, of talking trash about opponents. The "smaller moments," David T. Johnson calls these, where baseball is appreciated for its own sake, where players and viewers alike find "joy in the present moment."[11] This is a sentiment, by the way, that most of Linklater's other accounts of baseball, including *Inning by Inning*, share.

Baseball provides this ragtag bunch with a common purpose as well. Initially, this purpose is: not losing. Later, once the talented girl and rebel boy join, it becomes: winning. By the film's end, once the kids know how it feels to win, this purpose changes yet another time. Seeing the personal sacrifice each of his players makes for the team's success and the hurt it causes some of them, coach Buttermaker instructs them to enjoy the game, regardless of its consequences. Team spirit is valuable only in as far as it allows for each of its members to realize their full potential as well. This evolution seems to sum up Linklater's appreciation of baseball's qualities more generally: it is more important to know that you can win, to know what victory feels like, than to actually achieve it at any expense. The joy of playing for playing's sake is the game's highest reward. Indeed, across Linklater's oeuvre, those who play to win at all costs are consistently mocked. Coach Bullock's fanatism in *Bad News Bears*, for instance, is suggested to compensate for a lack of male prowess (his hand is crushed by Buttermaker in a handshake, whilst there is repeated mention of the too-tight shorts he is wearing). The overt, chauvinist nationalism framing the game receives similar mockery. The caricaturally muscular, aggressive behavior and misplaced bravado of pitcher Jay Niles (Juston Street) in *Everybody Wants Some!!* is implied to be related to a crippling insecurity. And *Dazed and Confused*'s senior O'Bannion's (Ben Affleck's) heinousness is said to be a result of his failure at school—he flunked his exams.

It is true that this attitude—an appreciation of the actualization of one's possibilities more than their achievement—appears across Linklater's oeuvre (indeed, it receives mention in relation to numerous other films in this very collection). Both John Pierson and Leslie Speed (2008) have interestingly compared this attitude with distinctly European intellectual and cinematic traditions, including the avant-garde and situationism, the movies of Luis Buñuel and Max Ophüls.[12] Speed persuasively suggests that its principal influence is Ernst Bloch's theory of utopianism. Bloch, he writes, citing Fredric Jameson, perceived utopia as "a manifestation of that primal movement toward the future and toward ultimate identity with a transfigured world" more than as a specific (non)place or object.[13] Indeed, its defining qualities were "expectation-affects" such as hope (as opposed, for instance, to necessity, inevitability, or even revolution). I would argue, however, that what *Bad News Bears* makes so plainly visible is that this European influence is as European as poststructuralism was supposedly French, or the American Dream a mere reinterpretation of Max Weber's protestant work ethic—that is to say, if the influence is European, it is so in a uniquely Americanized sense. For here, hope is conceived precisely in those terms we tend to associate with James Truslow Adams's future-oriented frontier mentality and every subsequent reiteration of the American Dream: melting pot, equal opportunity, work ethic, individual success, self-realization. What baseball teaches these kids is that if they put in the effort, that if each plays to the best of their uniquely individual—and differentiated—ability, the game will reward them as a whole; but that the reward isn't what they are playing for—it's the joy of the game. Indeed, watching Linklater's "European" humanism play out across the plate, the bases, and the field, I am reminded of a well-known quote by Philip Roth that prefaces nearly any cultural history of baseball and the American Dream I've come across:

> It seems to me that through baseball I came to understand and experience patriotism in its tender and humane aspects, lyrical rather than martial or righteous in spirit, and without the reek of saintly zeal, a patriotism that could not quite so easily be sloganized, or contained in a high-sounding formula to which one had to pledge something vague but all-encompassing called one's 'allegiance'.[14]

Rob Stone has argued that Linklater's films ask the viewers to reconsider their mythical notions of America and what it means to be American.[15] This may well be true, generally speaking, but I would suggest the baseball movies come to us with a different question: to believe in this myth more fully; not to do away with the idea of America altogether but its materialization past or present. For

Linklater, much like Roth, baseball provides us with the America that could be but is nowhere else to be found anymore (if it was ever at all): as communal as it is individualist, as generous as it is competitive, and as rewarding as it remains forever unfulfilled.

There are then, I think, two competing conclusions to be drawn from *Bad News Bears*' attitude towards team spirit and self-realization. The first is that the movie's presentation of baseball aligns with Linklater's "European" disposition elsewhere; it expresses his independently existing humanist utopianism. The second, conflicting conclusion is this: baseball—and all it represents culturally—is the framework within which we should understand Linklater's affinity with the sensibilities of the avant-garde, situationism, and the *Prinzip Hoffnung*, in the same vein that we might, for that matter, understand Roth's appreciation of sentiments that linger well beyond their origin or James Benning's obsession with static long takes. I don't know which of these conclusions is more viable, but it seems important to me to consider the possibility that baseball is more than a convenient coincidence; that baseball is itself an attitude or even, in Raymond Williams's words, a "structure of feeling": a shared sentiment as evasive and intangible as it is systemic which filters how we perceive ourselves and our relation to the world.[16]

Bad News Bears explicitly relates baseball's ability to foster community through purpose to empathy. The film suggests that the game's recontextualization and common purpose allows for an empathy toward others that they might otherwise not be able to extend. Indeed, it is both an inclusive and a productive affect, one that does not require any other sentiment than that of belonging to the same group (regardless of one's other differences); and which is perceived to contribute to that group's well-being. This empathy finds expression not, as it might in some of Linklater's more emotionally articulate films, in the explication of feelings or physical intimacy, but in an implicit appreciation of what others require to thrive on and off the field. Aggressive, foul-mouthed Tanner (Timmy Deters), who is—the film informs us early on—so antisocial that he gets into fights with the entire fourth class, is shown to care enough for his dreamy teammate Timmy (Tyler Patrick Jones) to take a punch for him. He further encourages nerdy Prem (Aman Johal) to stand up for himself by teaching him swear words. Hard-hitting Kelly (Jeffrey Davies) is a renegade who drives a motorcycle straight through a pack of kids. Yet once he is on the team, he expresses discomfort taking the spotlight from less talented teammates. To play baseball, it would seem, opens up another way of being-in-the-world.

AXEBALL

For the little leaguers in *Bad News Bears*, team spirit is an achievement: it is a delicate ecosystem the practice of baseball teaches them to grow, a healthy biosphere in which they in turn, as they come to understand, can flourish. The students in *Everybody Wants Some!!* have learned this lesson already: they value the idea of the team, even if, like Jake, they don't know any of the other members yet, or, like batters and pitchers, they don't necessarily understand or get along with each other. In this film, team spirit is defined at once by competition and, paradoxically, loyalty, though what they share is a distinct machoism: the collective's defining features are those of a particularly assertive masculinity, like monkeys fighting for the top branch (in one indicative scene, the players jump from high tree branches into the water, one of them beating his chest as he does so). I intend competition here as competitiveness amongst team players. This is not to say that their team spirit might not be expressed through competition with other teams, but since the film does not explicate as much (following the players in pre-season and off the field for the most part), I don't think we should speculate it is. As I mentioned above, the players are engaged in congenial but cutthroat games throughout. Amongst the games they play are table tennis, arcade games, foosball, basketball, living room netball, billiards, bloody knuckles, and various pitching and batting games. One game involves splicing baseballs mid-air with an axe, something which is as terrifying as it is indicative of the machoism running across all this. The students also compete in drinking and picking up women. These games are often superficially easy-going, laid-back even: the players are dressed in underpants or pajamas and are drinking throughout, whilst other members of the team—also dressed casually and with beer in hand—stand around mocking them. Yet as the matches progress, the players' faces harden, their smiles become grimaces, their movements turn erratic and aggressive as they shout and curse.

One of the games Jake is involved in is a morning game of ping pong. He competes with senior, all-American batter and pro-prospect McReynolds (Tyler Hoechlin). The game is presented through two scenes, which are intercut with images of teammates involved in increasingly physical living room netball so as to communicate to the audience both the prevalence and the bio-political function of the gamesmanship. The first scene cuts between action shots of Jake and McReynolds silently playing, a wide angle shot of three teammates drinking and watching, and a two-shot of two other teammates preparing a drink without paying much attention to the play. It is telling for the jovial atmosphere of the match that it is both soundtracked by and given equal screen time to the teammates discussing how to drink your liquor: it's all fun and games. The second scene on the contrary opens to aggressive banter between the players. "That's right, freshman," McReynolds says whilst looking his opponent straight in the eyes, "Yeah, you keep up that funky-ass spin shit. I've got you figured out, son." If the choice of words—"freshman," "son"——is intended to put Jake down, the stare suggests aggression is the means by which Jake can expect this to be achieved. After winning the point, Jake responds in a manner that communicates to McReynolds as well as the viewer that he understands—and is ready for the fight: "Are you feeling threatened yet?" Jake's retort is awarded with the laughter of the other players, a schadenfreude that expresses the libidinous excitement of hierarchies being contested here. As the scene progresses and the game looks to be decided in the freshman's favor, the façade of banter is dropped altogether. McReynolds verbally abuses Jake, shouts obscenities at the onlookers, and ultimately throws his bat at his opponent's head in anger before taking a swig of liquor and storming out. The anger is interesting here for two reasons. First, it shows how serious the players take these games, if not because they are top athletes who are instinctively competitive regardless of the sport, then because they understand that these games have a political function: they determine the group hierarchy. Second, McReynolds's anger signals to the others that he does not accept his loss nor the hierarchy it implies. Indeed, the first thing McReynolds reminds Jake of during their first batting practice, is the ping pong game, contextualizing and putting the pressure on their more important athletic interactions.

In *Everybody Wants Some!!* players are as competitive with one another as they are loyal to each other, however. The players may be engaged in a constant battle for dominance amongst one another, but they form a pack, a tribe, in relation to others. This is manifested when freshman pitcher Jay Niles, who is universally disliked by the others, gets into a fight in a club. Even though he does not count any friends amongst his teammates, he is to blame for the brawl, and supporting him might have consequences for the others—they will be expelled from the club—they still take his side in the scrimmage. Linklater—uncharacteristically—explicates the dynamic so that there can be no mistake about what has happened here. "It's crazy," Jake tells his teammate Finnegan (Glenn Powell) after they've been booted from the club, "we're fucking defending this guy." Finnegan responds: "it's all so damn tribal. It's the pack mentality, animal instincts."

Linklater suggests that this loyalty is as much a blessing as it can be a burden. Midway through the film, Jake is invited to a party by the girl he likes, Beverly (Zoey Deutch). Beverly is a theater major and the party is set to include costumes, cross-dressing, and plays. From his hesitancy in sharing the news of the party—he initially does not reveal the party's whereabouts—with others, it would appear Jake is keen to visit on his own, a decision that seems informed by his desire to make this a romantic evening as much as his feeling the baseball players will not mix well with the crowd. It's not, he says, when pressured by the others, that he does not want them to come. "I just implied you might be bored, that's all," which is code, of course, for the exact sentiment they accuse him of. "Let me get this straight," senior pitcher Nesbit (Austin Amelio), says to Jake, standing on his own, ready to head out the door, as much to the others, circled around him, "a freshman is trying to stop us from going to a party . . ." "Fuck it," Jake replies, defensively, to add awkwardly: "you guys can come if you like." "Oh no," Finnegan mock-cries, "I don't want us to embarrass you in front of all of your artsy-fartsy theater major friends," and so on, until Jake finally sees no other option than to beg his teammates to join him. The entire set-up, cutting back and forth between mid-shots of Jake and the team, with Jake standing at one end of the room, whilst the others are seated together at the other end, and with Jake having to defend his plans to the accusations and guilt trips of his teammates, suggests that if loyalty is what protects one against the outside it is also what imprisons one from it. Baseball's mode of being-in-the-world allows for individual pursuit only as long as it benefits the whole team, and if this enables one's self-confidence it also, Linklater here shows us, might run the risk of limiting one's development.

BEING MARK McGWIRE

Linklater is generally thought to be something of an outsider in the film industry. Neither his mode of filmmaking nor the movies themselves fit comfortably in either the mass-produced Hollywood glove nor the handcrafted mitt, even if some of them have been commercial successes and others are considered Indie staples.[17] It is surprising, in this respect, that his account and use of baseball appear rather conventional, aesthetically and ideologically. For if Linklater's connotation of the game with coming-of-age, masculinity, and the American dream are shared by most movies on the subject, so are some of the tropes through which he represents these. One can think here of the predilection for unlikely winners, the concern with father-son relationships, the celebration of comradery or brotherhood, the appreciation of the game's slow pace, or the emphasis on places where open fields are available (i.e., rarely urban settings).[18]

The director's most conventional ploy here, perhaps, is that he populates the stands, bleachers, and fields predominantly with white boys. In historical and sociological accounts of the sport, much is made of its ability to unite people from all cultural and ethnic backgrounds, even if this inclusivity was historically seldomly extended to and is still only occasionally available or in any case accepted by black Americans.[19] In the early twentieth century, baseball brought together immigrants from Germany, Italy, and Ireland, whilst it has invited in Hispanics in recent decades. Baseball has also long provided women with the opportunity to play organized team sports.[20] I don't know if any other sport in America prompts the words "democracy," "equality," and "melting pot" as much as baseball does.[21] Baseball movies, however, rarely reflect this project(ion). "Most," film scholar Aaron Baker notes, "prefer stories that construct a more monocultural image of baseball as defined only by the achievements of White males."[22] Latham Hunter adds that these males are more often than not "middle class," and tend to be from the suburbs or country as opposed to the inner city.[23] This goes for Classical Hollywood representations as much it does for recent attempts, a lack of progress out of sync with developments in reality.[24]

Baker suggests that one of the reasons baseball movies even today remain so concerned with white men is that they are stuck in the past. Certainly, baseball films appear to have a predilection for period settings. They are drawn to the heydays of the 1930s, 1940s and 1950s especially, eras which notably preceded the civil rights movement and women's lib. As Lester D. Friedman notes, we would do well to remember that "during this time so nostalgically invoked by so many Americans, Major League Baseball was a totally segregated sport."[25] Indeed, all the talk about baseball as a game of equal opportunities, individual achievement, and the American Dream would "have struck many Black players merely as empty platitudes with little applicability to their lives."[26] *The Natural* (1984), the genre's most iconic film about a middle-aged white rookie in the 1940s playing other white players in front of white audiences, might in this context also be said to be the most exemplary.

But even films set in the present nostalgically play out historical themes and sentiments. The game's "lack of rush, iconic tools made of wood and leather that symbolize America's pastoral past and inclination to celebrate the heroes of its storied history,"[27] Baker writes, momentarily turn any moment into a nostalgic memory of a pre-industrial, agrarian idyll where people felt at one with their surroundings. Baseball slows down, brings back to human scale, implements fair rules, and injects individual heroism into a Dream that many feel has spun out of control and out of reach. In baseball movies, the bat does not hit the ball forward but backwards, straight into a perceived (but obviously nonexistent, entirely imagined) past, to a time when people still believed in the American Dream—or in any case still believed in an American Dream to which they felt that they could claim ownership. Judging from the race and gender of most of the players, however, this nostalgic homerun shuts out African Americans and people of color more generally as well as women, the insinuation being that they are to blame for the Dream's current evaporation. Nostalgia is an aching for a past that never was, but it is also an inability to come to terms with the present that is;[28] in baseball movies, that inability often quickly takes on very worrying forms.

As Rob Stone has noted, Linklater's "universe" in general "is limited in being almost exclusively white, heterosexual, well-fed, and at least high school educated. His characters can get jobs, but choose not to."[29] In line with my conclusions regarding *Bad News Bears*' utopian spirit, I don't know in this respect whether his accounts of baseball are expressions of this "limited" mode of being-in-the-world, or might be argued—given their partly biographical status—to be explanations for it, showing us how the director sees the world from the perspective of a baseball player: from across an open, Texan field, a boy amidst other white, straight American boys with whom he shares a common ground if not necessarily a politics, an active participant but in one of the slowest games around; someone who appreciates the craftsmanship of a well-made leather glove even as the cars speed by in the distance. Yet whatever the relation between Linklater's oeuvre as a whole and the movies concerned, in however small part, with baseball, it is certainly true that here the sport, too, is a white, straight, middle class-ish country boys' game. Nostalgia, moreover, seems to be partly to blame, since *Bad News Bears* is an adaptation of a movie from the 1970s, whilst *Everybody Wants Some!!* is set in the early 1980s.

One could maintain, of course, that the *Bad News Bears* are made up of a variety of cultures, ethnicities, and classes. Amongst the players are shy Armenian Garo (Jeffrey Tedmori), nerdy Asian Prem, and African American Ahmad (Kenneth Harris), as well as two Hispanic boys from a working-class background. Yet I would maintain that the inclusion of these children only serves to naturalize the sport's whiteness. Awkwardly, they are the only players whose ethnic identities are made an issue of, often a comedic one. During the first team meeting, Buttermaker stumbles over Garo's last name Daragabrigadien, saying "what the hell, is that Aztec or something," whilst thinking it appropriate to greet Ahmad with "what's up bro." Later, Garo's cultural background is explicitly turned into a plot pivot when he confesses to Buttermaker that his immigrant dad does not want him to play the game, an alienation that is especially sensitive—and Garo seems particularly vulnerable—given the sport's association with father-son relationships. The color of Ahmad's skin, too, serves a running gag. Wearing a number 25 jersey, Buttermaker automatically assumes it is a reference to one of the great black players to have worn it. It isn't: it refers to Mark McGwire, who hails from the same region. This is a cross-racial loyalty that Buttermaker for unexplained reasons struggles to comprehend: "but he is white." Prem and the Hispanic brothers aren't confronted with their backgrounds as much as that they put forth stereotypical representations of their ethnicity. Indeed, Prem steps into the shoes of nearly every other Asian child in American movies from the late twentieth century in that he appears career driven and extraordinarily talented at mathematics, devising a computer program that makes statistical analyses of each and every game play and player records. The film does not inform us whether he plays the violin, too, but I would, frankly, not be surprised if this is a detail that was in the first draft of the screenplay. Similarly, the Hispanic brothers play no part in the movie other than as a running gag about their inability to speak English. In stark contrast, none of the white kids is ever asked about their cultural or ethnic background, nor are they stereotyped racially. This is not to say that they aren't caricatures, too; it is just, as I mentioned above, that their representations are allowed to move beyond the color of their skin into class and social groups.

In *Everybody Wants Some!!*, the baseball team consists almost exclusively of white, male players. Women do not play ball, nor do they seem to understand it (or much else, a few exceptions excluded). Only one of the protagonists is not white: Dale (J. Quinton Johnson). One might argue that the film's explicit whiteness and focus on men is a commentary on the genres the film plays—not so much as parody as through pastiche—with and within: the baseball film and the 1980s fratboy or college campus movie. Yet all the same, race and race relations are never explicitly problematized, though they are implicitly, if that is the word, acknowledged on a few occasions. On one of Jake's first team outings, five teammates including Dale are singing along to the Sugarhill Gang's 1979 hit song "Rapper's Delight," credited as the first commercial hip hop success. The sight of the four white guys over-shouting one another as well as Dale as they rap is a peculiar sight, especially in today's context. Later that evening, the team go to a country bar. Dale informs his teammates he feels uncomfortable heading there: "I don't know about this country bar, man." The implication here is, of course, that he is a black man and country bars tend to be populated with white people. But his reservations are instantly dismissed and depoliticized. "We're just gonna do a quick wardrobe change," one says, followed by a conversation about country music. No one mentions race. Linklater's decision to disavow the importance of race here seems informed by the naïve sense—prevalent, as Baker notes, in most baseball movies and indeed sports films more generally—that sport isn't about race, but fair competition and equal opportunity.[30] As Dale tells the freshmen: here, everyone "is on your own. And it's competitive man . . . If you want to succeed, shit if you really want to succeed, your only choice is to mentally toughen up." Baseball is a meritocracy, where success is achievable by everyone who plays well regardless of where they're from.

THE EMPIRE STRIKES THREE

Linklater presents baseball as a game that is inclusive, equalizes, values hard work but allows for joviality, and encourages individual achievement in the context of team spirit whilst promoting team spirit in terms of self-realization, Baseball isn't totalitarian, nor is it sanctimonious: some if its players behave poorly and get away with it. But it does not reward such conduct. Baseball shows the America as it might have been had everyone played by the rules, put in the effort, and valued one another for their contributions. It would seem, however, that this America does not include, or in any case was not made for, either African Americans and other people of color or indeed women, as both are sparse in numbers, marginalized narratively, and consistently portrayed as other. Baseball is a white boy's game—young ones as much as "old boys," and indeed it is precisely the interaction between the two that renders this exclusivity so problematic. Though Linklater's tone is ambiguous enough to leave undecided whether this exclusivity is a commentary on the genres adapted and/or appropriated or an authorial structure of feeling, baseball is presented as an apparatus which subjects its players as much as us, its viewers, not just to a view of America, but of all of us ourselves as Americans.

NOTES

1. I am grateful to Kim Wilkins for comments on earlier drafts of this chapter.
2. Robert Elias, *Baseball and the American Dream: Race, Class, Gender and the National Pastime* (Armonk, NY: M. E. Sharpe, 2001).
3. For a definition of baseball movies in the context of sports movies more generally, see Lester D. Friedman, *Sports Movies* (New Brunswick, NJ: Rutgers University Press, 2020), 40–68.
4. See Elias, *Baseball and the American Dream*.
5. Louis Althusser (1970), *On the Reproduction of Capitalism: Ideology and Ideological State Apparatuses* (later printing edition) (London and New York: Verso, 2014).
6. Elias, *Baseball and the American Dream*, 3.
7. Lawrence R. Samuel, *The American Dream: A Cultural History* (Syracuse, NY: Syracuse University Press, 2012), 9.
8. John Thorn, "Our Game," in *Total Baseball*, edited by John Thorn, Pete Palmer, Michael Gershman, and David Pietrusza (New York: Viking/Penguin, 1997), 6.
9. Aaron Baker, "Hollywood Baseball Films: Nostalgic White Masculinity or the National Pastime?" *Quarterly Review of Film and Video* (2021): 3.
10. For a discussion of these boys' historical, generic, and immature image of masculinity, see Mary Harrod's chapter in this book.
11. David T. Johnson, *Richard Linklater* (Urbana: University of Illinois Press, 2012), 94.
12. Cf. John Pierson, "Slacking Off," 2004, in *The Criterion Collection*, 21 February 2006; and Lesley Speed, "The Possibilities of Roads Not Taken: Intellect and Utopia in the Films of Richard Linklater," *The Journal of Popular Film and Television* 35:3 (2007): 98–106.
13. Speed, "The Possibilities of Roads Not Taken," 104.
14. Philip Roth, "My Baseball Years," *The New York Times*, 1973: 35.
15. Rob Stone, *The Cinema of Richard Linklater: Walk, Don't Run* (New York: Columbia University Press, 2018), 98.
16. Raymond Williams, *Marxism and Literature* (Oxford: Oxford University Press, 1977).
17. Cf. Johnson, *Richard Linklater*; Speed, "The Possibilities of Roads Not Taken"; and Stone, *The Cinema of Richard Linklater*.
18. Cf. Baker, "Hollywood Baseball Films"; Friedman, *Sports Movies*; Latham Hunter, "'What's Natural About It?': A Baseball Movie as Introduction to Key Concepts in Cultural Studies," *Film & History* 35:2 (2005): 7; Elizabeth Rawitsch, "'It's Strictly USA': The Performance of Ethnic Assimilation in Take me Out to the Ball Game," *Journal of Popular Film and Television* 39:3 (2011): 124–131.
19. Elias, *Baseball and the American Dream*; Susan Jacoby, *Why Baseball Matters* (New Haven, CT: Yale University Press, 2018). Friedman notes that baseball today draws fewer black and female viewers than NASCAR, which is generally considered the whitest sport there is.
20. Jacoby, *Why Baseball Matters*.
21. Cf. Samuel, *The American Dream*; Thorn, "Our Game"; G. Edward White, *Creating the National Pastime: Baseball Transforms Itself, 1903–1953* (Princeton, NJ: Princeton University Press, 1996).
22. Baker, "Hollywood Baseball Films," 1.
23. Hunter, "'What's Natural About It?'"
24. See Rawitsch, "'It's Strictly USA.'"
25. Friedman, *Sports Movies*, 49.
26. Ibid.
27. Baker, "Hollywood Baseball Films," 4.
28. Svetlana Boym, *The Future of Nostalgia*. (New York: Basic Books, 2001).
29. Stone, *The Cinema of Richard Linklater*, 5.
30. Baker, "Hollywood Baseball Films."

CHAPTER 6

Boyhood: Linklater's Testament of American Youth after 9/11

Timothy Shary

In 2002, Richard Linklater began shooting a film under the vague title of "The 12-Year Project." Its production would be audacious, and unprecedented: Linklater proposed to film for just a few days each year, in roughly one-year intervals, over the course of a protagonist's life from first grade to college, so that the audience would witness the character and his family (as well as the actors playing those roles) actually aging through the course of the story.[1] Linklater had shown his temporal and youthful enchantments in previous efforts such as *Dazed and Confused* (1993) and *Before Sunrise* (1995), yet what became *Boyhood* in 2014 was the most concerted and comprehensive depiction of coming-of-age ever attempted in cinema history, defying the *Bildungsroman* tradition that is so often invested in sentimentality and marred by melodrama. In dismissing a traditional short-term shooting schedule and resisting a conventional narrative structure, Linklater made *Boyhood* into a chronicle of youth untethered to industrial and generic confines that resulted in a certain timeless universality relating to the lives of American children in the early twenty-first century.

The protagonist of *Boyhood*, Mason (Ellar Coltrane), evolves through transitions from one year to the next that are often quite subtle, and some of which are detectable only by nuance. Even as Linklater shows Mason continuing through his school years, he eschews obvious markers such as captions or title cards to depict Mason growing through changes in friendships, fashions, and attitudes, resulting in a canny statement on the often unpredictable ways in which young people mature. We see Mason advance through his varying living conditions, his shifting social circle, and the visible fluctuations of his hairstyle. While his family relocates to different homes across southern Texas after his parents' divorce, we discern Mason's encroaching departure from boyhood itself as he moves toward high school graduation, leaving home, and going off to college. Linklater has said he "wanted the movie to seem like the memory of a young life, just rolling through time,"[2] and he captures that through this smooth growth of Mason on screen, void of many celebrated rituals that children have forced upon them, like holidays, vacations, and ceremonies. In fact, Mason has one just birthday in the story, his almost forgotten fifteenth, and Linklater even dodges Mason's actual graduation service. Further, we watch how Mason's slightly older sister and his estranged parents grow and transform across the same period, each on occasion voicing shared frustrations with the vicissitudes of life, resulting in many profound (and sometimes unexpected) statements on learning, psychology, family, sexuality, and economics in the current culture. As Boris Kachka concisely put it, Mason is "a deer caught in the headlights of working-class, broken-home America."[3]

The America in which Mason aged from childhood to manhood was rife with historical change as well. When the story begins in early 2002, less than a year has elapsed since the shattering events of 9/11, the consequences of which Mason primarily hears through his left-wing father. The U.S. was by then already involved in an assured yet undeclared war in Afghanistan, and within a few years would launch a far more dubious military attack on Iraq. Like many of his generation—who were slowly becoming known as Millennials—Mason grew up cynical and suspicious within the political atmosphere of the George W. Bush presidency, which was not alleviated by the election of Barack Obama in 2008. By then, the nation was in the grips of the Great Recession, which Mason observes as his working mother pursues a new career despite the resentments of multiple romantic partners, leading to upheavals in his education, housing, and social connections. American youth culture of the time was further impacted by the expansion of internet access, which was still something of a novelty when Mason started his schooling, and was completely integrated into daily life by the time he graduated in 2013.

Some of the directorial decisions about which events to record were essentially dictated by the shooting schedule. Linklater could only gather the cast and crew for a few days each year, and his budget was so low (merely US$4 million by the time the production wrapped) that staging large crowd events such as a graduation, or winter scenes involving conspicuous weather variables, could have been cost-prohibitive. Thus, Linklater usually portrayed just a few captured experiences in each year, from mundane moments of Mason attending school to a few more dramatic turns such as his mother Olivia (Patricia Arquette) leaving her second husband. This narrative method would indeed be rebellious within American movie traditions of conflict-and-resolution or even action-and-reaction, leading Gabe Klinger to adroitly claim that "the hidden aim of *Boyhood* is to dismantle that convention in mainstream narrative cinema that characters' lives have to be defined by prescribed momentous events."[4]

Boyhood demonstrates the extent to which Linklater allows the quotidian growth of his protagonist to flourish on screen in subtle bursts of curiosity, arbitrary memories, and casual concerns about the meaning of life. At the same time, I argue that what Linklater makes appear so seamless and natural on screen is, in reality, a methodically designed and cogently analytical statement on the momentary grace of childhood and the evanescent nature of time itself. As children, we do not have the perspective (nor the pressure) to consider life in full and can live in so many moments as they happen, unburdened by obligation and outcome, until adulthood gradually imposes its concerns about what we actually do in life and how long we have to do it, concerns that encroach upon Mason by the end of the film. Seen within the context of early twenty-first-century life, *Boyhood* is a wistful allegory for the development of American culture during a time of superficial security that is undergirded with doubts about the stability of nuclear family cohesion, the value of education and experience under capitalist limitations, and the roles of social institutions in shaping identities of gender, sexuality, nationality, and personality. Just as America started a new millennium with cautious optimism that suddenly turned to shocking anxiety within two years, Mason progresses through his boyhood curiosities and enforced schooling yet embarks on adulthood in the end with the same uncertainty he endured as a child.

THE DIRECTOR'S VISION

Richard Linklater was born in 1960 as America was gaining an altogether new perspective on the young consumers, protesters, and artists who would have more influence in cultural events than any other generational group in the century. He would grow up watching the Vietnam War unfold on television while the student revolts of the late 1960s were overtaken by reassuring complacency in the disco era of his later teens. Linklater witnessed an intriguing trajectory of youth representation at the movies throughout the course of his own youth: Hollywood moved from sublimating teenage sex with sun-and-surf movies like *Beach Party* (William Asher, 1963) and *Beach Blanket Bingo* (Asher, 1965) to celebrating outright druggy rebellion with *Wild in the Streets* (Barry Shear, 1968) and *Free Grass* (Bill Brame and John Lawrence, 1969) to recalling simpler times before all that turmoil in *American Graffiti* (George Lucas, 1973) and *Grease* (Randal Kleiser, 1978). These two 1970s hits were exceptions to the industry's otherwise derisory efforts to exploit the teenage audience during that decade, which resulted in forgettable fare such as *The Cheerleaders* (Paul Glickler, 1973), *Massacre at Central High* (Rene Daalder, 1976), and *Corvette Summer* (Matthew Robbins, 1978).

Indeed, the odd cycles of American youth cinema during the director's own formative years would find a certain realization in his formative features, made from the age of 31 to 36, the first four of which were single day-and-night narratives in the lives of (primarily) young people. *Slacker* (1991) was a mildly political response to the apathy that youth of the 1990s were accused of espousing; *Dazed and Confused* was a nostalgic tour of rebellious mid-1970s teens drifting through the drug culture of the time; *Before Sunrise* all but transferred the romantic longings of its characters into conversation; *SubUrbia* (1996) literally lined up disaffected young adults who find themselves in contemporary suspension without rebellion or nostalgia to relieve their anomie.

Curiously, Linklater's films about youth (which would later include *School of Rock* [2003] and *Bad News Bears* [2005] before *Boyhood*) would largely operate outside the generic limits of classic 1980s teen cinema as characterized by sex romps (*Porky's* [Bob Clark, 1981], *Risky Business* [Paul Brickman, 1983]), slasher series (*Friday the 13th* [Sean S. Cunningham, 1980], *A Nightmare on Elm Street* [Wes Craven, 1984]), and the sensitive films of John Hughes like *Sixteen Candles* (1984) and *The Breakfast Club* (1985). Such films, and the blockbuster success of family-friendly hits going back to *Star Wars* (Lucas, 1977), *Superman* (Richard Donner, 1978), and *E.T. the Extra-Terrestrial* (Steven Spielberg, 1982), would revitalize the sagging Hollywood box office and convince the studios in the 1980s to return to a heavy investment in youth movies as they had done in the 1950s with *The Wild One* (László Benedek, 1953), *Rebel Without a Cause* (Nicholas Ray, 1955), and *Gidget* (Paul Wendkos, 1959), though Linklater was not drawn to this impulse. He had spent much of the 1980s absorbing Classic Hollywood and foreign films, as his generational cohort drifted out of the decade with scant career opportunities and a critical incredulity about the state of American culture.

So when Linklater emerged as a talent in the early 1990s, the atmosphere of disenchanted "postmodern puberty" was ripe and ready for his forays into youth culture.[5] After *Slacker*, further Indie features proliferated to capitalize on the twentysomethings of Generation X who had been 1980s teenagers, including *Singles* (Cameron Crowe, 1992), *Clerks* (Kevin Smith, 1994), *Empire Records* (Allan Moyle, 1995), and *Reality Bites* (Ben Stiller, 1994), starring future Linklater collaborator Ethan Hawke. Meanwhile, Linklater moved away from youth themes by the end of the decade with his poorly reviewed Western gangster film *The Newton Boys* (1998), though his projects remained distinctly preoccupied with philosophical and moral matters, as seen in *Waking Life* and *Tape* (both 2001), which experimented with intriguing technologies of movie media as the young auteur ruminated on the metaphysics of reality (particularly perceptions of truth and identity) and the consequences of behavior (such as the impact of actions, and the duration of that impact). *Tape* suggested that he was still concerned with the legacy of youth— as its characters discuss and account for questionable behavior during their high school days—and during this time Linklater conceived the idea for *Boyhood*.

According to Nicole Sperling, "He was searching for a way to make a movie about childhood but was struggling to isolate one moment that defines it . . .

He'd grown up a child of divorce, moving around a lot, and was then still a relatively new father."[6] And as Linklater would say himself, this project "became a 12-year journey about coming to grips with my own childhood, while also understanding parenting."[7] Cinematic and literary attempts to render long passages in a life over time had been tried before, but Linklater's vision would represent an unparalleled attempt to cast Hollywood actors and relative unknowns for a production schedule that had never been attempted. The film would thus require an enormous leap of faith by its financiers, and the continuing commitment of its cast and crew.

The production of *Boyhood* then took place over thirty-nine total shooting days, which is actually typical for many Indie features, but those shoots were spread out over more than 4,000 days in real life, which was of course the radical difference.[8] This meant that enormous stretches of time would elapse between events for characters with coherent histories, thus placing a certain pressure on the actors to maintain some level of continuity in their performances despite significant changes in their lives, and it further placed a similar obligation on Linklater and his crew to maintain technical continuities for the duration.

Perhaps the biggest threat in that regard was the movie industry's encroaching rejection of film stock as a shooting medium, which had been standard since the earliest days of cinema in the 1890s. By the early 2000s, an increasing number of productions, particularly in the lower-budget independent realm, were moving toward less expensive high-definition digital video, and certainly by the time of production on *Boyhood* the use of video was an option. However, despite recently working with digital video on *Waking Life* and *Tape*, Linklater committed to the more familiar format of film stock when he started *Boyhood* in 2002, knowing he was somewhat gambling that the older medium would persist for the length of production. As he said from the start:

> I want the film to look like *one* film, not different technologies or different looks for twelve years. I want this to be seamlessly dissolving from one year into the next, just people subtly aging.[9]

Little did he realize what a calculated risk he was taking then: by the time *Boyhood* wrapped production in 2013 many movies were being shot on digital video (including major studio projects like *Oz: The Great and Powerful* [Sam Raimi], *World War Z* [Marc Forster], and *Gravity* [Alfonso Cuarón], which won the Best Cinematography Oscar that year), and by the time the film premiered the next year, roughly 90 percent of all movie screens in America were projecting digital images, not film.[10] Ashley Clark even suggested that Linklater's use of film in the digital era "operates as a quiet lament for a dying medium."[11] In an unintended yet parallel irony, Mason ages in the movie as the mode representing him is aging out of existence.

Beyond the technical realm, continuity would also be a vital concern in conveying the evolving story, from costuming to sets to vehicles and other props. Linklater could rely on the sartorial connections made over the years by his costumer Kari Perkins, who would persuade cast members to use their own clothes, or buy appropriate working-class attire at local Goodwill stores.[12] Set photographer Matt Lankes also provided an extensive visual record of the cast and settings each year, from which Linklater could plan certain features in the shooting of subsequent years' scenes.[13] The director had to make more advanced allowances for significant developments in the actors' appearances—particularly hairstyles, such as asking Coltrane to let his mop top grow long before a traumatic cut in the fourth year.

The unprecedented nature of these shooting conditions was evident at all levels of the production, giving pause to the financiers. After all, Linklater was not a blockbuster role model despite enjoying modest success with his films throughout the production period, particularly *School of Rock* in 2003. He began by looking for funding at large in 2001, and then approached the independent IFC Films, which had grown from the Independent Film Channel, both of which were owned by AMC Networks, the conglomerate that also owned the AMC and Sundance television channels. The President of IFC Films, Jonathan Sehring, became a key ally, since the company had supported *Waking Life* and *Tape*, and he agreed to a modest allocation of about US$200,000 for each year of shooting.[14] By the time the film was complete, the total budget would reach US$4 million, a humble figure for a film about working-class characters, even within the indie market, and more so compared to studio films that typically spend over US$100 million for stories about more glamorous figures.[15] By the summer of 2002, Linklater had assembled his principal cast and embarked on an uncharted excursion in cinematic storytelling.

THE SOCIAL-PERSONAL CONTEXT

Due to the unique production and radical narrative of *Boyhood*, any attempt to situate it within the generic cycles and patterns of Hollywood practices is difficult. The film is unlike any other youth comedy or drama, and lacks a big budget and splashy features, so it actually resists such positioning, and we must understand it as an artifact of evolution rather than a specific era. After all, the contexts of social history and industrial activity can be rather diffuse in a movie that is written and revised over the course of twelve years. *Boyhood* became a film influenced by these contexts as Linklater and his actors progressed through that time, beginning in the post-9/11 atmosphere that young Mason hears referenced in his father's political rants. Other timely developments influence Mason's own development, although true to childhood, none lasts for long. The

Harry Potter phenomenon that infused the experiences of many children from 1997 to 2011 (when those books and films were first being released) is apparent in some of Mason's prepubescent activities, but never recalled later. His use of technology moves from the bulky tabletop computers of the early 2000s to handheld smartphones in the early 2010s. And even his father's ongoing inducement for Mason and Sam to be fervent Democrat activists—flaunted when he has them canvas for Barack Obama in 2008—is gone by the time Mason is a jaded teenager and Dad (Ethan Hawke) has taken to selling insurance and driving a minivan for the sake of his new wife and baby son.[16]

The film thus implicitly shows how certain historical moments create backgrounds to Mason's life yet are in many ways disconnected from it. The same applies to the place of *Boyhood* within the genre of youth cinema because it enlists very few of the generic conventions that characterize teen movies (in terms of stock characters, dramatic conflicts, or appeals to adventure). Hollywood trends nonetheless continued to progress during the years the film was in development, none of which had any particular impact on its production. For instance, aside from the two *Harry Potter* references within the film, we see no evidence of the turn toward supernatural stories in teen cinema, which became abundant by the end of the 2000s with the *Twilight* pentalogy that started in 2008.

A similar indifference applies to the film's address of identity politics during an era in which young people felt increasingly pressured to abandon binary and restrictive labels (female/male, black/white, poor/rich) as they were simultaneously feeling more attuned to demographic categories (gender, sexuality, race, ethnicity, nationality, class, education) like never before. Mason thus has the privilege of his American, white, male heterosexuality, yet even as a working-class kid he is not brought to confront his place in society within these terms, nor does he consciously classify himself within the various collective ranks that so many young people have been compelled to adopt and refine over generations. Mason denies the facile branding that has been put upon so many young protagonists (hooligan, punk, jock, goth, nerd, rebel, stoner, dude), and, for that matter, he is clearly detached from much of popular culture by the time he is a teen, not embracing any particular musical styles, not enamored of particular artists, and not aligned with the busy zeitgeist of the early 2010s.

Boyhood could thus be released in 2014 with a protagonist and a story that were not beholden to current conditions in order to demonstrate relevance. The relevance of the film, and Mason's experiences within it, lay in its depiction of certain common qualities of youthful experiences that are not mired in passing cultural customs. Here is a rather comprehensive depiction of a child who, regardless of demographic, experiences the challenges of familial influence and inconsistency, the joys and frustrations of friendship, the mundanity of school, and the wonder of self-discovery—aspects that are universal to virtually everyone who comes of age. Mason may be a child of his time, while in so many ways he is representative of children across generations since the start of cinema, and *Boyhood* implicitly embraces the history of every youth film that had come before in its narrative events (troubles at home, fun with friends, going to school, discovering romance) and thematic ambitions (considering how children learn, adapt, play, communicate). At the same time, this sincere integration of youth genre interests is rendered in a sui generis style entirely its own, moving away from so many of the industrial expectations of Hollywood studios and even the emotional expectations of American audiences.

Youth culture was certainly in the throes of ongoing upheavals during the timeframe of the story. After the menacing terrorists attacks in 2001 left American children traumatized by the threat of harm from without, the ensuing news of constant combat in the Middle East gave them an impression of their nation in an endless state of war.[17] At the local level, youth had become accustomed to news of school shootings in recent years, which reached epidemic proportions in the decade before 9/11 (over 200 children shot in fifty-five incidents), leading to 'lockdown' drills implemented by many administrators. Alas, this morbid trend persisted with mass shootings (four or more murdered) at elementary schools (three from 2006 to 2022), high schools (five from 2005 to 2021), and colleges (six from 2001 to 2015).[18]

This culture of violence permeated children's entertainment with the increasing promotion of sadistic video games, as the expansion of the internet also gave youth unprecedented access to information and communication that adult authorities could barely monitor. Children's activities thus simultaneously acquired visibility—and exploitability—especially in the form of social networks that gained traction throughout the early part of the century. Suddenly children with computer access could proclaim themselves as individuals around the world, while local friends and rivals could also lay claim to their messages and images with no limit on critical commentary, giving rise to "cyberbullying" and its pernicious effects.[19]

And soon after these developments relocated the social pressures of school to home, young people began to literally embrace these communicative tensions with their bodies through the expansion of the smartphone in the late 2000s, which further burdened the population with a perceived need for ceaseless connection. Along the way, children were further targeted by a media industry eager to elevate them to adult status as consumers, which the internet only made easier through its proliferation of customized marketing.[20] While some cultural changes showed progress toward tolerance, such as the election of an African American president (2008) and the legalization of same-sex marriage (2013), the political prominence of youth was largely diminished because their characteristic causes—the environment, gender and racial equality, and education—continued to be treated with desultory lip service by most adult leaders.

Compared to Hollywood products since the 1950s that eagerly exploited youth stories, *Boyhood* stands as an inimitable testimonial about the maturation of youth without fanfare or phantasm. Mason—his name suggesting he is a builder—is an unassuming signifier of Middle America in the early twenty-first century, advancing from pre-digital expressions of creativity to cynical hesitation at the future to come. The film ultimately asks us to not worry so much about the future, after all. Just as Mason marches through moments that are rarely planned and most often out of his control, such is life, which goes on regardless of us. For children growing up in the wake of 9/11, who no longer lived with the fear of global nuclear annihilation like their parents but instead felt the paranoid pressure of politicians and news media increasingly warning citizens that terrorism could be around any corner, the 2000s provided weak reassurance that their future was secure. Mason initially enjoys an ascent to the supposed stability of middle-class family life only to see it collapse in the clouds of his two stepfathers' masculine arrogance and alcoholism, leaving him increasingly sardonic about his own opportunities in terms of relationships, labor, and society. His sense of identity evolves from embracing wonder to cautiously recognizing the corruption of power—in families, schooling, and even romance—despite hanging on to modest hopes.

When *Boyhood* began production, the concept of intersectionality had barely entered academic discourse, but by the time of its release, any critical viewing of the film, particularly with its encompassing title, would raise questions about the social traits of its protagonist and other characters. Linklater is clearly working from a white, male, heterosexual perspective, as embodied in Mason, and his lone demographic distinction in relation to most teens in other American movies and media is his working-class status, at least in the early and later years. He thus enjoys much automatic privilege that infuses the increasing frustration he feels about his thwarted expectations of life. By 2014, American youth had been elevated to far more conscious criticism of identity formations in relation to privilege and opportunity, so Mason's alignment with the dominant roles of race, gender, and sexuality can be viewed with a certain apprehension.

At the same time, the limitations of *Boyhood* in addressing a wider range of youth identities are motivated by Linklater's personal experience rather than an effort to normalize Mason's experience. The director not only grew up in South Texas with many of the same experiences as his protagonist, but his view of youth is largely guided by a 1970s sensibility affiliated with his own childhood years: upward class mobility is upheld as a noble objective for those willing to work for it, race and racial tensions are all but invisible in social life, and sexuality is unquestioned by a culture that offers no alternatives to heteronormativity. For all of his sensitivity and critiques, not to mention his father's liberal opinions, Mason seems barely conscious of the homogeneity that characterizes the population around him. His friends are all white, heterosexual guys who chase girls, drink beer, and smoke a little pot; he fits in at school by wearing common clothes and avoiding too much idiosyncrasy; he drives a nondescript vehicle, works a dull service job, and goes off to a generic college just like most of his brethren. Like other children, he grows up with an inborn acceptance of his social status that is waiting to be shattered as he becomes an adult and seeks further meaning for himself by middle age, just as his father did.

The evolution of Mason's identity thus proceeds with little attention to his roles within culture and much more emphasis on his roles within the personal relationships of his youth. *Boyhood* is actually filled with numerous demonstrable lessons about relationships, each of which corresponds to persistent aspects of childhood, and are naturally unrealized until adulthood. These relate to familial permanence, creative expression, romance and resilience, social standing, and that recurring Linklaterian concern about the immediate and entropic passage of time—the core concerns of the movie, and its testaments of youth.

TESTAMENTS OF YOUTH IN *BOYHOOD*

From the first scene in which Mason passionately explains the genesis of wasps to his mother until he leaves for college, Mason relies upon his mother to recognize his interests and ambitions, but nevertheless remains unable to articulate the significance of this relationship. The final scenes find him with new friends at college after he has left his high school friends behind, and we anticipate that they will be influential, but they do not hold the formative relevance of his parents. Even though his older sister Sam (Lorelei Linklater) becomes a more marginal figure in his life as he ages, she continues to play the vital role of leading the way into adulthood, introducing him to college and providing a paradigm of dating that can be 'chill' rather than the higher stakes he sustains with his first serious girlfriend.

As he moves across Texas over the course of the story, Mason's friends come and go, none of whom he mentions in later years. Even his stepbrother is summarily discarded and forgotten after his mother leaves his abusive first stepfather Bill (Marco Perella)—who is also never mentioned again—because they are not *real* family. Meanwhile, Mason's wastrel father reforms and becomes more reliable, maintaining a consistent (if sometimes distant) presence in his life, and he certainly has far more meaningful conversations with him than any of his friends. His mother remains the rock though, even if she crumbles a little in facing her own mortality. She gives Mason a model of determination and perseverance with little pressure, and though he leaves her nest at the end, he is clearly moving on with a sense of direction that is as poised and potent as his accomplished mother. Indeed, he has survived the endless ambiguity of time that so captivates Linklater, and though the future remains equally ambiguous, Mason has become the young man going west with a calm acceptance of his fate.

The Aristotelian adage, "Give me a child until he is seven and I will show you the man"—which inspired the British *Up* series (1964–2019)[21]—applies to our protagonist in many ways. When we first meet Mason at about this age, he is actively questioning life, finding unusual ways to foster his creativity (placing rocks in a pencil sharpener, spray painting in a tunnel), and wondering about the future of his family. For all his coolness, Mason has a lot on his mind. Linklater inserts small clues about Mason's further interests: in the fantasy worlds of *Harry Potter* that will factor into his questions about magic; in his quiet contemplations of a dead bird or his mother's contacts with new men that portend his uneasy understanding of life's changes; in the superficial attention he enjoys from girls that will eventually trouble his romantic relationships.

As a teenager, Mason paints a mural the size of a wall as "urban art," he detests taking pictures of a football game, and his musings on magic become "profound bitching" about the nature of technological influence. Linklater allows Mason's interest in photography to emerge rather organically though and does not labor to portray his early interest in visual design. Mason ultimately declines to take his first photograph to college with him, even though his mother still regards it dearly, because he sees by that point how he needs to put away childish things. As his photography teacher suggests, Mason's talents may not be evident in his work ethic, but they emerge in his energy and exploration.

Although Mason may not have the discipline that this teacher would like to see, the student has many exemplars of achievement to guide him, starting with his mother, and later his father. Both of his parents go back to school in their thirties to learn new career skills, and both become quite comfortable in their roles. Mason is initially frustrated by Dad's decision to sell his old muscle car, because he does not understand the greater benefit afforded by the practical minivan, which is Dad's destined symbol of accomplishment. In his later teens, Mason makes his own practical decisions, such as dismissing a potential promotion at his restaurant job, because the position is only a means to his goal of leaving altogether. His photographic talents help him secure a college scholarship, which is his real ticket out of town, and explain why he can leave his old snapshots behind. Linklater thus makes the equation between Mason's productivity and his potential. Like most young people, Mason is still seeking direction on the eve of adulthood, and he now has the ability to find his way.

Given Mason's youth for much of the story, he does not find himself interested in any kind of romantic relationship until late in the film. Along the way, however, he is witness to his mother's relationships with various men, including his father, which are all fraught with dilemmas that threaten to compromise her integrity. Olivia's relationship with her ostensible third husband (the story never clearly establishes they are married) also has its initial advantages—as a younger partner, Jim (Brad Hawkins) brings a certain verve to their new home together—yet before long, his own compromised integrity becomes a liability for the entire family. Crucially, Mason's final confrontation with him occurs immediately after he meets future girlfriend Sheena (Zoe Graham) at a party, suggesting some of the confidence he feels in letting this fake father know that he is developing an adult identity of his own. Nonetheless, Mason is later left to lament how his relationship with Sheena could not be sustained beyond its high school setting; her infidelity is inevitably with a college boy who offers more experience and less of the pessimism endemic to adolescence. When Mason later bemoans this breakup to his father, Dad tries to reassure him that Sheena did not represent the fulfillment that Mason anticipated, and we sense that this discovery will be the first of many that Mason learns in his further romantic life. By the end, he and Olivia are both without romantic partners, and yet both are better off in pursuing their own interests—though Mason is poised to take another chance.

While Olivia overcomes obstacles and moves on from bad decisions through her distinct determination, such triumphs seem somewhat lost on Mason and Sam, who, like most children, are preoccupied by their own interests, though we begin to see Mason's composure emerge in his teen years. He stoically resists bullies in middle school, he endeavors to fit in with his masculine cohort by boasting like his peers, he calmly resists Jim's criticisms of him, and he stakes out—and succeeds with—his own artistic style, despite his teacher's reprimands over his lack of discipline. When he leaves for college at the end of the film, Mason does not wear the mantle of a survivor or a victim; rather, he remains ever the intrigued explorer, taking in his new experience (now with his camera) and joining others in the exploration of new possibilities. Mason endures the uncertainty of the future with a trust in the present moment that celebrates Linklater's overarching commentary on time.

Mason's insulation is not a deliberate construction; rather, it seems to transform in a natural manner, as first he withstands the hostility of Bill, the disappointments of the family's many relocations, and the frustrations of young romance. He might swallow his contempt when Bill forces him to get his hair cut, or deny his pain when Sheena breaks his heart, until the impacts of these traumas emerge in more overt form later, usually with his parents. Olivia and Dad recognize their son's struggle to save face, which contrasts so dramatically to Sam's penchant for protest, and they also soothe him when he turns to them with his true feelings. This is a pattern that Mason will clearly need to break after he leaves home, for he will inevitably face more disappointments in adulthood on his own.

Linklater has not been didactic in his films; if anything, his characters seem to discover meaning through often random and certainly inconsistent means.

He does present Dad as a left-wing sympathizer who is himself sanctimonious in the beliefs he expresses to his children, but Mason's interest in specific politics is rather vague. Like virtually all teenagers, Mason and Sam are far more enchanted with the communal comportments of their friends and schools than they are by national events. The story cannot avoid politics though, as reminders are abundant beyond Dad's diatribes: Olivia's treatment by most men is patronizing, Jim is disillusioned by his role in the military, Mason detests the consumerist culture foisted upon youth, and their communities are awash in white pride. Within the conservative context of America (and particularly Texas) in the early twenty-first century, these conditions have been normalized, resulting in often unspoken recognition of social discord waiting to be exposed.

A more assertive yet subtle critique is reserved for religion in the film, specifically Christianity, as Linklater portrays his main characters within a largely secular milieu that belies the increasing divisions of devotion arising in post-9/11 American discourse. As jingoistic fears of Muslims gained traction, traditional Christian attributes became increasingly aligned with nationalism, a dubious development the religious right-wing seemed to embrace even more after the election of Obama in 2008 (further evident in irrelevant accusations about the president's connection to Islam). The absence of religion for most of the film, despite the presence that churches have in almost all Texas towns, gives way when Dad sheepishly submits to the expectations of his second wife's Christian parents in order to keep peace in his own home. Mason and Sam are clearly suspicious about his compliance, although they too consent to play along for the sake of propriety. Olivia espouses no religious beliefs whatsoever in the film, nor do her two husbands after Dad. Religion is thus a repressive and ultimately extraneous force in the lives of these characters. Linklater's upbringing in Texas would have certainly informed his sense for how prominent Christianity is within the culture, yet his marginalization of the topic is a critique in itself. The negligible visibility of religion in the film, as well as the minimal impact of politics, reveal Linklater's deeper faith in the influence of humans as individual agents compared to their supposed social synergy.

Linklater's fascination with the passage of time finds its perfect articulation in *Boyhood*, and Mason is an ideal avatar in the search for understanding how we can best grapple with the absolute uncertainty and inevitable procession of time. The film in the end is a sampling of moments that demonstrate the ageless maxim of Kierkegaard: "Life can only be understood backwards, but it must be lived forwards."[22] As Mason discovers his increasing sense of agency in life, he is able to make more decisions on his own, and yet finds himself always already subject to the confines of family, geography, society, and reality itself. The numerous changes of his childhood, across homes and schools as well as friends, have given him a stoic appreciation for the present he occupies. Most of life makes little sense as it happens, despite the efforts of so much structure that society applies to time, such as the twelve years of organized schooling enforced on youth.

Mason does not flail in fury at any potential frustrations. He quietly recognizes the "beauty in the mundane," as Ellar Coltrane observed about his character.[23] He respects the suspense that the future imposes, and as a consequence he is better able to experience his time than so many teenagers who restively confront their development into adulthood. In recognizing the primacy of the present, Mason does not seek the epiphanic breakthroughs so pervasive within conventional youth depictions. On the edge of adulthood, he has come to terms with time and its inexorable changes at a level that some adults never achieve.

Of course, this wisdom is bestowed upon Mason through Linklater's own experiences and education over many more years than his protagonist has lived. If *Boyhood* was the work of a much younger author, it may have indeed expressed more anxiety about the nature of change and the inconsistency of life. Instead, Linklater has created a character with the advantage of age, evolving within a world carefully constructed as a work of art that simultaneously celebrates liberation from the demands of structure. *Boyhood* is at once a collection of mere moments, and a demonstration of how each of those moments may signify so much and so little all at once. That significance is thus unclear and its value is unreliable. All that remains certain is this moment right now.

NOTES

1. In an interview from 2010 while Linklater was still in production, he curiously remarked of *Boyhood*: "I think time is sort of a lead character, if you wanted to get technical about it—the lead character of the movie." David T. Johnson, *Richard Linklater* (Urbana: University of Illinois Press), 148.
2. Richard Linklater, "Memories of the Present," in *Boyhood: Twelve Years on Film*, edited by Matt Lankes (Austin: University of Texas Press, 2014), 8.
3. Boris Kachka, "Ellar Coltrane Spent 12 Years Acting for Richard Linklater. Now What?" *New York Magazine* (June 30, 2014): http://www.vulture.com/2014/06/ellar-coltrane-on-his-12-year-movie-role.html
4. Gabe Klinger, "What is Boyhood?" *cinema scope 58 (2014)*: 8–17.
5. See my analysis of 1990s movies emblematic of this atmosphere: "Reification and Loss in Postmodern Puberty: The Cultural Logic of Fredric Jameson and Young Adult Movies," in *Postmodernism in the Cinema*, edited by Cristina Degli-Esposti (New York: Berghahn Books, 1999), 73–89. Specific to Linklater and the postmodern, see Mary Harrod, "The Aesthetics of Pastiche in the Work of Richard Linklater," *Screen* 51:1 (2010): 1–17.
6. Nicole Sperling, "One Actor, One Kid, 12 Years, One Film. 'Boyhood,'" *Entertainment Weekly*, July 17, 2014: 31–32.
7. Ibid.: 32.
8. Linklater claimed in an interview: "We started this film 4,207 days ago. We think that's the longest production in history." Emily Buder, "5 Things We Learned About Filmmaking from Richard Linklater's 'Boyhood,'" *IndieWire*, June 23, 2014: http://www.indiewire.com/2014/06/5-things-we-learned-about-filmmaking-from-richard-linklaters-boyhood-25035/
9. Michael Dunaway and Tara Wood, *21 Years: Richard Linklater* (Breaking Glass Pictures, 2014), DVD.

10. Helen Alexander and Rhys Blakely, "The Triumph of Digital Will Be the Death of Many Movies," *The New Republic*, September 12, 2014: https://newrepublic.com/article/119431/how-digital-cinema-took-over-35mm-film
11. Ashley Clark, "Film of the Week: *Boyhood*," *Sight & Sound*, August 2014: http://www.bfi.org.uk/news-opinion/sight-sound-magazine/reviews-recommendations/film-week-boyhood
12. Katy Steinmetz, "Everything You Need to Know About the Making of *Boyhood* Over 12 Years," *Time*, July 11, 2014: http://time.com/2974681/boyhood-movie-making-of-richard-linklater/
13. Many of these production images have been collected in Matt Lankes, *Boyhood: Twelve Years on Film* (Austin: University of Texas Press, 2014).
14. Steinmetz, "Everything You Need to Know About the Making of *Boyhood* Over 12 Years."
15. For detailed financial information on *Boyhood*, see "Boyhood (2014)," *The Numbers*, accessed June 20, 2017, *Nash Information Services*: http://www.the-numbers.com/movie/Boyhood
16. Mason is actually Mason, Jr. and his father is Mason, Sr. For the sake of concision and clarity, I refer to Mason, Sr. as "Dad."
17. Cecile Rousseau, Uzma Jamil, Kamaldeep Bhui, and Meriem Boudjarane, "Consequences of 9/11 and the War on Terror on Children's and Young Adults' Mental Health: A Systematic Review of the Past 10 Years," *Clinical Child Psychology and Psychiatry* 20:2 (2013): 173–193.
18. Many of these cases, and a trove of data, can be found in Laura Finley, *School Violence: A Reference Handbook* (2nd ed.) (New York: ABC-CLIO, 2014).
19. Sameer Hinduja is one of the most prominent scholars studying cyberbullying; among other works, see his book with Justin Patchin, *Bullying Beyond the Schoolyard: Preventing and Responding to Cyberbullying* (2nd ed.) (New York: Corwin, 2014).
20. A view of youth as more empowered by technology can be found in Yuya Kiuchi and Francisco Villarruel (eds.), *The Young Are Making Their World: Essays on the Power of Youth Culture* (Jefferson, NC: McFarland, 2016).
21. The famous British series began with *Seven Up!* in 1964 and has most recently resulted in *63 Up* (2019). A movie crew has been visiting most of the same fourteen people every seven years for decades, documenting their progress through life beginning at age seven, and tacitly examining the influence of British class and social structures on the influence of citizens' development.
22. Søren Kierkegaard (1843), *Papers and Journals: A Selection*, ed. and trans. Alastair Hannay (Hammondsworth, U.K.: Penguin, 1996), 161.
23. Ellar Coltrane, "Growing Up on Camera," in Lankes, *Boyhood*, 12.

CHAPTER 7

The (Un)bearable Weight of Gendered Genre: Richard Linklater's Post-*Boyhood* Masculinities

Mary Harrod

Since the release in 2014 of his multi-award-winning *Boyhood*, the once under-examined filmmaker Richard Linklater has come to greater public prominence and begun to attract amplified critical scrutiny. That film's innovative approach to filming the same child actor growing up in "real time" over nearly two decades won rapturous praise for its apprehension of the quick of transient life,[1] while its attention to the struggles of a single mother garnered a Best Supporting Actress award for Patricia Arquette at the 2015 Oscars and commendation of Linklater for feminism.[2] Yet rather than building on *Boyhood*'s overtly realist project, Linklater's subsequent work refuses to sediment into such easy classifications. This is perhaps not surprising for a director whose association with fare as varied as the experimental feature animation *Waking Life* (2001) and the mainstream blockbuster *The School of Rock* (2003) has always led audiences to expect the unexpected; the two films produced after *Boyhood* in any case appear on the face of it to initiate a major change of direction—if not a reactionary *volte-face*. *Everybody Wants Some!!* (2016) spends three days in 1980 following the social interactions of a college baseball team played by actors in several cases pushing a decade older than the characters they incarnate and who look "initially [. . .] so pristine as to seem not real."[3] Their principal activity is showing off, to each other and the opposite sex, and there are no substantial female roles—although in the tradition of lascivious "frat boy" films initiated by *Animal House* (Ramis, 1978), women do feature as underwear-clad mud-wrestlers, airheads fit to be subjected to jokes about "studying cunnilinguistics" and, on one occasion, a topless conquest in a small dark space.[4] *Last Flag Flying* (2017) casts three heavyweight, popular, older actors, Bryan Cranston, Steve Carell, and Laurence Fishburne, as Vietnam veterans Sal, Doc, and Mueller who reunite in 2003 in order to accompany Doc in transporting for burial the body of only his son killed in Iraq, propelling them on an all-male odyssey that gently echoes Vietnam War-era buddy road movies among the best-known of which are *Easy Rider* (Dennis Hopper, 1969), *Butch Cassidy and the Sundance Kid* (George Roy Hill, 1969), and *Midnight Cowboy* (John Schlesinger, 1969).[5] In line with the broad concerns of those films and more particularly with the cultural associations of military life, on their journey the protagonists of *Last Flag Flying* learn some difficult lessons about what Sal calls "be[ing] a man." Clearly signaling the film's concern with parameters of desirable performances of masculinity in this millennium, this phrase is articulated when Doc views his dead son's mutilated corpse ("you gotta be a man now"), and as such can be read as endorsing the traditionally desirably "masculine" quality of stoicism. Women, meanwhile, are even more absent from this diegesis: mise-en-scène and dialogue on the rare occasions they allude to them at all do so almost exclusively to situate women within a heterosexual economy associated with male pleasure and virility (exchanging fond recollections of frequenting female sex workers stands out), and only one somewhat more extended scene includes any female actress, Deanna Reed-Foster in the role of Mueller's wife. Little wonder, then, that some reviewers were put off by the masculinism of these films, and (it is reasonable to surmise) more specifically by their apparent nostalgia for retrograde constructions of this gender identifiable with earlier Hollywood genre cycles.[6]

This chapter interrogates in detail Linklater's post-*Boyhood* masculinities as constructed by the films in question, initially via a focus on their (fairly explicit) thematizing of manhood then through a thoroughgoing analysis of the inseparable question of their generic participations. In line with Christine Gledhill's observation that "in media genres, the genericity of social gender is put to fictional and dramatic use, making its aporias and contests visible and opening up multiple possibilities of generic-gender play and transformation,"[7] I argue that rather than simply endorsing backward notions of manhood that celebrate such once presumed natural male traits as aggression, competitiveness, love of hierarchies, territoriality, promiscuity, and pronounced homosociality,[8] *Everybody Wants Some!!* and *Last Flag Flying* underline the constructed nature of past-facing gender identities and ideals, in this case "the inherent minstrelsy of the gender/genre performance[s] of 'man.'"[9] Like John Alberti, I see genre and gender categories as closely co-imbricated in the context of cinema, where popular formats in particular reiterate and embroider on gender archetypes, in so doing staging and negotiating discursively legible identities through their broadly mimetic (though indirect) relationship with the profilmic world. For this reason, this chapter interrogates from a gender studies perspective the participation of *Everybody Wants Some!!* in U.S. youth films, as well as examining its engagement with both buddy road movie and bromance conventions and the sports movie, and it looks at *Last Flag Flying*'s creative use of tropes drawn principally from Westerns via buddy road movies and from the Iraq War movie subgenre. Such a perspective sheds light on the difficulties of unpicking the gender politics of the films under consideration, given their ritual deployment of conventions, aesthetics, and affects linked to earlier filmic and cultural modes. I ultimately argue, nonetheless, that it is at the level of generic and more generally stylistic form that these films' complex views of past ideals are most clearly expressed, through an ambivalent yet recurrent embrace of the overtly inauthentic trappings of former eras—the inescapable "weight" of socio-generic convention—as paradoxically a generative means of self-expression or actualization, and a legitimate route to potently felt human connection and identity formation in the present, that need not equate to retrograde politics. In making this claim, I sketch continuities between Linklater's most recent male-focused genre pieces and not only *Boyhood* but the director's earlier oeuvre more widely, which as a whole comprises a lucid intervention into cinema's potential to mediate human experience.

INTERROGATING MANHOOD

Everybody Wants Some!! has also been honored with the label "spiritual sequel," by Linklater himself describing its relationship not with frat comedies but to both *Boyhood* and the cult classic *Dazed and Confused* (1993).[10] This is most obviously a propos thanks to its focus on the beginning of college for its main character, Jake (Blake Jenner): the approximate moment at which both of Linklater's earlier youth-focused chronicles ended. *Last Flag Flying* picks up a different baton, as it adapts a 2005 novel written by Darryl Ponicsan as the sequel to his 1969 *The Last Detail*, re-scripted for cinema by Robert Towne and directed by Hal Ashby in 1973 (and starring Jack Nicholson); Ponicsan collaborated with Linklater on the screenplay for his adaptation. Yet to the extent that *Everybody Wants Some!!* can be seen as a coming-of-age story, in detailing an apparently key moment in young people's transition to adulthood, arguably so can *Last Flag Flying*, since it at least flirts with depicting later-life maturation. Apart from the central focus on the (typically) later-life challenge of learning to deal with loss, during their Odyssey between Virginia, Delaware, and New Hampshire the trio of erstwhile comrades-in-arms discuss for the first time an act of inadvertent cruelty in which they participated in Vietnam, when a fellow soldier died in agony because they had exhausted their unit's morphine supplies in recreational use: a crime for which Doc took the blame and spent time in a military prison. They also attempt to make some amends for their actions by visiting the dead man's mother and speaking of his bravery and achievements. Doc's status as some years younger than his companions, complemented by Steve Carell's association with arrested development in several films but most famously *The Forty-Year-Old Virgin* (Judd Apatow, 2005), positions his bereaved character as the focal channel for the coming-of-age arc. Stolid bravery as a viable means to face unbearable human truths is figuratively endorsed in the film's final sequence, where Sal and Mueller join Doc in carrying his son Larry Jnr.'s coffin to the burial site (on their shoulders) in military uniforms, before returning to their friend's home for the wake and seeing him apparently comforted by the day's obsequies—the *ne plus ultra* among rites of passage—and the discovery of a letter in which Larry speaks of his happiness to die "for his country."

However, on closer examination, masculine coming-of-age trajectories are held at arm's length if not entirely disavowed in both the films in question. This genre is most obviously concerned with a main character (or characters) who are "able to move forward in his or her life and mature into a 'new age.'"[11] Beginning with *Everybody Wants Some!!*, the temporal setting is deliberately chosen. In the first place, the film includes regular titles counting down the days and hours until classes begin. As such, its action takes place outside of the educational experience proper, at least inasmuch as this constitutes an officially sanctioned milestone in knowledge acquisition. More importantly, the deadline structure is rendered absurd by students' open disdain for learning (they discuss means to attain credits without working) and the anti-climax of the classroom scene itself, which closes the film with a professor writing the at once anti-epistemological and patronizing, faintly sci-fi inflected sentence "Frontiers are where you find them" on the board, at which point Jake and his teammate Plummer promptly settle down to sleep. The film counts down, in sum, not to better times but rather something like the nothingness eclipsing youth for Doc's son in *Last Flag Flying*. It should be acknowledged that teen and college films are not coterminous with the broader cultural "coming-of-age" genre that evolved from eighteenth-century German literary *Bildungsroman*. The sidelining or ridiculing of education itself is indeed typical of such films and especially the frat subgenre focused on hedonistic partying.[12] It is perhaps more striking given *Everybody Wants Some!!!*'s overlap with the sports movie genre that nor does much baseball appear in the narrative, let alone any competitive fixture that might have added a landmark moment of triumph or even "character-building" loss (as adumbrated in Linklater's earlier Little League baseball-themed *Bad News Bears* [2005]) later in the narrative; instead, these moments are limited to unstructured practice sessions colored by a bitter rivalry at odds with the ethos of teamsmanship or meaningful communal identity which the characters elsewhere profess to embrace. In both arenas (education and sport), in other words, Linklater's structural approach is quite explicit in pulling the rug out from under any real sense of "future potential"[13] still broadly associable with many American youth films (even if the normative heterosexual romance plot retains some promise). Indeed, the film's entire architecture beyond the intertitles is episodic and wandering, loosely hinging on three nights of partying. Secondly, the choice of 1980 is also ironic for a coming-of-age story set after the events of *Dazed and Confused*, given a character's iconic statement in that film that, "It's like the every other decade theory y'know. The '50s were boring, the '60s rocked. The '70s, ohmigod, they obviously suck. I mean c'mon. Maybe the '80s will be radical, y'know." The film speaks to generational identity flux if not crisis by having its central characters put on different clothes and personae for variously themed nights out (a disco, a country night, a punk concert, and a fancy-dress house party thrown by drama students), with Jake openly discussing the confusion this provokes in him: "It sort of begs the question of who we really are."[14] Extratextual knowledge, meanwhile, lends irony to the bright-eyed hopefulness of these intermittently bohemian and anti-authoritarian young people about any "radicalism" in the 1980s, which would turn out to be a decade dominated by a reinforced individualistic conservatism, against which the 1970s—whose influence is still much in evidence in the boys' long hair, sizable moustaches and sideburns, and cannabis-smoking—would be held up as a pinnacle of liberalism.

Although its characters demonstrate a greater change of attitude throughout the course of the film than do those of its forerunner, *Last Flag Flying* also rejects the possibility of true maturation into any social realm defined by the Law of the Father. In the first place, Sal's exhortation to Doc to "be a man now" directly following the viewing of the corpse can be read as applying not only to dealing with unpleasant emotions but more directly to refusing to blindly accept hegemonic narratives, especially those promoted by (U.S.) territorial state actors. This is because the dead man's injuries belie the (false) version of the events surrounding his death initially fed to Doc by the U.S. army. Rarely have "masculine" hierarchies been as literally recast as contingent than by Sal's comment moments earlier to Doc that: "You don't gotta listen to no colonels anymore." Soon afterwards, Doc takes Sal's advice to refuse an army burial "with full honors" for his son and take the corpse home himself. Equally strikingly, linear progress itself is spatially eschewed by the protagonists' itinerary, which first takes them to Arlington National Cemetery in Virginia to collect Larry Jnr.'s corpse, only to have them realize it is still at his base in Delaware (a detour Linklater refused his editor's advice to cut).[15] Augmented by the fact that the group are later forced to abandon their truck and take a train due to an absurd mix-up that sees Mueller fingered for terrorism, and indeed are left behind at a stop on one occasion, this meandering approach gently parodies the buddy road movie paradigm it has initially engaged—though not necessarily the buddy comedy (see *Planes, Trains and Automobiles* [John Hughes, 1987]), on which more later.[16] There is also a black irony to any coming-of-age story that takes the form of a journey leading to the grave (in Sal's words, "Everybody's always in transit, even when you're dead"), while the corpse that the trio visibly heft from one form of transport to another—with Sal even deriving gallows humor from play with the truck's forklift—is more likely to be interpreted as a grotesque literalization of the unendurable burdensomeness of certain ideals of U.S. masculinity, epitomized by the military as an agent of the nation's social and geopolitical identity, than as a metonym for martial heroism.

The very ideal of maturing with age is also sent up by specific elements of narrative, characterization, and dialogue in both films, through individual characters and by extension generations. In *Everybody Wants Some!!*, the pearls of wisdom imparted by the senior college students to new arrivals revolve almost exclusively around scoring "college pussy," and the dynamic is further travestied by a purposively ludicrous hazing scene involving freshmen gaffer-taped topsy-turvy to a wall while baseballs are fired at them. The fact that this moment echoes a similar scene in *Dazed and Confused* loudly enough for several reviews to have noted the parallel suggests another invitation to conclude that a college education has little effect on behavior in Linklater's intertextual universe. *Last Flag Flying* makes no bones about the need to read its "mature" men in relation to the increased prevalence of discourses of (white) male instability visible throughout the two decades preceding its release.[17] Donna Peberdy conveys the sense of what these discourses mourn by citing the character Ricky Roma (Al Pacino, Oscar-nominated for the role) from director James Foley's 1992 film adaptation of David Mamet's well-known play *Glengarry Glen Ross*, for whom "it's not a world of men. It's a world of clock watchers, bureaucrats, office holders . . ."[18] This suspicion of the corporate and technological sphere in favor of a nebulously defined "world of men" speaks to the implied worldview of *Last Flag Flying*'s Sal in particular, who despite viciously critiquing the military rhetoric surrounding both the Vietnam and Iraq wars (and so appearing a mouthpiece for Linklater's well-known anti-establishment views)[19] expresses nostalgia for life in the Marine Corps and, as a functional and unashamed alcoholic who earns a paltry livelihood through ownership of a bar and grill whose grill has "gone to rust," has rejected normative contemporary ideals of masculine worldly success. (Doc and Mueller's professions as stocking clerk at the Navy Exchange retail chain and man of the Church, respectively, also smack of mothballs.)[20] Cranston's totemic association through the television series *Breaking Bad* (AMC, 2008–2013) with the character Walter White, public service employee-turned-arch-criminal-drug lord and denizen of the deserts of the American West,[21] further informs this impression. Both he and his buddies are meanwhile portrayed as left behind by the technological revolution specifically, through a comical interlude during which Sal buys them all cellphones. If this act might appear to suggest "growth," reflexivity about successive ideals of masculinity relativizes the validity of any of these, as Sal declares, cowboy-style, "Barkeep, a round of phones for my friends here."

Indeed, *Last Flag Flying*'s occasional or indirect (by way of the road movie) references to the Western themselves signal a self-conscious interrogation of what it means to be a man during any era. Masculinity in classic Westerns tended to be very explicitly celebrated through an appeal to such values as the pioneer spirit and self-sufficiency; "[a]s portrayed in the Western and alluded to in the road movie, frontier symbolism is propelled by masculinity and a particular conception of American national identity that revolves around individualism and aggression."[22] However, further specifications are elusive, since a key feature of this genre's more enduring cultural work—especially in the postclassical period—has also been to interrogate masculinity as a continuum of positions whose respective claims to legitimacy wax or wane in varying contexts and especially at different historical moments.[23] One of the most famous films to exemplify this aspect of the genre, the John Wayne-James Stewart vehicle *The Man who Shot Liberty Valance* (John Ford, 1962), proves a particularly suggestive comparison point for *Last Flag Flying*. In it, Wayne plays a small rancher who metes out vigilante justice to violent criminals like Valance, pitted against Stewart's progressive lawyer. The film was made at a time when the older Wayne's currency as an ideal of tough masculinity was being devalued and for all his character's ability to check individual eruptions of disorder, he is negatively associated with obsolete aspects of Western masculinity such as an anti-egalitarian suspicion of education and democracy, and of civic life as such.[24] Yet, *The Man who Shot Liberty Valance* depicts U.S. history as based on the very myths of masculine strength embodied by Wayne: in the much-quoted words of a newspaper writer near the end of Ford's film, "when the legend becomes fact, print the legend." This closing emphasis problematizes through irony that film's focus on the need for male leadership to modernize, since Stewart's educated figure can only institute "civilized" ways more progressive than the brute force employed by Wayne's character to keep law and order because he is (falsely) mythologized as a murderous sharpshooter. Likewise in *Last Flag Flying*, not only is tough, military masculinity mocked and held in contempt by Sal and the film as a whole when it is revealed that the U.S. Army's offer of a hero's burial for Larry Jnr. is founded on lies, but the alternative Sal initially proposes—that the best route "is never the lie"—is equally undercut, when the men visit the mother of the man who perished with them in Vietnam and cannot bring themselves to go through with telling her he died arbitrarily and in agony. In this way, the possibility of acceding to greater, more responsible adult manliness through looking life's difficulties in the face, which elsewhere appears a worthwhile ideal, is thrown as heavily into doubt as "the illusion of historical inevitability" in what David T. Johnson calls Linklater's anti-Western, *The Newton Boys* (1998).[25] Indeed, associable as it is with masochism (at one point Doc says "I don't want to make it easy on myself"), such a stance is just one more in a list of masculinities ripe for puncturing through dark comedy, when Mueller observes, "Morphine *is* addictive," only for Sal to smartly riposte, "Yeah, so's pain."[26]

GENRE AS/AND GENDER

The above example points toward the stakes of considering gender identities through the prism of U.S. genre in Linklater's recent male-focused diptych: the multiply inflected and shifting terrain of identity formation that is revealed when we unpick the intricate ways in which models of masculinity are interwoven with story structure, character type, and iconography. In this section I will show, however, that the (sub)genre that best accounts for and illuminates the masculinity on display in *Last Flag Flying* is a successor to the Western: the Iraq War movie, combined in a sometimes-awkward admixture with the ("mature") buddy comedy. The latter genre in turn provides the principal lens through which I view *Everybody Wants Some!!*, overlaid by the aforementioned college variant (while, like the road movie in *Last Flag Flying*, the sports movie format turns out for the most part to be, if not a red herring, an inverted shadow genre). My key argument is that gendered genre tropes are exaggerated in both films in such a way that they address the viewer through a pastiche mode embracing ostentatious imitation I have previously identified in Linklater's films outside the present, more genre-focused perspective.[27] I begin with the later film since the strategy is more obvious here, being worked out substantially through plot and dialogue, while (in line with the substantially semantic determinants of the U.S. youth film) *Everybody Wants Some!!*'s self-consciousness is often more a question of style, especially visual.[28] In both cases, however, this approach is significant for Linklater's apprehensions of "manhood," in that by highlighting their representations' imitative status in general, the films in the process highlight the artifice of gender, as famously described by Judith Butler. A reading whereby genres pastiche themselves perfectly encapsulates Linklater's engagement of long-standing popular (and other) cinematic forms in the service of ongoing aesthetic resonance and affective meaningfulness even in their very constructed-ness, contingency, and inherent tendency toward ideological obsolescence; and this view can also be extended to these films' portrayals of masculinity.

Cinema Scope journalist Sean Rogers has observed that Linklater is not a director to shy away from having characters state his "theses" or points of view and I have already suggested that at times Sal expresses truistic liberal critiques of the U.S. military from a nonetheless "wise"—seasoned but humorously distanced—and sometimes righteously angry perspective.[29] Thus in a parody of 1960s and 1970s rhetoric, colored by bathos, "I was ready to kill me some Commies in San Diego but they never showed up," while what the army and government tell you is quite simply "a pile of crap." Sal is an anti-hero, spouting offensive views of women (in one gratingly awkward scene over a semi-formal lunch he tells the wife of Mueller, who has now become a Reverend, that his girlfriend has "other talents" than cooking) and puerile homophobic jokes (to Mueller, whose first name is Richard, "you like Dick?"). Yet just as Rick Zinman discusses the (somewhat overlooked) theme of paternal avatars in *Boyhood*, Sal can be likened to the highly flawed father figure who still ultimately has something to offer played by Ethan Hawke in the earlier film and several other Linklaterian examples, among which *School of Rock*'s Dewey Finn is the most salient.[30] The examples demonstrate well my point about the desirability (and impossibility) of throwing the proverbial baby out with the cultural-generic bathwater in which it is inevitably coated, even if the latter is a little off-color. And once more, Cranston's persona is crucial to this effect: *Breaking Bad* creator Vince Gilligan reputedly cast the actor for his "ability to be both loathsome and sympathetic"[31] and certainly Cranston's much-touted likeability and comedic gifts are key to offsetting Walter White's increasingly execrable behaviors in that series, as they are to setting Sal up as the primary identification figure in *Last Flag Flying*. Broader aspects of plot and mise-en-scène meanwhile contribute to a highly negative view of the U.S. army and foreign policy. As touched on, while Doc is told his son was killed protecting his comrades, it is revealed he was in fact shot in the back of the head while buying (with unsubtle, nationalistically—and neoliberally nuanced—irony) "cokes" for the men.[32] More evocative than such details alone, however, is the appearance of the sterile space from which Doc collects his son's body and learns the truth (via Sal, from an indiscreet soldier): as one review notes, the aircraft hangar's bare whiteness not only conveys cold bureaucracy but also the impossibility of obfuscating horrors.[33] Further, the colonel in charge himself is so pale that, with dark hair and (seemingly) eye make-up, he personifies the deathly visage of the outmoded institution (Figure 7.1).

This view is important from a generic perspective because the defining feature of the Iraq War film is its centralization of critiques of war, including through subtle elements of wry parody, building on but intensifying this impulse in Vietnam films: a kinship also ostentatiously figured in this film by the protagonists' identity as veterans of the earlier conflict.[34] As Sal observes, "Every generation has its war," while the response from the soldier, Washington, tasked with accompanying the men and corpse on the train to the burial site (played by L. Quinton Johnson, who also starred in *Everybody Wants Some!!*), "You're there for your brothers and that's what really matters," is a cliché of the genre particularly redolent of Kimberly Peirce's *Stop-Loss* (2008).[35] While that film also coincides with Linklater's in partially exploiting a road movie

Figure 7.1 The colonel's pallor in *Last Flag Flying* suggests the U.S. army's waning vitality as a viable social institution

structure—but on another journey, effectively, to nowhere—the setting of events off the battlefield and a focus on a bereaved family are also frequent tropes reproduced by Linklater's "familiar template."[36] One more specific commonplace deserves special attention for its over-deterministic engagement of questions of masculinity: the ironic repurposing of the iconography of the U.S. flag—and actual or implied flagpole, as transparent phallic signifier of patriarchal nationalism. Ironic deployments of this symbol are central enough to the genre to feature on several films' posters, while *In the Valley of Elah* (Paul Haggis, 2007), centralizing another grieving father (Tommy Lee Jones) who unearths a comparable cover-up about the inglorious circumstances of his "heroic" son's death, closes with the disillusioned protagonist lowering the stars and stripes from a pole on his front lawn. Linklater goes one step further by referencing the national flag in his title, thus drawing fairly explicitly on a heavily compromised generic repertoire of associations around U.S. military prowess. Moreover, if Robert Eberwein has identified a linkage between male sexual and military failure in Iraq War films (in which he includes both Gulf conflicts) and particularly explicitly in *Jarhead* (Sam Mendes, 2005),[37] here too *Last Flag Flying* is self-conscious and tongue-in-cheek, as virile penile function provides the subject of a comical exchange between the central trio and young Washington, where Sal muses ruefully: "I had a Johnson that would stand up and watch me shave [. . .] now it watches me pull up my socks." Cranston's impression of his member through silly voices and even a ramrod pose (reversing the usual synecdoche whereby the phallus represents the man) make the sequence all the more laughable—indeed, Carell's well-known comic persona emerges as Doc is barely able to speak for guffawing.

Through such humor, which in revolving around discussion of female conquests in a male-only space directly engages buddy comedy tropes, Linklater moves beyond the crescendo of condemnation and disgust to which the oddly anti-war war film (sub)genre of the Iraq War movie has built and which it nonetheless so heavily references. Likewise, his final sequence reverts to an ambivalent endorsement of the meaning of American masculinity connoted by the stars and stripes, as Doc reverses his decision to bury his son in civilian clothes, opting for a military burial performed by Sal and Mueller, who join the deceased in being decked out in full uniform. This ceremony is a pastiche of the hero's send-off to the extent that it has been established that Doc's son was shot in the back of the head while purchasing refreshments; the source of masculine "heroism" in material behaviors (let alone biological-reductionism) becomes irrelevant and meaning lies in the discourse and not the historical "reality" it purportedly celebrates. Thus a slow-moving camera and a predominance of medium shots as well as some overhead ones emphasize the elaborate choreography of proceedings, including the folding of the flag to be given to Doc (Figure 7.2), yet Sal states simply: "I don't know how grateful the nation is or how much the President regrets your loss and all that, but here it is, your country's flag." In sum, while the epic stature of virile, nationalistic masculinity (and indeed Christianity, through ceaseless mockery of Mueller's faith) has been thrown into doubt at every turn by the film, the trappings of this identity and the rituals in which it is embedded are shown to be meaningful as much as anything from an experiential perspective, underlined by cutaways to Doc with a trembling lower lip and Levon Helm's soulful, country-accented "Wide River to Cross" in the score, in a mise-en-abyme of the mode of address of the whole film.

Figure 7.2 The generic choreography of emotion is embraced by *Last Flag Flying*'s climactic funeral sequence

Noting that critic J. Hoberman has seen postclassical buddy films as picking up the homosocial dynamics of the Western, most obviously when they also update horseback motion as transport on wheels, Maria San Filippo characterizes the 1970s phase of that genre as tragic but identifies comedy with post-1980s variants.[38] *Last Flag Flying* sit somewhere between the two modes such that the film puts more than one period of cinematic memory into productive dialogue—notably about gender identities—consonant with postmodern discussions of pastiche that emphasize "engaging the history of art and the memory of the viewer in a re-evaluation of aesthetic forms and contents through a reconsideration of their usually unacknowledged politics of representation."[39] The jostling of different sensibilities linked to different generic cycles reinforces the film's own concern with transience, obsolescence, and anachronism and may also produce an effect similar to that described by Elena Gorfinkel in reference to temporally disjunctive American independent films wherein the viewer "becomes aware of his or her own historical position, caught between different periods, in a region of illegible temporality and mobile film historical space."[40] *Everybody Wants Some!!* more fully embraces comic distance in service of the drive underpinning both films to "invite[s] spectators to engage affectively, *though not [. . .] uncritically*, with history."[41] Specifically, in "nail[ing] the pressure that guys come under to act cocksure when they aren't really that sure at all,"[42] Linklater wrings humor from the performativity of vigorous, "red-blooded" youthful masculinity epitomized by the college sportsman—the emblematic jock of frat comedy. Here, the film wears its generic agenda on its sleeve to the extent of verging on caricature: at one point Jake tells fellow freshman Brumley (Tanner Kalina) not to be so desperate (for senior peer approval) and the latter responds, "Desperate for pussy!", while Jake elsewhere draws attention to the way in which "everything round here's a competition" and Finnegan (Glenn Powell) to the fact that "It's all so fucking tribal," as the young men while away their time pursuing sometimes intense or violent sporting and leisure activities, from ping pong to hitting a baseball with an axe to games of "bloody knuckles."

Everybody Wants Some!! resonates particularly loudly, however, in the specific context of the "bromance" strain of buddy movies consolidated in the mid-2000s by (namely) comedies such as *Wedding Crashers* (David Dobkin, 2005), *I Now Pronounce You Chuck & Larry* (Dennis Dugan, 2007), *Superbad* (Greg Mottola, 2007), and ensemble films by Judd Apatow.[43] Homing in on this period, San Filippo identifies a newly invigorated drive in such comedies to "defamiliarize the compulsory monosexuality that governs our logics of desire" by modelling "heteroflexible conceptions of millennial masculinity and gender relations."[44] Importantly, for San Filippo these films refract rather than repudiate the need for boundary-policing of heterosexual and homosexual categories linked to fear of the latter in earlier cycles. This observation corroborates Alberti's identification of subtle yet anxiety-ridden displays of homophobia in contemporary bromances; yet San Filippo, following Andrew Horton, emphasizes the way in which comedy's liberation from realism nevertheless allows it to play with and within liminal spaces outside conventional norms and *Everybody Wants Some!!* appears on balance adventurous with regards to the possibility of bisexuality, not retardataire. If Brumley's "desperation" to impress other men is signaled once through dialogue, homoerotically-tinged homosociality saturates the actors' physical performances, as they repeatedly slap each other on the backside; Brumley—sounding suspiciously like Bumley, in a possible frat-style joke fitting for the film's autobiographical derivations from Linklater's own youth as a college baseball player—is notably tactile in interactions with his peers. While some commentators took umbrage at male point of view shots of female derrières in the film, these can be read as part of the film's meta-referentiality to frat buddy comedy, while Hannah Jane Parkinson rightly points out that the flesh offered up throughout the film for our gaze is overwhelmingly male, apparently prompting one commentator to dub *Everybody Wants Some!!* "the gayest [film] of 2016."[45] Though low-level, cartoonishly graphic homophobia peppers jovial competitive banter earlier in the film ("I heard her call you a cock-jockey," "I heard cock-gobbler!"), later Jake and another team-member are apostrophized to admire Roper's (model Ryan Guzman) behind in tight trousers as he twerks and pouts over one shoulder, hazing includes duping new arrivals into putting their face near each other's be-jock-strapped anuses, and teammate Dale's (Johnson) possible Freudian slip "Temptation my asshole!" is humorously echoed as a mock-shocked interrogative by Finnegan. As in the Van Halen song its name cites, *Everybody Wants Some!!* apparently elevates sexual conquest ("getting some") to the status of principal motivation, yet the equal structural weighting accorded to performing virile masculinity between men blurs boundaries; in this context, the title's nondiscriminatory ethos evokes proto-queer relationalities.

Casting and styling are key aspects of *Everybody Wants Some!!*'s playful distancing-through-exaggeration of the psychosexual dynamics common to college films and indeed teenpics (of which they are often seen as a subset). I have already alluded to the choice of actors for the most prominent roles significantly older than the characters they are playing, which is a cliché of onscreen teen narratives; thus Guzman and Tyler Hoechlin (playing McReynolds) were twenty-nine while Powell was twenty-eight and Jenner twenty-six in 2016.[46] Not only was Wyatt Russell, playing self-styled spiritual guru-type Charlie Willoughby, 30, but through this character the film winkingly recognizes the tendency by having it revealed that Willoughby *is* in fact a thirty-year-old posing as a college baseball player in order to endlessly defer growing up. The echo here of Ben Affleck's overgrown high school hanger-on O'Bannion from *Dazed and Confused*, who in turn recalled John Milner (Paul Le Mat) from ur-teenpic *American Graffiti* (George Lucas, 1973),[47] constellates intergenerational exchange within the text alongside intertextual examples of the same phenomenon. More to the point, the glorification of the actors' athletic physiques includes their youthful but fully grown maleness. Exceptionally tight costumes are well chosen here to convey visually the pressure to fit bodies into social molds rather than vice versa. In the case of Brumley, his outfits are moreover exaggeratedly childish, usually consisting of school-boyish shorts and long socks, at odds with his slouchy young adult posture and the light moustache that dusts his upper lip, despite his teammates openly mocking the latter's volume to further highlight liminal maturity. Pairing such features with a baby face and slight overall chubbiness accentuated by snug vest-tops (Figure 7.3), Brumley embodies graphically the weight of manhood, by embracing the larger-than-life generic frat comedy tropes of both caricatural physical precocity and life-stage-confusion. He simultaneously does so by triangulating these with homoeroticism, when we note on-screen male polysarkia's linkage to not only immaturity but also effeminacy and "queer fat," or a representational tendency to signify queerness through corpulence.[48]

Referencing (at times ill-fitting) types chimes with *Sight and Sound* reviewer Pamela Hutchinson's aforementioned appraisal of characters' unreality, which she ties to their perfect appearances and in particular the film's use of primary colors in depicting them: another prosaicism of the U.S. teen genre.[49] This perspective underlines the kinship between *Everybody Wants Some!!* and Linklater's forays into rotoscoping, *Waking Life* (2001) and *A Scanner Darkly*

Figure 7.3 Tanner Kalina's Alex Brumley (left) is the face of queer fat in *Everybody Wants Some!!*, in a scene where his housemates suggest losing at cards means he must fellate a moose

(2006), where real actors' performances were drawn over to render them as animations for the final cut. The comparison is, however, not simply a question of artifice; just as the animated films troubled categories of realism,[50] so does *Everybody Wants Some!!* emphasize iconicity and indexicality as inseparable—as suggested by my stress on graphic embodiment as part and parcel of the instantiation of ostentatious imitation. It is worth noting that *Last Flag Flying*, too, alongside its discoursing on U.S. foreign policy, acknowledges that it is the corporeal nature of the experiences shaping subjectivities that makes it particularly difficult—and undesirable—to reject the cultural drifts and tenor of the spatio-temporalities in which they occurred. Thus military identity is rendered as a corporeal selfhood when Sal says he has always identified with the green "race," meaning the Marine Corps, over the white one and admits his nostalgia for a period otherwise characterized as barbarous, dehumanizing, and ideologically meaningless if not negative.[51] Similarly, he maintains that the U.S.A. remains "a great country" (presumably, in terms of cultural heritage) even if its government is dishonest. Put differently, however cynical the postmodern sensibility of these films may be about grand, collective narratives, individual identities are colored by group ones: a tension classically explored by war, teen, and sports films alike, where the desire to shine—or simply survive—coexists restlessly with the need to collaborate.[52]

CONCLUSION: ONTOLOGIES OF THE LIGHTNESS OF BEING

Sal's statement about national ideologies bears comparison with *A Scanner Darkly*'s melancholic interrogation of a U.S. society in which comforting truths had been radically undermined, which was figured through that film's destabilizing of ontologies.[53] In my earlier discussion of that film, I read this phenomenon through Butler's account of post-9/11 U.S. melancholia, and her writings prove equally apposite for these later Linklater films. While *Last Flag Flying* self-evidently participates in male melodrama, several reviews identified a comparable, perhaps unexpectedly melancholic, affect to *Everybody Wants Some!!*.[54] This derives from an awareness of transience much closer to that of *Boyhood* than the film's upbeat action might suggest. As *The Observer* put it, "Linklater [. . .] looks on the puppyish, peach-skinned beauty of these college athletes in a way that no jockish campus jaunt of the 80s would have done: a celebratory gaze, in one sense, but laced with awareness that this too shall pass."[55] And if the seemingly formula-driven college film proves simultaneously connected with vital existence, defined by mutability, it might be noted that despite its unique intervention into the time-bound, shifting texture of the latter domain, conversely, *Boyhood* repeatedly acknowledges the inescapably culturally mediated nature of everyday existence—after all, time is a manmade invention. Thus, Mason's desire to stay off screens is belied by aspects of that film's mise-en-scène, most obviously as deriving from his identity as a budding photographer.[56]

The reconciling of "direct" and mediated experience as largely indistinguishable in the way they act upon and are inscribed on the body in Linklater's work further echoes Butler's nonetheless culturalist theories of gender (a detail sometimes left out of reductive accounts of her work), for instance in her assertion that embodied sexuality shapes cultural intelligibility from the outset.[57] While in *A Scanner Darkly* the deferral of indexical embodiment to an inaccessible space outside the text heightens a melancholic sense of loss, in contrast and as I have also argued for *Dazed and Confused*,[58] the three male-focused films (including *Boyhood*) discussed here come closer to Richard Dyer's appraisal of pastiche imitation as able to communicate a sense of living "permanently, but without distress, within the limits and potentialities of the cultural construction of thought and feeling";[59] or, the need to fit into gender and other molds is bittersweet but ultimately bearable in these narratives. Nowhere is this more in evidence than in *Everybody Wants Some!!*'s upbeat soundtrack highly evocative of the late 1970s to early 1980s period yet nonetheless over-identified with mediations of it: for instance, The Knack's "My Sharona" with which *Everybody Wants Some!!* opens was the theme tune to Gen-X classic *Reality Bites* (Ben Stiller, 1994). Some critics have suggested the film sloughs off aesthetic and character-driven fakery in favor of greater authenticity in its latter half but I see this as a false binary for Linklater—thus Finn's supposed revelation of his "true self"[60] later in the film when he archaistically reads books by Beat Generation hero Jack Kerouac, smokes an attention-grabbing pipe, or wears a kaftan (Figure 7.4) on the contrary illustrates the impossibility of getting away from culturally conditioned selves (as well as containing another visual joke about links between youthful and aged selves). Similarly, Willoughby may discuss finding your identity "between the notes" in Pink Floyd's "Fearless" but just as those aspects of this film that might appear unusual for a mainstream Hollywood comedy—the contempt for learning despite the educational setting, in-your-face homoeroticism and backbiting among friends—in fact redeploy conventions in sometimes innovative ways, even guitarist Dave Gilmour's interstitial moments exist entirely within the framework of the pentatonic scale's recognizable structures.

Such an apprehension speaks to the uniquely acute evocation by Linklater's films not so much of the lack of distinction between "subjective" and "objective" realism in the age of widespread digital mediation as the utter meaninglessness (by definition) of embodied subjectivity unshackled from discursivity in the first place.[61] Even when they are living out a version of Linklater's own "directly" experienced past, characters have no need to be rotoscoped in order to appear

Figure 7.4 Finn's (Glenn Powell's) costuming in *Everybody Wants Some!!* expresses both the provisionality of identity and generational confusion

ersatz performers subscribing to the dictum "fake it to make it." On the other hand, the role of the living, feeling body recurs in discussions of representing living creatures even as entirely animated copies in his work (Steven Shaviro's discussion of Linklater's *Waking Life* and *A Scanner Darkly* repeatedly references the [un]touchability of memory)—and indeed beyond.[62] Yet the conflation of bodily-emotive and culturally constructed experiences of gendered and all selfhoods in Linklater's films goes beyond even influential theories of embodied film address focused on the haptic, which preserve the binaristic vocabulary of surface *versus*, rather than *as*, "depth."[63] This corporeally articulated yet culturally determined conception of both life and the cinematic experience may well be his work's most important contribution toward evoking the provisionality of not just masculinity but all identities, while championing such flimsiness as a nonetheless valid (because it is the only possible) mode of being in the world.

NOTES

1. Manohla Dargis, "From Baby Fat to Stubble: Growing Up in Real Time," *The New York Times*, July 10, 2014: https://www.nytimes.com/2014/07/11/movies/movie-review-linklaters-boyhood-is-a-model-of-cinematic-realism.html; Mirhan Tariq, "'Boyhood': Richard Linklater's Extraordinarily Unique Commitment to Beauty of Real-Life," *Hollywood Insider*, October 29, 2020: https://www.hollywoodinsider.com/boyhood-linklater-review/
2. Amy Taubin, "Headline Acts," *Film Comment*, March–April 2016: 64. "Real time" is Dargis's approximation for the gradual way in which we see *Boyhood*'s main actor age

with the character. See also the statement by the American Film Institute honoring the film for its "snapshots of a life lived" (in Timothy Shary, *Boyhood: A Young Life on Screen* [London and New York: Routledge, 2018]).
3. Pamela Hutchinson, "*Everybody Wants Some!!*" *Sight and Sound* 26:6 (2016): 60–61. Linklater's following film, *Where'd You Go, Bernadette* (2019), also explicitly broaches feminist-accented topics around female self-realization.
4. *Animal House* is invoked by more than one reviewer of *Everybody Wants Some!!*, although like me, Wendy Ide suggests the similarities are superficial. Wendy Ide, "Everybody Wants Some!! Review – Jocks Away," *The Observer*, May 15, 2016: https://www.theguardian.com/film/2016/may/15/everybody-wants-some-review-linklater-freshmen-campus. Other examples of this genre include *Revenge of the Nerds* (Jeff Kanew, 1984), *PCU* (Hart Bochner, 1994), *Van Wilder Party Liaison* (Walt Becker, 2002), *Road Trip* (Todd Phillips, 2000), and the cross-generational variation *Old School* (Phillips, 2002).
5. The fact that Cranston's role was originally offered to *Easy Rider* star Jack Nicholson—who had featured in *Last Flag Flying*'s predecessor *The Last Detail*, discussed in the next section—suggests a certain self-consciousness about this lineage. Philip Horne, "It Shouldn't Happen to a Vet," *Sight and Sound* 28:2 (2018): 10–11. For further discussion of buddy road movies of the liberationist era, see Maria San Filippo, "More than Buddies: Wedding Crashers and the Bromance as Comedy of (Re)Marriage Equality," in *Millennial Masculinity: Men in Contemporary American Cinema*, edited by Timothy Shary (Detroit: Wayne State University Press, 2012), 182–183.
6. On *Everybody Wants Some!!*, see Eileen Jones, "Nobody Wants Some," *Jacobin*, May 5, 2016: https://www.jacobinmag.com/2016/05/richard-linklater-everybody-wants-some-mumblecore/; or Jean-Loup Bourget, "*Everybody Wants Some!!*" *Positif* 663 (May 2016): 54. Hutchinson, "*Everybody Wants Some!!*" 61, in an otherwise positive review, also finds the film to be marred by its "straight-white-maleness." The lukewarm reception of *Last Flag Flying* is best exemplified by its lack of critical coverage for a Linklater film, while Peter Bradshaw's (2018) review in *The Guardian* calls it "generic" and an "oldster roadtrip."
7. Christine Gledhill, "Preface," in *Women Do Genre in Film and Television*, edited by Mary Harrod and Katarzyna Paskiewicz (London and New York: Routledge, 2017), x.
8. See R. W. Connell, *Masculinities* (2nd ed.) (Berkeley and Los Angeles: University of California Press, 2005), 46.
9. John Alberti, *Masculinity in the Contemporary Romantic Comedy: Gender as Genre* (London: Routledge, 2013), 24.
10. In Hannah Jane Parkinson, "'Jocks get a bad rap': What *Everybody Wants Some!!* Says About the Modern Man," *The Guardian*, May 13, 2016: https://www.theguardian.com/film/2016/may/13/everybody-wants-some-richard-linklater-boyhood
11. Selbo in Alistair Fox, *Coming-of-Age Cinema in New Zealand: Genre, Gender and Adaptation in a National Cinema* (Edinburgh: Edinburgh University Press, 2017), 5.
12. Robin Wood, "Party Time or Can't Hardly Wait for that American Pie: Hollywood High School Movies of the 90s," *CineAction!* 58 (2002): 4–10. I have also argued elsewhere that *Dazed and Confused* mimics teenpic classic *American Graffiti* (George Lucas, 1973) in eschewing narratives of progress. Mary Harrod, "The Aesthetics of Pastiche in the Work of Richard Linklater," *Screen* 51:1 (2010): 21–37.
13. Catherine Driscoll, *Teen Film: A Critical Introduction* (Oxford: Berg, 2011), 29.
14. It also briefly flirts with exploring such confusions at the level of its own cinematography, by using a split-screen phone device redolent of even earlier cinematic decades for a phone-call between Jake and the object of his affection, Beverly.
15. Horne, "It Shouldn't Happen to a Vet," 11.
16. Cf. Ryan Gilbey, "*Last Flag Flying*," *Sight and Sound* 18:2 (2018): 66.

17. See: Sally Robinson, *Marked Men: White Masculinity in Crisis* (New York: Columbia University Press, 2000); Raya Morag, *Defeated Masculinity: Post-traumatic Cinema in the Aftermath of War* (Oxford: Peter Lang, 2009); Donna Peberdy, *Masculinity and Film Performance: Male Angst in Contemporary American Cinema* (London: Palgrave Macmillan, 2011), 7; Claire Sisco King, *Washed in Blood: Male Sacrifice, Trauma, and the Cinema* (New Brunswick, NJ: Rutgers University Press, 2011).
18. Peberdy, *Masculinity and Film Performance*, 1.
19. Linklater has been seen as a poster child for Generation X, whose members are typically often associated with independence and critical thinking. His most blatantly ideological film is surely *Fast Food Nation* (2006), inspired by Eric Schlosser's eponymous book interrogating how destructive food cultures have reshaped U.S. identity.
20. A hackeneyed critique of religious belief is nonetheless rehearsed by Sal, who says in anti-hierarchical spirit that in a world that includes child rape, genocide, and 9/11, it's God who should be explaining himself to him and not the other way round.
21. See Mark Bernhardt, "History's Ghost Haunting Vince Gilligan's New Mexico: Genre, Myth, and the New Western History in Breaking Bad," *Journal of Popular Film and Television* 47:2 (2019): 66–80.
22. Shari Roberts, "Western Meets Eastwood: Gender and Genre on the Road," in *The Road Movie Book*, edited by Steven Cohan and Ina Rae Hark (London and New York: Routledge), 45. It should be noted that such values were heavily questioned, negotiated, and revised by the late 1960s buddy road movies cited in this article.
23. John White, *Westerns* (London and New York: Routledge, 2011), 43.
24. Robert B. Pippin, *Hollywood Westerns and American Myth: The Importance of Howard Hawks and John Ford for Political Philosophy* (Castle Lectures in Ethics, Politics, & Economics) (New Haven, CT: Yale University Press, 2010), 76–77.
25. David T. Johnson, *Richard Linklater* (Urbana, Chicago, and Springfield: University of Illinois Press, 2012), 51–52.
26. The (North) Eastern U.S. setting of the action also literally and self-evidently distances *Last Flag Flying* from traditional Westerns. Despite the East Coast setting, Linklater has discussed his intentions to target Republicans disillusioned by the status quo, with Doc's home in swing state New Hampshire offering an obvious example of this demographic in the East—a comparable one to that represented by Walter White, whom Morgan Fritz describes as "not so much directly conservative as emblematic of the new enraged petty bourgeoisie of the so-called Tea Party." Morgan Fritz, "Television from the Superlab: The Postmodern Serial Drama and the New Petty Bourgeoisie in *Breaking Bad*," *Journal of American Studies* 50:1 (2016): 176. See also Horne, "It Shouldn't Happen to a Vet," 11.
27. Richard Dyer, *Pastiche* (London: Routledge, 2007), 1; Harrod, "Aesthetics of Pastiche."
28. On the semantic determinants of the post-1980s genre, see Elissa Nelson, "*The Breakfast Club* as Archetype: Revealing the Tropes of the Teen Film as Genre," Paper delivered at SCMS Conference, March 30–April 3 (2016), Atlanta, GA. The syntactic variety tolerated by youth films is also a running theme of the seminal work of Timothy Shary in this area.
29. Sean Rogers, "*Everybody Wants Some!!*" *Cinema Scope* 17:67 (2016): 77.
30. Rick Zinman, "Richard Linklater's *Boyhood* and the Problem of Aging in Film," *Senses of Cinema* 91, July 19, 2019.
31. Eric San Juan, *Breaking Down Breaking Bad: Unpeeling the Layers of Television's Greatest Drama* (CreateSpace Independent Publishing Platform, 2013), 20.
32. The fact it is once suggested these were a local brand does not invalidate the reference to Americana.
33. Gilbey, "*Last Flag Flying*."

34. For a full discussion of the Iraq Wars on film, see Robert Eberwein, *The Hollywood War Film* (Hoboken, NJ: Wiley-Blackwell, 2019), 122–135.
35. Mary Harrod, *Heightened Genre and Women's Filmmaking in Hollywood: the Rise of the Cine-De* (London and New York: Palgrave Macmillan, 2021).
36. Michael Koresky, "Last Flag Flying," *Film Comment* 53:6 (November/December 2017).
37. Eberwein, *The Hollywood War Film*, 131.
38. San Filippo, "More than Buddies," 182–183.
39. Linda Hutcheon, *The Politics of Postmodernism* (New York: Routledge, 1989), 96. Hutcheon uses the term "postmodernist parody" (and even contrasts this with a Jamesonian notion of "blank" pastiche) but describes practices I am subsuming, following Dyer, under the wider umbrella of pastiche.
40. Elena Gorfinkel, "The Future of Anachronism: Todd Haynes and The Magnificent Andersons," in *Cinephilia: Movies, Love and Memory*, edited by Marijke de Valck and Malte Hagener (Amsterdam: Amsterdam University Press, 2005), 155.
41. Ibid., 153, my emphasis.
42. Parkinson, "'Jocks get a bad rap.'"
43. On bromances see also Tamar Jeffers McDonald, "Homme-com: Engendering Change in Contemporary Romantic Comedy," in *Falling in Love Again: Romantic Comedy in Contemporary Cinema*, edited by Stacey Abbott and Deborah Jermyn (London: I. B. Tauris, 2007), 146–159; Alberti, *Masculinity in the Contemporary Romantic Comedy*, 25–43; and, on *Superbad* specifically, Celestino Deleyto, "The Comic, the Serious and the Middle: Desire and Space in Contemporary Film Comedy," *Journal of Popular Romance Studies* 2:1 (October) (2011).
44. San Filippo, "More than Buddies," 183.
45. Parkinson, "'Jocks get a bad rap.'"
46. The choice of Jenner for the role also explicitly alludes to teen TV through the actor's starring role in *Glee* (Fox Television, 2009–2015) and there is a sense here of cinephile Linklater branching out to position his diegesis in a new media intertextual web. Such a view appears particularly appropriate when we consider the database-like elements of the sequence where the protagonists of *Everybody Wants Some!!* attend differently themed social events in succession, literally trying on different outfits or selves at each. As Marsha Kinder has pointed out, of course, "interactivity did not begin in cyberspace" but is present in more subtle forms in fiction dating back many centuries. Marsha Kinder, "Designing a Database Cinema," in *Future Cinema: The Cinematic Imaginary after Film*, edited by Jeffrey Shaw and Peter Weibel (Cambridge, MA: The MIT Press, 2003), 351. Indeed, Linklater's *Before Sunrise* (1995) (and to an extent its sequels) plays with a "garden of forking paths" narrative structure—such that here too the director positions his work, for all its innovation, in relation to earlier generations as well as multiple cultural forms. See: Jorge-Luis Borges, *El jardín de los senderos que se bifurcan* (Buenos Aires: Editorial Sur, 1943).
47. Harrod, "Aesthetics of Pastiche," 24.
48. Caetlin Benson-Allott, "The Queer Fat of Philip Seymour Hoffman," in *Millennial Masculinity: Men in Contemporary American Cinema*, edited by Timothy Shary (Detroit, MI: Wayne State University Press, 2012), 200–222.
49. Gemma Edney "Un Vrai 'Teen Film' Français? The Contemporary Adolescent Genre in French Cinema," in *Screening Youth: Contemporary French and Francophone Cinema*, edited by Romain Chareyron and Gilles Viennot (Edinburgh: Edinburgh University Press, 2019), 7.
50. Steven Shaviro, "Emotion Capture: Affect in Digital Film," *Projections* 1:2 (Winter): 70.
51. The derivation of *corps* from the Latin for *body*, *corpus*, highlights the extent to which identification beyond the social is encouraged by the institution.
52. As Linklater has put it, "What is individuality?", in Johnson, *Richard Linklater*, 144.

53. Harrod, "Aesthetics of Pastiche," 24.
54. Tim Grierson, "Everybody Wants Some: Dazed and Confused, Again," *The New Republic*, March 29, 2016: https://newrepublic.com/article/132145/everybody-wants-some-dazed-confused; Andriana Sotiris, "*Everybody Wants Some!!* is a Coming of Age Drama that Sidesteps the Genre's Pitfalls," *Socialist Worker* 2504, May 17, 2016: https://socialistworker.co.uk/art/42745/Everybody+Wants+Some%21%21+is+a+coming+of+age+drama+that+sidesteps+the+genres+pitfalls
55. Guy Lodge, "Everybody Wants Some!!; Green Room; Author: The JT LeRoy Story; Whiskey Tango Foxtrot and More – Review," *The Observer*, September 18, 2016.
56. David Rudd, "'Life Doesn't Give You Bumpers': A Coming or Going of Age in *Juno* and *Boyhood*," *Quarterly Review of Film and Video* 37:6 (2020): 593.
57. Judith Butler, *Bodies that Matter: On the Discursive Limits of "Sex"* (New York: Routledge, 1993).
58. Harrod, "Aesthetics of Pastiche," 26–27.
59. Dyer, *Pastiche*, 180.
60. Hutchinson, "*Everybody Wants Some!!*" 61.
61. Shaviro, "Emotion Capture," 70. It is noteworthy that not employing self-consciously digital, typically multi-media aesthetics is one point on which Linklater's engagement with the Iraq War in *Last Flag Flying* deviates from many examples of the genre, as first noted by Garrett Stewart in "Digital Fatigue: Imaging War in Recent American Film," *Film Quarterly* 62:4 (Summer, 2009): 45–55.
62. Ryan Pierson, *Figure and Force in Animation Aesthetics* (Oxford: Oxford University Press, 2019), 134. In his book on the practice, Ryan Pierson cites rotoscoping artist Mary Beam's perception that "when I rotoscope I can touch whales."
63. For instance, Laura Marks's well-known description of how "[haptic visuality] tends to move over the surface of its object rather than plunge into illusionistic depth, not to distinguish form so much as to discern texture." Laura U. Marks, *The Skin of the Film: Intercultural Cinema, Embodiment, and the Senses* (Durham, NC: Duke University Press, 2000), 162.

CHAPTER 8

Stories So Far: Romantic Comedy and/as Space in *Before Midnight**

Celestino Deleyto

In one of the most often quoted lines from Richard Linklater's *Before* trilogy—*Before Sunrise* (1995), *Before Sunset* (2004), and *Before Midnight* (2013)—Céline (Julie Delpy) locates God in "the little space in between" people. The dialogue with Jesse (Ethan Hawke) in which this line appears takes place in Vienna when they first meet in *Before Sunrise*. For Céline, this is an intimate space, the glue that brings the bodies and souls of people together. From a generic perspective, in the *Before* trilogy, this "little space" seems to evoke romantic comedy, the genre of intimate protocols and short distances. But, in a different sense, this space is not so little: it expands and contracts in major ways in the course of the eighteen years that the story lasts. It is a transnational space that comprises the cities of Vienna and Paris and the region of Messenia in the Peloponnese. It includes also all the places in which the characters have lived or visited (some mentioned, some not) at least in the two nine-year intervals between the films, if not beyond them: the trilogy sparks this particular kind of imagination in spectators, who feel compelled to fill in the gaps between the three brief moments in the lives of the characters depicted by the films. In other words, Céline's "space in between" is both intimate and transnational—in part, intimate because transnational. In this chapter, I would like to explore this intimate/transnational space in the third of the films, *Before Midnight* from the comic perspective offered by the trilogy and this film in particular.

The very prominent different national origins of the lovers in the trilogy—Céline French, Jesse American—have, surprisingly, gone practically unmentioned in the abundant scholarship on the films. It is as if critics had implicitly agreed on the irrelevance of this difference—reluctant, perhaps, to admit that such things matter anymore in a supposedly borderless world. However, we do not live in a borderless world and borders as well as national differences continue to matter. If anything, as Cooper and Rumford affirm, borders proliferate today more than ever before.[1] In this chapter, therefore, I want to stress the narrative importance of the transnational couple—not primarily through human interaction but rather through an exploration of the spaces in which their relationship develops. These spaces are, as we shall see, the result of a cinematic rendering of the geographical and social spaces in which the story is set: Vienna, Paris, the southern Peloponnese. As a whole, the trilogy offers a remarkably accurate if subtle perspective on Europe and the process of transnational European integration in the eighteen years and three decades that the films span: from the 1990s to the 2010s. It could be argued that the process of European integration and its ups and downs in the three decades—from early ambitions of progress toward political union, through subsequent, often failed, attempts at bringing it to fruition, to the growing tide of nationalist retrenchment and magnification of internal and external difference—are the trilogy's deep, if almost invisible, structuring principle. The trilogy exists in this historical reality and develops a rich, comic perspective on the continent's social and geopolitical space. While the three films share a common European space, the specificities of the three places and times in which their respective actions happen are such that they demand individual consideration. For this reason, this chapter will focus only on the third instalment, *Before Midnight*, and on the intersection between social space and comic perspective, one that encompasses the little space of romantic comedy but also, as will be seen, a larger comic space. After a brief theoretical discussion of this intersection and its particular manifestation in the film, I first explore the production of the southern Peloponnese as cinematic and transnational space offered by the film and then examine its comic perspective. Taking issue with those interpretations of the movie that consider it more melodrama than comedy, I focus on Céline and her relation with space as a conduit for the film's comedy and on Delpy's performance in three specific scenes. Finally, the chapter ponders on the significance of a cultural text that looks at the recent history of Europe through a comic lens.

THE COMIC PERSPECTIVE AND THE SOCIAL SPACE

Classical comic theory developed along two lines: the Aristotelian tradition that inscribed comedy within the realm of the social and described its goal as corrective, and early twentieth-century anthropological speculations on the origins of the genre in fertility rituals and seasonal celebrations. Once the ritual turned into theatrical performance and then into narrative, it would produce, among other manifestations, Old and New Greek comedy and, many centuries later, Shakespearean and romantic comedy. What transpired from this history was not only a series of generic clusters but also a particular way of looking at the world—a "comic view," with humor, laughter, *eros*, resilience, the impulse of survival and the renewal of life as its main characteristics. In recent film theory, Andrew Horton and Joanna Rapf include variants of these two trajectories among their six "observations" on the genre: comedy as a way of looking at the universe and as "one of the most important ways a culture talks to itself about itself."[2] These two insights bring together the location of comedy in the realm of the social and the comic as a particular perspective on the world.

In one of the first books on film comedy, Gerald Mast had argued that, apart from "comic plots," what characterizes the genre is a "comic climate," through which "an artist builds signs into a work to let us know that he considers it a comedy and wishes us to take it as such."[3] Among these signs, he lists certain types of characters, comic dialogue, and cinematic techniques of mise-en-scène, framing, editing, and performance. He concludes that what may not be a comic plot in itself can be turned into comedy through the cinematic articulation of this comic climate. This notion helps Mast to explain why the same story can produce a relentless melodrama in Eric von Stroheim's film version of *The Merry Widow* (1925) and a musical comedy in Lubitsch's 1934 adaptation of the original operetta.[4] In a previous work, I have posited a similar concept as one of the central elements of romantic comedy: the comic space of the genre. Drawing on Northrop Frye, Deborah Thomas, and others, and starting from the comic worlds of Shakespearean comedy and its Renaissance predecessors, I have defined the space of romantic comedy as a magic space of transformation that allows intimate desires to be expressed in a less inhibited way than in the social space of everyday relationships, one that protects characters from social pressures and repression and may help them mature.[5]

The comic space is one of the ways through which comic texts negotiate a culture's conversation with itself. This conversation is carried out precisely through the deployment of a magic space in which anything can happen, where love, but also friendship and sociability, can flourish and where a comic perspective on the world around us is the only requirement. This transformation of social into comic space tells us as much about the society and the historical time in which the text exists as about the text itself. We may read the comic space as a way to understand the social space but also as a way to remember, more generally, that every story is susceptible to a comic angle and, further, that our grasp of our place in society and history would be incomplete without it. (To illustrate with a brief example, *Trouble in Paradise* [Ernst Lubitsch, 1932] transforms a social space of stifling sexual protocols and inhibitions and, secondarily, social unrest as a consequence of the financial crisis of the early 1930s into a magic space in which desire, if subject to its own contradictions and crises, successfully overcomes social repressions, which are duly (and hilariously) ridiculed. The film both enters in conversation with the social debates of its time and insists that a comic lens such as the one it applies to its view of society is essential not only because social critique is important for a society to progress but also because our lives would be sadly incomplete without the capacity to laugh at the world around us.)

This comic space does not erase the dramas, conflicts, and grim realities of the world, and is thus firmly rooted in everyday experience, but it entreats characters and spectators to find comedy and appreciate its value in the midst of those grim realities. Classical theorists have tried to describe this comic principle in various ways, from the expression of the human capacity to endure, to resist, and to keep going to the insistence to make game of "serious" life.[6] It is present in Freud's view of humor as a victorious assertion of the ego's invulnerability and defiance of the world,[7] and is also behind Horton and Rapf's assertion that in the world of comedy, nothing is sacred and nothing human is rejected.[8] Comedy is celebratory, anarchic, and iconoclastic. Because it demands our right to laugh at everything and find joy in life even against all odds, Bakhtin's description of medieval carnival continues to be one of its most comprehensive expressions: a time of the year in which everything is permitted, hierarchies are upended, the low becomes high and the high low, a moment in which people laugh at everybody and everything, with a laughter that is both satirical and festive. Carnival occurs on the border between art and life, a form of play that becomes a way of life.[9] The combination of celebration of life and defiance of death, of iconoclasm and joy, is the guiding principle in the construction of the comic space and of comedy's approach to the social world. In *Before Midnight*, we find joy and laughter in a space which is made up of a multitude of individual and communal stories, crucially including, as will be seen, those that tell of transnational encounters, intercultural alliances, and mixed social groups as well as individuals. For the duration of the film, spectators are asked to look at this transnational comic space as joyful, without denying its many problems and contradictions.

My focus on space in the analysis of comedy can be framed within the more general notion of the spatiality of cinema. As Mark Shiel suggests, film is more a spatial than a textual system, by which he means that the deployment of space is more important than the narrative. As such it is particularly adept at illuminating the dynamics of lived spaces.[10] The spatiality of romantic comedy is part of this spatial turn that the cinema has shared in recent times with other disciplines, including geography, philosophy, art history, and literary studies. In spatial theory, space is not a backdrop for human action but something produced by humans. Most influentially, Henri Lefebvre sees space as socially produced through both discourse and social practices.[11] For her part, geographer Doreen Massey laments the split between space and time that in the course of the twentieth century relegated the former to synchrony. Space is often seen as immovable whereas time lasts, flows, changes. She argues that space and time are inseparable. Space is as mobile and subject to constant change as time: never fixed but constantly flowing. The commuter that looks from the train window at the same place every day does not see exactly what they saw the day before. When we travel, we do not only travel through space but also across earlier trajectories and ongoing stories. Places constantly change. For example, adults' dreams of returning home to find the location of their childhood are illusory.[12] She describes space as a simultaneity of stories-so-far and a multiplicity of durations.[13] We perceive space through stories and our understanding of a place is the aggregate of all the stories that have occurred in and have been told about that place. With this in mind, I will argue that cinematic space—both in the sense of the fictional or fictionalized location in which the characters are placed and of its formal construction—is, as Antoine Gaudin argues, a dynamic phenomenon produced by the film and one that is located in history.[14] Both in its changeability and its constructedness, cinematic space is no different from social space.

Therefore, the social space that comedy transforms into a comic space is not only constructed through social practices and discourse but also through time and history. It is the sum total of the stories associated with a particular place. These previous stories are incorporated into a dynamic cinematic space, however indirectly or invisibly. When a comic text transforms a social space, it is contributing a comic view of that space and prompting spectators to add the necessary comic perspective to their understanding of it. That is, comedy offers an interpretation of the social world, a social world which exists in real places. As John Rhodes and Elena Gorfinkel argue for film in general, part of the power of comedy lies in its explanatory power of real places, their history and the stories that make up what those places are.[15]

The social space turned comic space in the *Before* trilogy is Europe. Far from a static reality, Europe was, in the eighteen years' interval between the releases of the three films, characterized by rapid change and fiercely contradictory impulses and discourses, the meeting point of a plurality of stories. In the early 1990s, Europe was in the throes of what appeared to be an epochal transformation. As such it became part of the space of *Before Sunrise*. Since then, from their small place in culture, the three films have traced, in often indirect ways, a history of vigorous hopes and growing frustrations. Beyond the interpersonal relationship they narrate, the three stories are transnational stories, created within the context of the uneven process of European integration, and participating in what Randall Halle has called a transnationalization of European culture.[16] The first two films are, in industrial terms, essentially U.S. products, while *Before Midnight* was produced by Faliro House, a Greek company that has participated in the production of both Greek and U.S. films. The three of them, although more directly in the case of *Midnight*, participate in this cultural process, while adding, through Jesse's presence, an American perspective to a trans-European movement in which the cinema was, as Halle asserts, fully integrated.[17]

A transnational Europe becomes, then, the general space of the trilogy. As a result, the films do not only create a very distinct, if unstable, comic world but also cast their comic view on the idea of European integration and the series of crises and setbacks undergone by the continent during the eighteen years between the first and the third, and further into the future. In the next sections, the article explores some of the stories-so-far that are used as part of the construction of the comic space of *Before Midnight* and suggests the ways in which the film contributes, through its comic space, a comic view of Europe as the site of intense and sustained transnational mobilities.

WELCOME TO KARDAMYLI

The three films of the trilogy are set in locations where, as Maria San Filippo says, "history looms large."[18] The three show a sharp awareness of history in their construction of space but, I argue, it is their recent history as part of a changing European reality that is gradually brought to the forefront. The first two films had used Vienna and Paris to construct vivid comic spaces at two different stages in the transnationalization of European culture—early optimistic belief in greater political integration and turn-of-the-century setbacks—which provided an apt environment for the blossoming and re-awakening of transnational romantic desire between the protagonists. Given the conceit of two characters walking and talking under the intense scrutiny of the camera, the space around and beyond them could have receded into invisibility and irrelevance, yet Linklater often suggests otherwise. Most apparent are the two montage sequences, at the end of *Before Sunrise* and the beginning of *Before Sunset*, of the places visited by the characters, once they have become separated in the first film, and before they get together again in the second. Beyond more specific meanings about the desolation of Vienna once the lovers have gone their different ways and the hope in the tentative reunion of the couple in Paris, this is a direct warning to spectators not to ignore the centrality of space in the trilogy, a warning that is spelled out in *Before Sunrise* when Céline describes the painting by Georges Seurat "La voie ferrée" as a world in which the environment is stronger than the people, humans appearing to dissolve into space in his paintings.

In general terms, Linklater had, by the time of *Before Midnight*, developed a strong sense of space in his films. Critics have highlighted and described the director's realistic approach to cinematic representation, including the films of the trilogy, and have mentioned his use of "real" locations, the simplicity and transparency of his cinematic style, the recurrence of long takes, and the realistic performances he elicits from his actors among other techniques as some of the ways to implement this approach.[19] From *Slacker* (1990), Linklater's brand of 1990s "American" realism has been the organizing principle of his constructed spaces.[20] In the trilogy, these same formal strategies are also the tools through which the European spaces are imbued with a comic perspective. At the same time, the trilogy's depiction of space is, as in Massey's theory, closely linked with temporality. The spectators are ushered into the different European locations as Jesse and Céline walk through them and they are revealed to them and us in the course of their wanderings. In this, Linklater's creation of filmic space from the real places in which the films were shot reminds us of the role of the road in the paintings of Paul Cézanne, in whose landscapes the bend of the road constantly alters our point of view and heralds the irruption of the new.[21] In *Before Midnight*, as the couple discover the southern Peloponnese, like Cézanne, from the road, Linklater, Delpy, and Hawke create a rich and evocative comic space through a deep engagement with the real places where the story is located and a remarkable alertness to their historical, social, and cultural realities, both past and present.

By now familiar with the presence of transnational Europe at a crucial period of its history and its bearing on the romantic developments in the ongoing relationship, we come to *Before Midnight*. In the summer of 2012, when the film is set, things have changed in the fictional world: the brief summertime encounters in European capitals of the previous two instalments have given way to a stable relationship and a family. The transnational romance which in the two previous films had produced cliffhanger endings rather than serious conflicts—Will they meet again in six months? Will he miss his flight back to the U.S.?—is now threatened by transnational realities. Living in Paris, Jesse has been separated from his son Hank (Seamus Davey-Fitzpatrick), who lives in Chicago with his mother and only sees his father during the holidays, and he begins to find the separation unbearable. In the course of the film, this brings Jesse and Céline to the verge of breakup. In keeping with the trilogy's open endings, the film leaves the couple's conflict unresolved. In the meantime, the dream of Europe as a geopolitical reality in which borders would work as sites of encounter and exchange rather than exclusion and repression has suffered serious blows: first the series of national resistances culminating in the failure of the European Constitution to be implemented in 2005, and then the financial crisis of 2008 which, having originated elsewhere, hit the continent hard, with populist nationalisms on the rise and transnational aspirations on the retreat throughout the Union. The filmmakers set their third episode in Greece, the country that was most seriously affected by the economic crisis and that, together with Spain and Italy, came to epitomize the depth of the divide between North and South within the continent. The refugee crisis of 2015, again with Greece as its epicenter, intensified the North/South chasm and dampened the dream of transborder tolerance. Thus, the transnational couple in crisis is thrown right in the middle of one of the fault lines of the transnational European project.[22] The social space has changed in eighteen years and the most recent stories that have accumulated have brought it further away from the already fragile optimism of the first film.

Jesse and his family have been invited to a writers' retreat in a house in the southern Peloponnese. For the central part of the narrative Linklater breaks the pattern established in the two previous films and in the long initial scene of this one, when, in the central section of the movie, Céline and Jesse share an important segment of the story with other characters. These are the people staying in the house in what seems to be the last day of Céline's and Jesse's holiday. They are the host, a British writer called Patrick (Walter Lassally), married couple Ariadni (Athina Rachel Tsangari) and Stefanos (Panos Koronis), Patrick's friend Natalia (Xenia Kalogeropoulou), his grandson Achilleas (Yiannis Papadopoulos), and the latter's partner, French actor Anna (Ariane Labed). The ebullience and extroverted behavior of these characters, as seen particularly during the dinner scene but also in previous conversations between the men in the garden and the women in the kitchen, transcend realism and become part of the process of transformation of the social space into a comic space. At the same time, the transnational make-up of this group is reinforced by extra-filmic elements that reinforce the credibility of the resulting comic space.

The central section of the film was shot in Kardamyli, in the Messenian Gulf, in the house of popular travel writer and ex-British Army Officer Sir Patrick Leigh Fermor, who had died the previous year. Born in London, Fermor traveled on foot from Holland to Constantinople, then settled in Greece, before joining the British Army and playing a central role in the abduction of a Nazi general in Crete, an episode that was made into the film *Ill Met by Moonlight* (Michael Powell and Emeric Pressburger, 1957). He then continued to travel around the world and, in his later years, lived between England and the Kardamyli house. The fictional host of the house, Patrick, is also a writer, played by first-time actor and celebrated British cinematographer Walter Lassally, who, among other accolades, had won the Academy Award for *Zorba the Greek* (1964). Born in Berlin, he moved to London as a boy, a refugee from Nazi Germany, and lived in Crete for the last two decades or so of his life. Athina Rachel Tsangari, who plays Ariadni, is a film director who had recently garnered some critical success in the festival circuit for her film *Attenberg* (2010) and had made her only previous acting appearance in *Slacker*. She was also co-producer and an important presence throughout the production of *Before Midnight*.[23] Panos Koronis, who plays her husband Stefanos, is an actor and director of commercials. He lived in Los Angeles for a long period of his life, where he was a theater director. He would appear again in Tsangari's next film as director, *Chevalier* (2015), also produced by Faliro House. Natalia is played by Xenia Kalogeropoulou, a celebrated stage actor in Greece, who trained and made her debut in London. Ariane Labed is a

French-Greek stage and screen actor, who spent her childhood between Greece, Germany, and France. She was the protagonist of *Attenberg*, in which she plays a young Greek woman and for which she received several awards. In *Before Midnight*, she is a French stage actor, who has played Perdita in Shakespeare's *The Winter's Tale* at Epidavros.

Thus, the film features a transnational cast with a certain artistic pedigree and a location with transnational connotations. The action takes place in an atmosphere in which border crossings, particularly around Europe, are an everyday fact of life, various languages are casually used, and people are comfortable in a mixed social environment. The Greece embodied in these characters is very distant from that of the people demonstrating every day at Syntagma Square in Athens against the Greek and European authorities' handling of the financial crisis and its terrible consequences for the population at approximately the same time in which the film was conceived, shot, and released. By contrast, these are Europeans who appear to live in a social bubble while the crisis is raging outside and putting the European project in jeopardy. Despite being removed from the realities of discontent in the country, this is, however, a believable space. It is shot in real, recognizable locations, if relatively distant from the most popular tourist sites. We see the family drive from Kalamata Airport to the writers' retreat and then, in the evening, walk to a seaside town where they watch the sunset and check in at a hotel. The filmic space is made up of various localities in the Messenia region. These include the seaside towns of Kardamyli and Pylos, the small village of Platsa and the medieval fortification of Methoni, certainly not within walking distance of one another but—placed within an approximate 100-kilometer range—sharing a common history as part of a centuries-old single geographical reality, that of the southern Peloponnese.

Are Céline and Jesse at all aware of any of the stories-so-far that, following Massey, have gone into the creation of this space? Some of the filmmakers' comments suggest that, as part of the film's realism, they are. In the "Making of" documentary that accompanies the DVD of the film, Hawke mentions Eros, a password for love and desire. The god does not figure in the film, he says, because he does not need to: the whole movie is dominated by Eros, both because it is a film about love and because it takes place in Greece. "That's what Greece does to you," he concludes. Linklater relates this effect to the country's ancientness, which adds to the "little [. . .] paradise [the characters] find themselves in at the beginning."[24] Close analysis of some moments will suggest that, as the couple traverse the various spaces, they are aware of the stories they evoke, even if they do not voice their sense of growing enchantment at the place.

A brief account of the various locations the characters first drive and then walk through may reveal important slices of the region's fraught past and of the weight of history in their present realities. Kalamata is the port where the Franks disembarked at the beginning of the thirteenth century on their way back from Constantinople during the Fourth Crusade, eventually conquering most of the Peloponnese. The Mani peninsula, where Ariadni was born, was the destination where local Greeks kept retreating and fortifying themselves after various invasions, starting with the Slavs in the sixth century. The little chapel in Platsa stands for the impact of the three-and-a-half century long presence of the Ottoman Empire in the region but also represents the continuing religious conflicts between the Latin and the Orthodox churches in the medieval period and beyond. Methoni was for many centuries one of several Venetian strongholds and witness of the expansion of the Republic as a trading power and a political actor in Eastern Europe and the Middle East. Ancient Pylos, as old as Mycenaean Greece, and as such mentioned in the *Iliad*, witnessed the medieval rule of the Franks, the Venetians, and the Ottomans, and, centuries later, became the site of the Battle of Navarino, where the Franco-British-Russian alliance defeated the Turco-Egyptian fleet in 1827, thus paving the way for the independence of modern Greece.[25]

Thus, the sunny, quiet places that Céline and Jesse visit are the result of a cacophony of voices from the past. These are stories of invasion and conquest, of transnational encounters and cultural exchanges: of the alleged purity of the Maniots, who sometimes claim a direct line with the ancient Spartans; of the Tzakones, probably the children of Slavic invaders and Greek women who remained in the peninsula long after their ancestors had gone; and of the *gazmoules*, the descendants of middle- and lower-rank Frankish soldiers and Greek women in the thirteenth century. They tell us of the city of Mystra, built as a fortification by the Franks in the foothills of the Taygetus Mountain Range, that became the capital of their province and was later turned by the Byzantine Despots into the most important cultural center of the Empire at the end of the fourteenth century. They are made up of the voices of Western crusaders, Venetian traders, Ottoman rulers, Catalan and Albanian mercenaries, Greek lords and slaves, Orthodox bishops, and local farmers. They evoke political, military, and economic powers that thrived, declined, and disappeared, and a varied assortment of peoples who lived through long periods of relative dearth and prosperity. Thus, the geographical place chosen for the location of *Before Midnight* is the sum total of a series of trajectories and a never-ending succession of micro-histories that offer important insights into the history not only of modern Greece but also of the continent, and that may ultimately explain the desire for and the difficulty of a pan-European project at the beginning of the twenty-first century. In admittedly indirect ways, the parallels between the teeming voices from the past and the Kardamyli group proliferate. That this accumulation of stories so far may be constructed by the film as the magic space comedy may seem a hopelessly misguided cultural operation, but the long history on which the space of the film is based offers as many reasons for celebration as it does for distress. Seen through a comic lens, it is all a matter of perspective.

É UNA FESTA LA VITA

These words, uttered by Guido (Marcello Mastroianni) in the final scene of Federico Fellini's *Otto e Mezzo* (1963), encapsulate the comic perspective. They may also serve as a description of the comic space of *Before Midnight*. Yet, for all the complexity of this comic space, most commentators have avoided defining the film as a comedy or, in some cases, have actively opposed it.[26] While Philip Horne concedes that "there could be tragic or comic readings of what happens in the film,"[27] Rob Stone considers its shift toward the melodramatic to be the film's main asset.[28] James MacDowell has persuasively suggested that what had started as a romantic comedy in *Before Sunrise* eventually becomes an ongoing romantic melodrama, climaxing "in the bitterness and recrimination of *Midnight*," one that, additionally, adopts a misogynistic point of view in the gender conflict and finally leads the spectator to a "desolating ending."[29] Yet, in a later essay, he finds more hope in a nuanced analysis of the ending in which the characters are left at the moment of resolving an argument.[30] San Filippo explains the ending as "a present made possible by, however tentatively, making peace with both one's past and future."[31] Still more affirmatively, Carolina Amaral, who also regards the trilogy as a love story in three parts, describes its plot as the unfolding of an amorous encounter.[32] The last half-hour, in which the relationship is threatened, does not attempt to destroy the couple: it rather embraces it in its complexity and ambiguity, thus, succeeding at portraying love in its duration. She argues that love is not threatened by obstacles but, rather, by a superficial "safe" view that promises love without risks. The ending offers a new beginning and thus shows the couple's ability to restart their history indefinitely, a way to inscribe both the eternity of the happy ending and the passion of the first encounter within narrative duration.[33]

Melodrama and comedy, obstacles and new beginnings, then, coexist in the movie as part of "the struggle to keep love alive,"[34] like they coexist in romantic comedy in general. While we may agree that the film's ending is up for interpretive grabs, and its resolution, left once again outside the text, may ultimately depend on the nature of our investment in the story, we should be warned against allotting too much importance to the endings of romantic comedy. In comedy, attraction and rejection, hostility and affinity are all part of the ride and of the fun of being alive.[35] And, as Maria San Filippo reminds us, contemporary romantic comedy is as much about *un*coupling as it is about couple formation.[36] It is the erotic and life-affirming ride that counts and that continues to attract.

In *Before Midnight*, various contemporary iterations of the battle of the sexes are subjected to a comic perspective. The dinner scene makes this explicit: set against Greece's "ancientness," the characters discuss various ways of understanding intimate scenarios: from Natalia's touching evocation of the uniqueness and durability of the love for a special person to Achilleas and Anna's belief that the idea of a love that will last forever is a thing of the past—just not practical. Between them, the two middle-aged couples, Ariadni and Stefanos, Céline and Jesse, recreate the battle of the sexes with an emphasis on men's continuing sense of entitlement and privilege—Ariadni apparently more amused and resigned and Céline more frustrated by persistent inequality and male selfishness and self-centeredness. Throughout, however, the comic impulse remains palpable, with the specialness of the transnational group conferring a privileged way of discussing conflicts and the characters and sympathetic spectators deriving pleasure from being part of the conversation. Patrick verbalizes this feeling when he deflects the focus away from romantic love and says that ultimately it is not the love of a person that matters but the love of life, as concise a statement as we could find of what comedy is, uttered by the closest we get to an authorial figure in the story.

The emotional impact of this scene hangs over the rest of the film, even though, as we approach its final part, at the hotel, the divergences and quarrels that threaten the couple begin to gain ground. As MacDowell argues, in this section Céline deploys a feminist critique of the couple's relationship: she describes the burden of a centuries-long history of female subjugation in Jesse's attitude to her career, her own anxieties about motherhood, the rational/emotional typecasting, and other well-known forms of patriarchal programming.[37] For this critic, the film is ultimately unwilling to take the woman's side in the gendered conflict, tilting the scales in Jesse's favor and denying us direct access to her point of view.[38] Yet, as MacDowell himself later argues, Céline takes the initiative at the most important moments in the film and she—not Jesse—becomes the embodiment of several dimensions of the comic perspective.[39] There are three such moments in the final part of the film: the visit to the little chapel, the moment when they reach the seaside at the end of their walk, and the final minutes of the film.

The chapel is, as we have seen, a minuscule microcosm of the history of the area, including religious conflict. Jesse has been told by the caretaker that it was the Turks that scratched out the eyes from the Byzantine icons on the walls. In the DVD commentary, the filmmakers acknowledge that the long history of conflict between Greece and Turkey was in their minds when scripting and shooting this scene and they were wary of striking the wrong note. In the film, however, Céline starts with a dismissive remark about the power of religious miracles and then goes on to turn the hostility between the two countries into an obscene line: "I'll never suck another Turkish cock," invoking the spirit of carnival and reminding us that "comedy is sacrilege."[40] She then mocks Jesse, who appears a little nervous about her audacity, and calls him "a closet Christian." Given the rise of religious fundamentalism and the extreme right, Céline's defiant comic spirit is timely, a reminder that, as Sypher asserts, the irreverence of carnival is a sign of wisdom.[41] Her relatively gentle poke at Jesse here will become openly sarcastic later in the hotel room when she, for example, mocks the chasm between the admiration he constantly courts from younger women and the reality of his serious limitations as a lover. In the meantime, through her comic intervention in the chapel, she is, then, both victim of the social evil of sexism and Aristotelian agent of change.

Céline's sarcasm in the hotel room moves her and the film away from comedy and brings the story to the verge of abandoning its comic vision, a dark moment that is not at all unusual in comedy. However, we find her again as a comic agent at the end of the film. A few minutes after she dramatically leaves the room saying, "I don't think I love you anymore," Jesse joins her on the terrace by the sea and initiates a playacting game: he is a traveler from the future with a message for Céline from her 82-year-old self. She is initially unwilling to participate and twice asks Jesse to stop playing and remember instead what she has just told him upstairs. He finally gives up and they seem to have come to a stalemate, she firm in her rejection and he warning her that he will not keep trying forever. However, Céline has one more surprise up her sleeve for us and for Jesse. Delpy's performance is crucial and worth considering here: a lesson in transitioning from melodrama to comedy, and a reminder of the simultaneity in people's experience of the tragic and the comic spirit. Her acting is minimalistic. After Jesse's attempts at reconciliation run out of steam, a tense silence ensues: Céline frowns trying to keep her tears in check, swallows, looks away, reaches down for something on her leg, touches her hair, crosses her legs and her arms, breathes out almost imperceptibly, turns to look at Jesse while he is looking away, looks away again as he turns back to her (reminding us of the scene at the record shop booth in *Before Sunrise*, and opening up a possibility of hope). Then she turns her head once again, not quite looking at him, and speaks: "So, what about this time machine?" In the course of thirty-seven seconds Céline has traveled a long road between the melodrama described by MacDowell and Stone and the playful world of comedy. As she speaks, it cannot be said that she is enjoying the game yet, but she has come to the realization that it is a game worth playing. Finally, she is ready to engage in her favorite performance: the admiring "dumb blonde" that mocks her partner's view of his own irresistible appeal for young women. This is an abridged version of the more extended performance she had already put on at the dinner table: "Wow, you're so smart . . .," to everybody's delight. The impersonation is again pure Aristotelian comedy but, seemingly devoid now of the biting sarcasm of the previous iteration, it highlights the eroticism and the delight of play, even as it continues to ridicule patriarchal sexual protocols. It suggests that, against all odds, the comic spirit will prevail. Nothing has changed magically, and the jury is still out on the future of the couple (and of the family), but Céline is back, as it were, in the realm of comedy. By the time the camera pulls away from the characters and, in the purest romcom fashion, frames them surrounded by the social world represented by the other tourists having drinks by the sea, Céline and Jesse have relaxed. She then utters the final line of the film: "Well, it must have been one hell of a night we're about to have," verbalizing not only the dynamic in love between instant encounters and duration described by Amaral but also the upside-down world of comedy, here upturning temporal logic for the sake of the comic game. Whatever may happen after the final fade-out, spectators remain firmly in the comic space.

Delpy's performance of Céline's transition at the film's close is the continuation of a previous moment in the film: the couple's contemplation of the sunset before arriving at the hotel. If the final performance takes place in the little space between the characters, in this earlier case Céline's interaction is not primarily with her partner but with the wider space of the southern Peloponnese and, I would argue, with Europe at large. It is as if, following Patrick's statement in the dinner scene, Céline had come to realize that the little space where she had placed her idea of god is not so little after all, and that intimacy between people is only a manifestation of a larger kind of comic engagement with the world around us. The sequence, less than a minute long, is constructed with Linklater's customary transparency: a medium two-shot of Céline and Jesse looking at the sunset is interrupted twice by shots of the sun setting, one from their approximate position and another from behind them. Recalling the ending of Eric Rohmer's *Le rayon vert* (1986) (minus the green ray), another summer film taking place in another coastal European town, the film subtly breaks the relative democracy of the two-shot and highlights Céline by giving her the initiative and by having the soft orange light of the sun falling primarily on her. On the surface, this seems an isolated moment, the last micro-episode in their walk, but Delpy's performance and the visual rhetoric that surrounds it invest it with greater significance. As she narrates the imminent disappearance of the sun behind the stretch of land across the harbor, Céline takes a deep breath and smiles, looks at Jesse, who smiles back, then her smile becomes more wistful and finally disappears when the sun is gone. She looks again at Jesse. She wants her partner to read what is going through her mind and her heart, but she is unreadable for Jesse. This is a moment of communion with her environment. She turns back to the sun, an almost imperceptible smile momentarily back on her face, and then lowers her eyes and picks up her drink. The microscopic wonders of the performance suggest a solemnity that exceeds an emotional reaction to the setting sun. Rather, they convey the wisdom that she has gained in the course of the narrative. The slow movement of the sun— "it's still there, it's still there . . . it's gone"—visualizes Céline's earlier preoccupations with mortality in the three films, but it also suggests her gradual understanding of the temporality of space and of the value of the transnational in Peloponnesian, Greek, and European history as seen through a comic lens.

GIA ENA TANGO

We may compare Céline's communion with her environment in this moment with a similar one in a slightly later film, Fatih Akin's *In the Fade (Aus dem Nichts*, 2017). Katja (Diane Kruger) has travelled from Germany to Greece in pursuit of the neo-Nazi couple who have killed her husband and child in Hamburg. Once she has located them, she decides to plant a home-made bomb in the caravan where they are hiding, but at the last minute she changes her mind and goes back to the house by the sea that she has rented. Sitting on the deck, looking out at sea, she notices that, for the first time since the terrorist attack, her period has returned. Kruger's performance, comparable in its understated excellence to Delpy's in *Before Midnight*, suggests that Katja cannot accept the return to normality that her period indicates. With her family gone there is only one way ahead for her. The location, Schinias Beach, near Athens, is not so distant from the Kardamyli seaside, and the Attica region is the product of a comparable accumulation of stories-so-far as the southern Peloponnese, yet, surrounded and overwhelmed by death, Katja is impermeable to comedy. Her acquired wisdom consists in the acceptance of the finitude of existence. In contrast, Céline is going through a crisis that might lead not to death but to the end of love, but her absorption of the exuberant social space around her has taught her that life is a precious thing, to be enjoyed while it lasts, and that the world, with its inequities and sufferings, is also a laughing matter.

A slightly different point of comparison is explicitly offered by the film, in one of many intertextual references in the trilogy, in this case to *Viaggio in Italia* (Roberto Rossellini, 1953). Continuing the recurrence of death in the couple's conversations pointed out by critics as one of the trilogy's most recurrent topics, Céline mentions a memory of a black-and-white movie she saw as a teenager in which a couple walk through the ruins of Pompeii looking at bodies that have been there for centuries, forever caught in their sleep, intertwined in one last embrace.[42] *Viaggio in Italia* is another film about a middle-aged couple in crisis. Absorbed as they are in their marital problems and their desire to end their relationship, the characters isolate themselves from the social space of Naples, until, in the last minute, they become overwhelmed by the teeming life of the Italian city and reach a reconciliation, however fragile. This reference may be taken as an anticipation of Jesse's and Céline's trajectory but Rossellini's film is not a comedy and its social space, however richly portrayed, is not a comic space. In *Viaggio in Italia* the characters are, as it were, on their own. In contrast, *Before Midnight* constructs a rich canopy around the couple and, through Céline's vision and Delpy's performance, it plunges its spectators in an unrepentant comic world. This comic world is once again condensed, after the final fade-out and as the credits start to roll, in "Gia Ena Tango," a melancholy song about lost love turned into exhilarating experience by the wondrous voice of famous Greek singer Cháris Aléxiou and by the relentless appeal of popular music. Whatever may happen to the couple beyond the film's ending, its space remains resolutely comic. Just as importantly, the song is a reminder of the geographical specificity of its discourse on the future of the continent.

For what both *Viaggio in Italia* and *In the Fade* share with Linklater's trilogy is their trans-European identity and their awareness of themselves as European cultural objects. With English George Sanders and Swedish Ingrid Bergman as the married couple, and Rossellini as director, the trip the characters take in the former may be seen as a response to the feeling of exhaustion and uncertainty as the continent was beginning to face the future after the all-too-recent realities of genocide and destruction of the Second World War. More than sixty years later, *In the Fade* traces a very different map of Europe that links Germany and Greece, with Turkey implicit in the mix, and describes a European Union beset by its own incapacity to deal with difference and the external Other and threatened by a clandestine alliance of racist, ultra-nationalist, neo-Nazi groups. *Before Midnight* exists in the same geopolitical space as the latter, with the present of transnational culture in Europe as its structuring principle. However, unlike in the other two, the same transnational culture becomes the engine of comedy. Linklater's realistic method rules out any temptation of naïve optimism, yet it insists to turn the European project, like the frail eighteen-year-old relationship it protects, like the century-long history that precedes it, into a comedy into which we enter with our eyes fully open. What Céline sees in the fading orange light of the sunset is a map of Europe crossed by lights and shadows, but she has become the most powerful agent of comedy and, as such, she asks us to defy darkness and embrace the enduring joy of transnational European encounters from the vantage point of the continent's southern margins.

NOTES

* Research towards this article was funded by Spain's Ministerio de Ciencia e Investigación, project ref. FFI-2017-83606 (245–237) and the Diputación General de Aragón, ref. H23_20R. Thanks are also due to Danae Satchel, Ignacio Deleyto, Betty Kaklamanidoy, Andrés Bartolomé, Marimar Azcona, William Brown and Evangelos Katafylis.

1. Anthony Cooper and Chris Rumford, "Cosmopolitan Borders: Bordering as Connectivity," in *The Ashgate Research Companion to Cosmopolitanism*, edited by Maria Rovisco and Magdalena Nowicka (London: Ashgate, 2011), 261–264.
2. Andrew Horton and Joanna E. Rapf, "Introduction: 'Make 'em Laugh, make 'em Laugh!'" in *A Companion to Film Comedy*, edited by Horton and Rapf (Malden, MA and Oxford: Wiley-Blackwell, 2013), 2–4.
3. Gerald Mast (1973), *The Comic Mind: Comedy and the Movies* (Chicago: The University of Chicago Press, 1979), 9.
4. Ibid., 12.

5. Celestino Deleyto, *The Secret Life of Romantic Comedy* (Manchester: Manchester University Press, 2009), 30–38.
6. Robert W. Corrigan, (1965) "Introduction: Comedy and the Comic Spirit," in *Comedy: Meaning and Form*, edited by Robert W. .Corrigan (New York: Harper & Row, 1981), 8; Wylie Sypher, "The Meanings of Comedy," in *Comedy*, edited by Wylie Sypher (New York: Doubleday & Company, 1956), 38.
7. Sigmund Freud (1927) "Humour," in *Art and Literature*, Vol. 14 of The Penguin Freud Library (Harmondsworth: Penguin, 1961), 428, 433.
8. Horton and Rapf, "Introduction," 4.
9. Mikhail Bakhtin (1965), *Rabelais and his World*, trans. Helene Iswolsky (Bloomington: Indiana University Press, 1984), 7–8.
10. Mark Shiel, "Cinema and the City in History and Theory," in *Cinema and the City: Film and Urban Societies in a Global Context*, edited by Mark Shiel and Tony Fitzmaurice (Oxford and Malden, MA: Blackwell, 2001), 6.
11. Henri Lefebvre (1974), *The Production of Space*, trans. Donald Nicholson-Smith (Oxford and Malden, MA: Blackwell, 1991).
12. Doreen Massey, *For Space* (Los Angeles, London, New Dehli, Singapore, and Washington, DC: Sage, 2005), 124.
13. Ibid., 24.
14. Antoine Gaudin, *L'espace cinématographique: Esthétique et dramturgie* (Malakoff: Armand Colin, 2015), 9–10.
15. John David Rhodes and Elena Gorfinkel, "Introduction: The Matter of Places," in *Taking Place: Location and the Moving Image*, edited by Rhodes and Gorfinkel (Minneapolis and London: University of Minnesota Press, 2011), x.
16. Randall Halle, *German Film after Germany: Toward a Transnational Aesthetic* (Urbana and Chicago: University of Illinois Press, 2008), 6.
17. Ibid., 93.
18. Maria San Filippo, "Growing Old Together: Linklater's *Before* Trilogy in the Twilight Years of Art House Distribution," *Film Quarterly* 68.3 (2015): 53.
19. Robin Wood, *Sexual Politics & Narrative Film: Hollywood and Beyond* (New York: Columbia University Press, 1998), 323; Rob Stone (2013), *The Cinema of Richard Linklater: Walk, Don't Run* (2nd ed.) (London and New York: Wallflower Press, 2018); Leger Grindon, "Taking Romantic Comedy Seriously in *Eternal Sunshine of the Spotless Mind* (2004) and *Before Sunset* (2004)." in Horton and Rapf, *A Companion to Film Comedy*, 197; James MacDowell, "Comedy and Melodrama from *Sunrise* to *Midnight*: Genre and Gender in Richard Linklater's *Before* Series," in *After "Happily Ever After": Romantic Comedy in the Post-Romantic Age*, edited by Maria San Filippo (Detroit: Wayne State University Press, 2021), 47.
20. Stone, *The Cinema of Richard Linklater*, 16–17.
21. Guillermo Solana, *Cézanne: Site/Non-Site* (Madrid: Museo Thyssen-Bornemisza, 2014), 44.
22. See Stone, *The Cinema of Richard Linklater*, 3–4, 131.
23. Ibid., 131–132.
24. Philip Horne, "Passing Through," *Sight & Sound* 23:7 (2013): 32.
25. See: Steven Runciman (1980), *Lost Capital of Byzantium: The History of Mistra and the Peloponnese* (London and New York: Tauris Park, 2009); Siriol Davies and Jack L. Davis, "Greece, Venice, and the Ottoman Empire," *Hesperia Supplements* 40 (2007): 25–31.
26. Stone, *The Cinema of Richard Linklater*, 134–136; MacDowell, "Comedy and Melodrama."
27. Horne, "Passing Through," 32.
28. Stone, *The Cinema of Richard Linklater*, 135.
29. MacDowell, "Comedy and Melodrama," 49, 62.

30. James MacDowell, "Romance, Narrative, and the Sense of a Happy Ending in the *Before* Series," in *Before Sunrise, Before Sunset, Before Midnight: A Philosophical Exploration*, edited by Hans Maes and Katrien Schaubroeck (London and New York: Routledge, 2021), 190.
31. San Filippo, "Growing Old Together," 53.
32. Carolina Amaral, "Do encontro à duração: amor na trilogia *Antes do amanhecer*, *Antes do pôr sol* e *Antes da meia-noite*," *Intexto* 50 (2020): 147.
33. Ibid., 157–158.
34. Sukhdev Sandhu, "*Before Midnight*," *Sight & Sound* 23:7 (2013): 71.
35. Celestino Deleyto, "Humor and Erotic Utopia: The Intimate Scenarios of Romantic Comedy," in Horton and Rapf, *A Companion to Film Comedy*, 193.
36. Maria San Filippo, "Introduction: Love Actually: Romantic Comedy since the Aughts," in San Filippo, *After "Happily Ever After,"* 3.
37. MacDowell, "Comedy and Melodrama," 54.
38. Ibid., 55–57; see also Stone, *The Cinema of Richard Linklater*, 134–136.
39. MacDowell, "Romance, Narrative," 189.
40. Sypher, "The Meanings of Comedy," 38.
41. Ibid., 37.
42. Wood, *Sexual Politics & Narrative Film*, 322, 328; David T. Johnson, *Richard Linklater* (Urbana, Chicago and Springfield: University of Illinois Press, 2012), 88; Stone, *The Cinema of Richard Linklater*, 121–123.

PART 3

Style and Meaning

CHAPTER 9

Empathetic Effort in *Where'd You Go, Bernadette* and *Bernie*

Kim Wilkins

An illuminating exchange occurs between a teenage girl and her father in the second half of Richard Linklater's 2019 film, *Where'd You Go, Bernadette*. Faced with the devastating reality that her mother, Bernadette (Cate Blanchett), has willfully absconded from the family before Christmas, Bee (Emma Nelson) pleads with her father, Elgie (Billy Crudup) to embark on a search and rescue mission to reunite the trio. In response to Elgie's claim that Bee's proposal would prove futile as "there's just no way one person can ever know everything about another person," Bee insists: ". . . it doesn't mean you can't try! It doesn't mean I can't try." Bee's heartfelt declaration crystallizes a thematic preoccupation traceable across much of Linklater's oeuvre. From the ongoing negotiations of romantic intimacy in the *Before* trilogy (1995, 2004, 2013) to mediations between divergent masculinities in *Last Flag Flying* (2017), Linklater's films tend not to celebrate interpersonal comprehension so much as the efforts characters expend toward empathy: their attempts at "feeling-with" another, in Alex Neill's formulation.[1] In this chapter, I analyze two of Linklater's films whose narratives explicitly foreground these acts of empathetic understanding: *Bernie* (2011)—which centers on the 1996 murder of the octogenarian millionaire, Marjorie Nugent (played by Shirley MacLaine) by her much younger companion, Bernie Tiede (played by Jack Black)—and *Where'd You Go, Bernadette*—which follows an eccentric but devoted mother and architect who willfully disappears in the lead-up to a family trip to Antarctica.

There are numerous other-oriented emotions at play across Linklater's oeuvre that enact interpersonal reconciliations (particularly sympathy), however I emphasize the role of empathy precisely because—as Bee notes—the achievement of interpersonal understanding is often acknowledged as fraught or impossible and yet it is nonetheless pursued in these films as a key component of story. While the majority of literature on cinema and empathy attends to the relationship between film viewers and fictional characters (particularly within the cognitive tradition) my focus in this chapter is precisely on the expenditure of empathetic effort between characters within Linklater's films.[2] Although empathetic acts are found in many of Linklater's films, *Bernie* and *Where'd You Go, Bernadette* have been selected as case studies as both narratively foreground empathetic effort by centering on attempts to understand drastic, and perplexing, actions committed by eccentric characters: supposedly unpremeditated murder and a sudden deliberate disappearance paired with the abdication of a filial role, respectively. As such, *Bernie* and *Where'd You Go, Bernadette* are uniquely positioned to investigate the empathy expended in attempting to reconcile these acts and others' reactions to them, be they by a close-knit small-town community or a family unit. That is to say, *Bernie* and *Where'd You Go, Bernadette* fundamentally adopt Bee's charge "to try." Indeed, that characters acknowledge the potential futility of their ultimate goal—as Bee does—and nevertheless persist in its pursual evinces a spirit of empathetic generosity. One of the ways in which this effort manifests is, in characteristic Linklater form, through conversation.

DIALOGUE OR CONVERSATION?

In a 1999 article for *Film Quarterly*, Todd Berliner outlined the distinct dialogue conventions by which most mainstream American films abide: dialogue either enhances the plot or provides pertinent background information; dialogue progresses along direct lines often with characters winning or losing a scene or interaction; conversations generally stay on topic with both or all characters listening to one another; unlike real people, characters tend to speak with clarity and without error; and films that depart from these conventions usually do so for narrative purposes, that is, violations tend to highlight something essential to the film.[3] Berliner's account of American mainstream film dialogue is predicated on a strict adherence to Hollywood cinema's long, and reductive, characterization as a storytelling form strongly oriented toward narrative closure most commonly associated with the work of David Bordwell.[4] As such, the overall importance of these mainstream dialogue conventions is a sense of security in understanding that all utterances are relevant to the film story.[5] While less determined by strictly linear, plot-driven understanding of storytelling, Sarah Kozloff extends this conception of narrative-centered dialogue in her book-length study of film dialogue, where she firmly establishes its primary conventional function is to serve to communicate aspects, or the development, of narrative.[6] As such, exchanges between characters are designed to be overheard—or eavesdropped on—by the audience who utilize the information relayed to aid their comprehension of story. Kozloff groups the functions of film dialogue into primary and secondary categories: the first constituted by functions that are fundamental to a film's narrative ("anchorage of the diegesis and characters, communication of narrative causality, enactment of narrative events, character revelation, adherence to the code of realism, and, control of viewer evaluation and emotion") and the latter constituted by non-narrative functions such as aesthetic effect, ideological persuasion, and commercial appeal (exploitation of the resources of language, thematic messages/authorial commentary/allegory, and the opportunity for "star turns").[7] As she notes, these categories explain broad general uses and are not exclusionary in that one bit of dialogue may serve multiple purposes, and as such they can be nuanced in their outcomes. Nevertheless, the delineation of mainstream American film dialogue as overwhelmingly narratological in function—that is, in service of facilitating comprehension of causality in narrative trajectories that are always aimed toward closure and resolution, *pace* Berliner—has maintained its position in film studies textbooks. There dialogue is typically understood at the formal level as plot beats and the functional level as narrative information.[8]

While Linklater's dialogue does generally participate in the narrative-centric impetus assumed of Hollywood cinema, there are also exchanges between characters that lay bare a more thematic function than those highlighted by these formalist studies of mainstream film dialogue. These sequences focus on moments in which a character realizes they *do not know* how another feels and from this acknowledged position of ignorance extends "an offer of conversation" geared toward empathetic understanding, as Sherry Turkle puts it.[9] Such conversations, in Turkle's terms, are "an offer of accompaniment and commitment. And making the offer changes you. When you have a growing awareness of how much you don't know about someone else, you begin to understand how much you don't know about yourself."[10] Conversation, in Turkle's sense, sits in stark contrast to the term's formalist conceptualization in studies of filmic speech. Kozloff writes: "Given that a scene presents conversation, three alternatives exist: monologue (a character talking out loud with no-one else present), duologue (two characters speaking to each other), and polylogue (more than two characters talking)."[11] My approach to conversation in this essay differs to Kozloff's useful categories. More than instances of "talking" or "speaking," my focus is specifically on the nature of exchanges in which characters are encouraged to speak freely by the promise of a listener whose aim in the interaction is empathy.

Empathy, as Alex Neill writes, is an "other-focused" emotional response, in which one "[comes] to share [another's] feelings, to feel with him; if he is in an emotional state, to empathize with him is to experience the emotion(s) that he experiences."[12] In Neill's sense, empathy can thus be separated from other other-focused emotions, such as sympathy, which is characterized as feeling for (rather than with) another such that "one's response need not reflect what the other is feeling, nor indeed does it depend on whether the other is feeling anything at all."[13] Neill writes:

> in empathizing with others, we come to know how things are with them, by seeing the world from their point of view, as they see it, and feeling as they feel. In short, we come to understand them better; so that we are better placed to understand why they have reacted and behaved as they have done, and to predict how they will react and behave in the future.[14]

Although Neill suggests that often empathy is not effortful—rather something that "happens to us"—conversations in Linklater's films at times operate differently. They function as concerted attempts to understand *how things are* with another. Thus, while the moments of interpersonal exchange under examination adhere to the formal characteristics outlined by Kozloff, their textures and function are more aptly aligned with Turkle's "offer of conversation." Although empathy is not—as her description implies—inherently altruistic or compassionate,[15] these conversations exhibit "a kind of intimacy" that affords more than the acquisition of "information" in the form of facts or kernels that enable narrative comprehension. Instead, they are attuned to different types of information concerned with emotional and experiential states that may provide insight into how another thinks or feels.[16]

Take, for example, a tender exchange between Bee and Bernadette that occurs one-third into the film. To this point, Bernadette has been characterized as a charismatic and deeply flawed, eccentric, architectural genius. She is quick-witted, entitled, incredibly judgmental, and, as her interactions with "Manjula" (a Russian criminal network attempting to defraud the family under the guise of a virtual personal assistant based in Delhi) reveal, casually racist. She is plagued by insomnia, agoraphobia, social anxiety, and, as is often the case in films about creative geniuses, the brilliance of her own mind. Yet, despite her many faults and eccentricities, Bernadette is a devoted and, by all accounts, brilliant mother to the intelligent, confident, and utterly unpretentious, adolescent Bee. The two women share an intimate bond and vehemently protect one another from what each perceives as the other's vulnerabilities to the outside world. For Bernadette this is a hangover from Bee's infancy, as she was born with little hope for survival due to a congenital heart defect, while for Bee, this is the recognition of her mother's unstable mental state and incompatibility with normative societal expectations for success.

The sequence comes after two inciting events: one episode in which Elgie happens upon an unconscious Bernadette splayed across a sofa in a pharmacy storefront—the result of insomniac-induced exhaustion—and a second in which Bernadette expresses exceeding pride for Bee's efforts in choreographing an elephant dance for a group of first-grade students. The sequence begins with the two women driving in dark, rainy Seattle. In a shot-reverse-shot formation, the women are shown singing along to Cyndi Lauper's "Time After Time" with theatrical abandon. While car singalong sequences are frequent occurrences in American cinema, they are often performed for comedic purposes ("Bohemian Rhapsody" in *Wayne's World* [Penelope Spheeris, 1992]), to exhibit group cohesion ("Tiny Dancer" in *Almost Famous* [Cameron Crowe, 2000]), or to showcase a star turn (Miley Cyrus in *The Last Song* [Julie Ann Robinson, 2010]), here the sequence proposes a separate emotional itinerary. As Bernadette and Bee perform the song with practiced gestures, and harmonies, "Time After Time" is presented as part of a collection of memories and experiences shared between intimates: a suggestion amplified by the close and private spatial proximities of the car.

Bernadette hits a high note in the chorus and suddenly stops. "Oh, Bee," she sighs. Employing classic pathetic fallacy, Bernadette is seen beyond the rain-stained glass biting her lip as tears well in her eyes. Recognizing her mother's vulnerability, Bee leans forward in an attempt to make eye contact with her mother. With one hand on the wheel, Bernadette wipes her face with her elbow. With a generous smile, Bee offers, "See, Mom, this is why I didn't want you to come to the elephant dance." Bernadette chuckles, sighs, and looks to the road ahead. Nodding, she states with absolute candor, "I just need you to know how hard it is for me sometimes." She wipes a tear from her eye. Bee reaches out to her mother across the car, turns her shoulders square to face Bernadette, inches forward, and places her hand on her chin to indicate that she is listening. "What's hard?" she asks. Bernadette glances at her daughter, smiles reassuringly and looks back to the road. "The banality of life," she answers. Bee glances downward. Her eyes shift from a warm upward gaze at her mother's tear-stained face to a subtly complicit smile. Bernadette glances back at Bee and, regaining composure, adds, "but I retain the right to be incredibly moved by those little things no-one notices, ugh, for better and worse." Bee remains in a listening pose, silent. Still gently smiling, she waits. The camera switches to a two-shot outside the car: rain pelts the windscreen. Unlike the Seattle weather, Bee is unable to simply emote in attunement with Bernadette. Bernadette flashes a look at Bee and appears to recognize the emotional space her daughter has left her to fill in the conversation. Unable, or perhaps unwilling, to delve further into her emotional fragility, Bernadette—and the film—shifts register. "It's not going to stop me taking you to the South Pole," she declares, matter-of-factly. Bee shakes her head with incredulity and informs her mother that they are not going to the South Pole, but the Antarctic Peninsula. The understated humor in Bee's fervent clarification of the difference between the two geographic locations pivots the moment from bare vulnerability back to a comedy of wit in preparation for the proceeding sequence's visual comedy in which the neighborhood babbitt, Audrey's

(Kristen Wiig) house is flooded during an excruciatingly pretentious prospective kindergarten parent soiree, due, in part, to Bernadette's deliberate decision to allow a hill slide to occur between their respective properties.

To be clear, although Bee and Bernadette's exchange evinces an effortful attempt at empathy located in Turkle's "real" conversations, the sequence conforms to the formal conventions associated with mainstream Hollywood cinema rather than appealing to a naturalistic style. It does not, for instance, give the impression of improvisation—as in the case of a filmmaker like John Cassavetes—nor do the women misspeak, mumble, or interrupt one another in the manner associated with Robert Altman's dialogue experimentations.[17] Rather, each line is delivered with clarity and precision—designed to be registered by the eavesdropper, as Kozloff puts it.[18] This is unsurprising as *Where'd You Go, Bernadette* is a mainstream Hollywood film not only in its industry location but also its adherence to its formal narrative conventions.[19] Indeed, the scene demonstrates the tight bond between mother and daughter and explicates Bernadette's mental state, and as such could be read as providing background information. Yet, as Bernadette frequently vocalizes her own neuroses in monologues masquerading as emails to Manjula and in self-deprecating diatribes packaged as witty quick-fire addresses to Elgie, this explication is largely redundant. Neither is it necessary to demonstrate the intimate bond between Bee and Bernadette. The shared theatricality of their in-car singalong for a woman like Bernadette, whose self-presentation is peculiar precisely because of her outward emotional paucity, immediately signals a shared intimacy reflected in the enclosed space of the vehicle. Furthermore, the sequence does not establish a winner or loser, nor does it "stay on topic." So, how then are we to understand this exchange in terms of the conventions of mainstream American film dialogue outlined in the extant scholarship?

As Berliner explains:

> [it is] a peculiar characteristic of Hollywood dialogue that, although characters speak in ways that emphasise their conflicting objectives, together their dialogue contributes to a unified purpose. Although a character will appear to be striving to achieve his or her goals, the scene's dominant purpose overrides the character's individual contributions to the dialogue.[20]

Bee and Bernadette's conversation can indeed be accounted for in these terms. Its importance is less centered on the content of either woman's utterances than on the function of their exchange. In fact, the important "lines" of this exchange can be reduced to two sentences: Bernadette: "I just need you to know how hard it is for me sometimes"; and Bee: "what's hard?" As this exchange ends on an open—and for Bernadette unanswerable—question it places the act of conversing without a set, achievable goal at its center. It highlights the spaces afforded an interlocutor to explain their position, thoughts, or emotions, without any obligation toward clarity or comprehension. Indeed, Bernadette's reply "the banality of life" is such a hackneyed line (iterations can be found spilling from the mouths of privileged intellectual characters across the annals of American film culture) that it suggests that she offers it as knowing deflection. After all, Bernadette is a wealthy, white, attractive, educated artist whose genius has been consecrated by that most coveted of American creative achievements, the MacArthur grant. Moreover, she is (mostly) supported by a family that adores her despite her self-destructive habits. Given her background, what could possibly be so "hard" for Bernadette?

The deflection in Bernadette's pivot thus seems to incorporate a degree of self-acknowledgment: an answer that Bernadette might deem satisfactory is beyond her capabilities. Of course, as Turkle notes, "conversations carry more than the details of a subject."[21] Questions may be posed in the hope of clarification, yet the answers received are not always self-evident or conclusive. Bernadette's response requires Bee to consider what is meant rather than simply what is said. As such, Bernadette's deflection can be read as a direct contradiction of Berliner's assertion that "movie characters usually listen to one another and convey what they mean [and] efficiency is achieved by packing dialogue with story information and eliminating the digressions that clutter real speech."[22] Bernadette cannot convey what she "means" for she does not appear to precisely understand her emotional or mental state herself. Attempting to explain this inability to express her mental and emotional state to Bee would threaten to undermine Bernadette's overarching drive to protect her daughter from what she perceives as life's dangers and disappointments. Thus, Bernadette employs a response in alignment with what Sianne Ngai describes as the disempowering nature of "ugly feelings," such as paranoia, irritation, and anxiety that, unlike more powerful negative emotions such as anger, lack cathartic release. By contrast ugly feelings "tend to produce an unpleasurable feeling about the feeling"[23] which consequently privileges reflexive responses that indicate the subject's perception of their original feeling as unwanted. Bernadette turns a deeply personal question into a broad, and insurmountable, existential conundrum. In doing so, Bernadette repositions herself not as emotionally vulnerable but as intellectual to a fault. Yet, Bee's sincerity, taking immediate pause from their joyous musical moment to focus solely on her mother's emotional state, undermines this attempted reflexive turn. By leaning forward in her seat to bid eye contact with her mother, Bee physically demonstrates her desire to understand Bernadette. Her knowing, complicit smile in reaction to Bernadette's deflection demonstrates that while she may not fully know her mother's emotional or mental state, she is close enough to understand the tactics Bernadette employs in her guardedness. Bee may get as close to knowing her mother as possible, but direct access proves elusive. Here the car setting performs a dramatic function as it denies the possibility for Bernadette to return Bee's focus, enabling and reflecting her inability to respond directly. For their safety, she must remain focused on the road.

Bee's attempt to understand cannot be realized as it would in a classical dialogue sequence. As Karel Reisz and Gavin Millar explain:

> Frequently dialogue scenes are shot something like this: (1) two characters are shown talking to each other in medium or long shot to establish the situation; (2) the camera tracks in towards the characters or we cut to a close two-shot in the same line of vision as shot (1);(3) finally, we are shown a series of alternating close shots of the two players—usually over the opposite character's shoulder—either speaking or reacting. At the main point of interest, close-ups may be used and the camera generally eases away from the actors at the end of the scene.[24]

The focus on the interpersonal, that is character-to-character, connection may be read into the shot itinerary of the sequence in question. Linklater holds on the two women in a medium close-up. However, as the shot is framed from outside the vehicle the heavy rain gently obscures the image, leaving them slightly out of focus. There are no over-the-shoulder shots nor a conventional action-reaction sequence as the scene does not revolve around a main point of interest that can be resolved by its end. Bernadette is framed in profile and Bee frontally as she smiles lovingly and waits for her mother to finish speaking. In resisting the dialogue scene shot repertoire outlined by Reisz and Millar, the sequence is not presented as a discrete narrative unit but as an open and ongoing thematic issue precisely because the nature of the conversation's topic cannot be closed off or concluded. This is attempted conversation in Turkle's idealized conception, where face-to-face exchanges are "the most human—and humanizing—thing [people] do" as being "fully present to one another, we learn to listen. It's where we experience the joy of being heard, of being understood."[25] Although Bee and Bernadette's conversation does not result in the joy of being understood, Bee's act of waiting is an instance of empathetic effort: the willingness to listen rather than speak, even if—indeed especially if—the speaker cannot, or cannot fully, articulate their feelings or thought processes.

Although largely within the domain of conventional American film dialogue, the difference between this type of exchange in Linklater films and the study of film dialogue surmised by Berliner, I suggest, can be understood by the common conception of "dialogue" as a term that specifically denotes the written speech of literary, theatrical, or film characters. As such, dialogue tends to be apprehended first and foremost as constructed speech that is authored and performed as a formal element and less considered in its textures and thematic functions.

It is unsurprising, then, that many studies of film dialogue have tended toward diagnosing stylistic dialogue in particularly verbocentric films as either part of a tradition or character type, such as the Hawksian woman associated with the screwball comedy, or the product of "literary" filmmaking as in the cases of David Mamet, Charlie Kaufman, or Noah Baumbach. Alternatively, this stylistic dialogue is considered as an authorial hallmark as in the various case studies of Jeff Jaeckle's collection, *Film Dialogue*, or Jennifer O'Meara's focus on a subset of male American indie auteur darlings—Richard Linklater included—as filmmakers whose work is characterized as verbally experimental, in her recent book, *Engaging Dialogue: Cinematic Verbalism in American Independent Cinema*.[26] These auteurist studies are productive for conceptualizing dialogue as a crucial component of filmmaking style. Indeed, many critics and scholars identify Linklater's verbocentricism, to borrow O'Meara's term, as a key authorial hallmark.[27]

As O'Meara's study demonstrates, Linklater is a distinctly verbocentric filmmaker; however, like his oeuvre itself, which ranges from non-linear independent films to Hollywood genre entertainment, his style of dialogue is hardly consistent. While a subset of Linklater's films have been characterized as "wordy"—the celebrated "walking and talking" *Before* trilogy (1995, 2004, 2013), the tripartite confrontation that governs his chamber play, *Tape* (2001), the interwoven drop-in conversations that comprise *Slacker*'s (1990) organizational structure, or the lucid-dream philosophical musings that similarly motivate the animated *Waking Life* (2001)—his debut, *It's Impossible to Learn to Plow By Reading Books* (1988), is decidedly reticent. Linklater's filmography moves between verbose over-intellectualization, regionally specific Texan vernacular, teen and youth lingo, children's speech, and the particular patterns of a variety of immigrant and non-English speakers. It is not that specific textures are evident across Linklater's dialogue nor, as my analysis of *Where'd You Go, Bernadette* demonstrates, that his work bucks all conventions outlined in formalist accounts of American film dialogue, but rather that at times the aim, or purpose, of dialogue in his films is antithetical to the notion of "closure" and "comprehension" assumed by these accounts precisely because it is not driven by the sort of narrative information exchange that presupposes a strictly linear cause-and-effect trajectory. Rather, in a manner similar to many exchanges in John Sayles's humanist realist cinema, Linklater's conversations often take the form of what Tim Dean calls relational discourse: interactions not primarily predicated on the exchange of facts or "data" in service of knowledge acquisition or narrative advancement, but rather built around social functions such as the desire to strengthen relationships or build trust.[28] That Bernadette allows herself the vulnerability to admit to Bee she finds it "hard [to be her]" is evidence of such trust. In return, Bee's commitment to listen demonstrates her side of a conversation as an attempt to understand the inexpressible rather than a synthesis of gathered information that could conceivably amount to the comprehension of fact. Indeed, it is Bee's bodily and facial gestures that both offer Bernadette the opportunity for open expression and demonstrate her intimate familiarity with her mother's deflection tactics. The scene proposes a glimpse into what might be understood as an act toward understanding that, as evinced in Bernadette's deflection, can never eventuate, let alone visually materialize, and yet is nevertheless wholeheartedly attempted. The conversation does serve a unified purpose, but one that is primarily thematic rather than in service of propelling the story forward toward its conclusion.

UNPLANNED SPEECH, AND TRYING TO EMPATHIZE WITH A MURDERER

While the intimacy between Bee and Bernadette enables the empathetic substance of their conversation to be primarily portrayed non-verbally, there are instances in both *Where'd You Go, Bernadette* and *Bernie* in which the attempt to understand another is conveyed explicitly through lengthy passages of dialogue sparked by open-ended questions. The most prominent example in the former occurs when Bernadette chances upon a former college mentor, Professor Paul Jillinek (played by Laurence Fishburne), who simply asks "what [she's] been doing in Seattle for twenty years?" Although the question—undoubtedly familiar to anyone who has experienced a reunion after a lengthy period of separation—is posed casually, Bernadette responds by launching into a long, unbroken monologue about her life. Indeed, the sequence presents a wealth of story information. The speech begins as an entertaining diatribe against Seattle—which Bernadette condemns as an urban planning catastrophe and creative wasteland—then, without breaking rhythm or wavering timbre, details her inability to recover from a significant professional disappointment due to the emotional carnage wreaked by the devastation of experiencing multiple miscarriages, the lingering trauma of learning that Bee's "chances for survival were miniscule" at birth, and, finally, ends by understatedly expressing her pride in Bee, and sadness at her imminent departure for an interstate boarding school. Paul's eyes fix on Bernadette as he listens. His expression shifts from amusement to concern, to sympathy, and finally compassion. Linklater heightens the gravity of Bernadette's revelations by incisively cross-cutting between her monologue and Elgie as he delivers a similarly lengthy, but decidedly more measured, account of Bernadette's downward mental trajectory to a therapist (played by Judy Greer). By cutting between the intersecting monologues, Linklater intimates a tête-à-tête between the couple that perhaps should—but does not—take place. As such, in lieu of listening to Bernadette's unraveling account of traumas with the view to empathy, Elgie's parallel monologue functions as commentary on her eccentric actions from the outside view of a mostly sympathetic partner. If, as Jane Stadler posits, "empathy brings us into relation with others by centrally involving us in their lives, and it offers a felt, experiential understanding of their situation, their values, and the impact of their lives,"[29] Elgie's speech makes clear that he feels *for* Bernadette rather than *with* her.[30] For instance, Bernadette's devastating disclosure that repeated miscarriages—compounded by the near loss of Bee at birth and her subsequent chronic illness—upended her intention to fully recover "from the ass-whooping" of a dramatic professional disappointment is intercut with Elgie's calmly sorrowful portrayal of their marriage as "drifting." As such, the sequence not only highlights a needed conversation through its editing itinerary, but by contrasting Bernadette's revelatory conversation with Elgie's more measured explanations it showcases the fissure between Bernadette's revelation of lived experience and Elgie's sympathetic but misdiagnosed perception of her interior state.

However, not only does the monologue recount Bernadette's tumultuous history—and thus, its narrative purpose is in part an explanation for her behavior and demeanor—but its frenetic pace and emotional pivots engenders an impression of unplanned and unrestrained speech. Indeed, despite her practiced quick-witted eloquence, the increasingly grave information Bernadette divulges as her monologue gains pace appears to outrun her thoughts, acquiring its own momentum, only to turn around and catch her unprepared for its emotional impact. In this sense, Bernadette's monologue can be placed in dialogue with Heinrich von Kleist's opening charge in "On the Gradual Production of Thoughts Whilst Speaking":

> If there is something you wish to know and by meditation you cannot find it, my advice to you, my ingenious old friend, is: speak about it with the first acquaintance you encounter. He does not need to be especially perspicacious, nor do I mean that you should ask his opinion, not at all. On the contrary, you should yourself tell him at once what it is you wish to know.[31]

Following von Kleist's thesis that the discovery of thoughts often occurs during a speech rather than prior to it, Bernadette's unplanned monologue to Paul functions as an experiential account of the previous two decades' ordeals, and her discovery of their cumulative weight in the present. It is precisely this function of uninterrupted speech in the presence of another—that is, its capacity to function as a means of working through complex emotions—that underpins both *Bernie*'s narrational strategy and thematic concern with empathetic effort.

Bernie's story is straightforward. After developing a close relationship in the wake of her husband's death, Marjorie Nugent—a moneyed yet parsimonious and bitter octogenarian—is murdered with an armadillo gun by Bernie Tiede, an affable, community-minded, and beloved assistant funeral director, who then conceals her corpse in a large home freezer and proceeds to spend her fortune until he is caught nine months later. The film's narrational strategy divides this story onto two converging tracks. The first is an expository documentary-style collection of direct-to-camera accounts by members of the Carthage community collectively referred to as "the gossips"[32] (fictional characters played by local non-actors with the recognizable exception of Matthew McConaughey as DA Danny Buck). The gossips offer reflections to interview questions, displayed to the audience via kitschy title cards, in open-ended form from locations around the town—homes, park benches, the police station, funeral parlor, church, the town diner. The gossips' responses are often edited such that they appear in conversation with one another, similar to Bernadette and Elgie's absent exchange but to different effect. For instance, the question "Is Bernie Gay?" provokes conflicting reactions that seemingly amount to debate. One man seated at the diner raises a knowing eyebrow as he characterizes Bernie as "a little effeminate" and points out his penchant for theatre and preference for the company of elderly women rather than those within a normatively acceptable dateable age range. The man's euphemistic description is then sharply contrasted with Lenora (Kay Epperson)—a prominent gossip—who swipes at the air as if to shoo the suggestion away. She indignantly declares "You know, I heard that he was gay, but he was such a good Christian man . . . everybody thought, how could that be? That dog don't hunt. Nah." A series of other answers detail town-talk of Bernie being "a little light in the loafers" or outright declare his homosexuality, before returning to Lenora's increasingly fervent Christian denial of this possibility. As such, the editing strategy transforms a series of monologues into a polylogue, in Kozloff's configuration. However, unlike the editing strategy that intimates conversation between Bernadette and Elgie, this polylogue is comprised of intersecting personal reflections about Bernie from a temporal position in which he is already incarcerated, and thus absent from the community. The effect created is a splintering of the Carthage community's collective compassion for Bernie into its individualized components: the effort each exerts toward empathy and their respective value systems—including varying degrees of religiosity, conservatism, and homophobia—in which such efforts are grounded.

The second track is a fictionalization of the murder plot, in which Jack Black and Shirley MacLaine portray the perpetrator and victim, respectively. Although *Bernie* engages many of the recurring traits of true crime stories—variegated accounts of events and people, insinuation of hidden financial woes or professional difficulties, implication that non-heteronormativity is inherently entwined with homicidal tendencies, and the genre's implicit white gaze inculcated by a conspicuous focus on both white killers and victims[33]—the divergent accounts of Bernie and Marjorie's relationship are not, as they may be in that genre, indicative of discontinuities in evidence nor do the variations in character assessments amount to a kaleidoscopic portrait of an unlikely killer. *Bernie* is not a murder mystery, nor is it, unlike the true crime genre, concerned with police investigative procedures in a manner that "invites viewer judgment on matters of justice."[34] Although the fictionalized account of Bernie's and Marjorie's ill-fated relationship portrays the murder at the fifty-minute mark, it is clear from the gossips' interview responses that Bernie has already committed and confessed to homicide at the film's outset. Thus, Bernie's culpability as an empirical and legal fact is never in question. The question is how the Carthage community may continue to love Bernie in spite of his heinous act. It is this conundrum—the justification of love in the face of the morally reprehensible—that the gossips attempt to resolve in Bernie's absence on the interview track. In concert with von Kleist's discovery within unplanned speech, the gossips each offer complex individualized emotional responses in coming to terms with the compassion they feel for a convicted killer. Following Aristotle's analysis in *Rhetoric*, Martha Nussbaum defines compassion as "a painful emotion occasioned by the awareness of another person's undeserved misfortune."[35] Its cognitive requirements are

> the judgment of *size* (a serious bad event has befallen someone); the judgment of *nondesert* (this person did not bring the suffering on himself or herself); and the *eudaimonistic judgment* (this person, or creature, is a significant element in my schemes of goals and projects, and end whose good is to be promoted.[36]

Nussbaum states that empathy is not equivalent to compassion, nor (in its moral neutrality) is it necessarily a predicate for its generation. However, as empathy involves "an imaginative reconstruction of the experience of the sufferer" it is a mental ability that is highly relevant to compassion.[37] Indeed, as the townsfolk explain their compassion for Bernie, what emerges in their speech are invariably attempts to imaginatively reconstruct his experience.[38]

Bernie is first introduced as almost benevolent: a man blessed with "the ability to make the world seem kind" as one elderly woman (played by Marjorie Dome) puts it. Curiously, this characterization does not shift following his arrest. Instead, the threat of his conviction is uniformly framed by the townsfolk as unfair: a misdoing on the part of American law enforcement with unduly grave ramifications for "poor Bernie." As Katrina G. Boyd adeptly surmises:

> *Bernie* is the anti-*Rashomon*; despite their varied explanations for the murder the numerous gossips basically agree on the preferred outcome for Bernie. In fact, with DA Danny Buck Davidson (Matthew

McConaughey) the obvious exception, the consensus is that Bernie should not "be punished too much" for murdering spiteful old Mrs. Nugent.[39]

Indeed, following Bernie's unforced tearful confession—"I know I done wrong and I must atone for my sins"—the townspeople harangue Danny Buck with pleas to waive standard legal procedures and express their "hope to be on the jury" so they may "vote to acquit" regardless of any evidence that may be revealed at trial. Thus, the Carthage community experiences pain at their recognition that convicting Bernie will amount to his immense suffering in incarceration. A conversation between Bernie and Lenora on the fictionalized murder plot track in the film's final moments highlights the complexity and texture of this compassion.

The scene takes place at Beeville maximum-security prison where Bernie is serving a life sentence. A low chatter is heard while the camera tracks along rows of inmates in visitation booths, seeking out Bernie among the uniformed crowd. Bernie's wan voice is heard as he unconvincingly attempts to reassure his visitor of his well-being—"it's not as bad as you think"—seconds prior to his appearance on-screen. The roving camera stops and fixes on an over-the-shoulder shot of Bernie. His visage belies his words. His once (overly) animated face is now resigned. His downcast eyes no longer seek contact with his companion's. The warmth and intimacy Bernie's facial gestures sought to offer the bereaved at the film's opening have drained away. He continues "I'm the choir director, teaching four classes. I'm in the craft shop most of the day . . ." then adds with a flattened intonation: "I miss my freedom." The camera cuts to Lenora, who listens intently. Nodding, she offers Bernie a validating statement "Well, sure you do, honey." His sad eyes lift to hers. The conversation shifts pace as Lenora enthusiastically details a letter she penned to the warden requesting Bernie's day-release in the event of her death. Resting his face in his hands, Bernie answers Lenora's zest with a heartened smile. Just as the two embark on a more upbeat exchange, a guard appears behind Bernie and silently enforces the conversation's end. With glassy eyes, Bernie tenderly informs Lenora "I cannot tell you how much it means to me that I am still in your prayers." She reaches across the table, takes his hand in hers, and declares Carthage's unwavering love for him, as well as her own ("I love you, baby"). Then, adopting a maternal tone, insists "You need to take care of yourself and be real careful because I think this could be a dangerous place." As Bernie rises to return to his cell, she reiterates her instruction to the guard "You take care of him." The tenderness of Lenora's visit—both her comforting words and gestures—asserts her position (and that of the Carthage community she represents) that even if guilty as convicted, Bernie is, like a child, too innocent for such punishment. However, if the townsfolk recognize that Bernie committed murder, the question they attempt to reconcile in their to-camera reflections is: how can Bernie's incarceration be understood as undeserved misfortune?

As Nussbaum writes, in feeling compassion we either "believe the person to be without blame for her plight [or], though there is an element of fault, we believe that her suffering is out of proportion to the fault."[40] As the "onlooker has to see the disaster as falling on the person from the outside" as a cognitive process assigning blame is highly malleable.[41] There are moments in which some gossips outright deny Bernie's guilt. However, as Lenora's visit demonstrates, for the majority of Carthage townsfolks Bernie's suffering is considered as unjustly disproportionate to his crime. Indeed, in the process of verbally comprehending their compassion for Bernie, the gossips mentally recuperate him as a victim—first of Danny Buck, and more severely of Marjorie Nugent: who subsequently is framed as a woman whose innate evil was so immense it drove a fundamentally virtuous man to murder. As Bernie's colleague explains with a decidedly considered vocal tone:

> You got this sweet guy. You got Bernie, who's just the nicest fellow I ever met. Known him for a little while now, and then you got Mrs Nugent, who is not nice. Not nice to a large degree. Just evil. So you've got this sweetness and this evil and they're kinda battlin' each other and you know that somethin' at some point's gotta give, somethin's gotta break, and she was just more evil than he was nice, I guess, and he just exploded.

In its appeal to rationalism, this response displays an effort to understand an unfathomable act by transforming it into a supposedly logical outcome of a set of circumstances that upholds the speaker's established binary between virtue (Bernie) and sin (Marjorie). This reformulation functions as Nussbaum's third requirement for compassion: eduaimonistic judgment. As she writes:

> the person must consider the suffering of another as a significant part of his or her own scheme of goals or ends. She must take that person's ill as affecting her own flourishing. In effect, she must make herself vulnerable in the person of another . . . But human beings have difficulty attaching others to themselves except through thoughts about what is already of concern to them. Imagining one's own similar possibilities aids the extension of one's own eduaimonistic imagination.[42]

Indeed, it is implied in the funeral director's explanation that if even Bernie, with his innate goodness, could not win out against Marjorie's inherent malevolence, any individual in the same situation would have killed her. This assertion is made clear by the subsequent gossip, who with sad acquiescence affirms "we're all capable of that dark moment if we ever get angry enough." Then, as if to prove her point, the next two townsfolk's responses detail—without trepidation—alternate methods of murder (casting Marjorie's body into the ocean from Bernie's airplane, smothering her with a pillow and claiming cardiac arrest brought on by a heart condition) that would have enabled Bernie to avoid being charged. These latter statements are undoubtedly intended to be received as darkly comedic—both an enactment, and parody, of Nussbaum's assertion that compassion is "most frequently taken to provide a good foundation for rational deliberation and appropriate action, in public as well as private life"[43]—the sequence's overall texture—transitioning from "shock!" and "fuckin' unbelievable!" to a state in which others imagine their actions in Bernie's position. The act of homicide—an aberration to one's humanity—is thus recast as a natural, shared human reaction when faced with someone "mean and ornery."

However, the humor that colors the townsfolks' attempts to convince themselves that Marjorie's murder was inevitable and Danny Buck that he should "leave poor Bernie alone" performs more than a tonal function. It highlights the schism between wishing to understand Bernie's actions as universal and human and the efforts toward empathy that would allow them to inhabit this position. In the end, truly understanding Bernie proves as impossible as ceasing to love him. In the film's final moments, the reconciliation of Bernie's actions and a community's love for him is deferred to a higher power. A gossip (Marjorie Dome) provides the final words:

> I don't care what he did. Yes, I do care. It was wrong. But I believe that if Bernie were truly sorry for what he did and would ask God's forgiveness, God would forgive him. And after all, that's all that really matters. I will miss him. All of us will.

Bernie walks—chest out and head high—back to his cell. Heavy barred gates lock behind him. He does not look back. An epilogue showcases footage of the real Marjorie Nugent and Bernie Tiede.

(*IN*)CONCLUSION

Concluding with Bernie imprisoned for a murder he is both seen committing and confessing to, the film adheres to the classical conventions of Hollywood storytelling that mainstream film dialogue is taken to primarily aid. As Bordwell famously—and contentiously—puts it, Classical Hollywood narratives end with "a decisive victory or defeat, a resolution of the problem and a clear achievement or nonachievement of [the protagonist's] goals."[44] *Bernie* concludes by affirming Bernie's guilt following his attempt to cover up Marjorie's murder and resolves in reaffirming his beloved status in Carthage as unchanged. Similarly, *Where'd You*

Go, Bernadette's frenzied final act, in which Bee and Elgie miraculously locate Bernadette in Antarctica and grant her permission to pursue her artistic needs away from the family unit, resolves in allowing her to act on what is identified as the crux of her malaise—her need to create. And it is precisely Bee's and the Carthage townfolks' attempts at empathy that enable these resolutions. Without Bee's commitment to try to understand her mother, or the Carthage gossips' attempts to understand their love for Bernie in light of his actions, these resolutions could not occur.

And yet, these narrative resolutions do not facilitate the closure of the thematic concerns that underpin either film. Bee never learns "what's hard" for Bernadette and the Carthage gossips never truly understand why Bernie killed Marjorie. They do not come to understand "how things are with" these eccentric characters. Character-to-character empathy is the "goal" presented in both *Where'd You Go, Bernadette* and *Bernie*. However, rather than framing this goal in terms of its achievement or non-achievement, both films conclude with the acceptance that fully understanding another may be impossible yet there is value in trying. Acceptance, however, is not equivalent to closure—instead it is the resolve to continually expend effortful attempts at understanding. The conversations I have analyzed in this chapter are instances of these efforts toward empathy. In these interactions, the space between the self and unknowable other is not perceived as a hopelessly unfillable void but as an asymptotic gap. While the gap can never fully close, it grows smaller with every attempt. For Bee and Bernadette the attempt is less the parley of vulnerability through the vocalization of intimate thoughts than listening to more than what is said, and for the Carthage community it is the affordance of "talking through" their compassion and love for a convicted murderer.

In vastly different ways, both types of conversation—the darkly comic diverging voices that comprise the chorus of Carthage gossips' asserting Bernie's worthiness and the non-verbal reassurances of love between filial confidants—privilege inconclusiveness in a manner that draws attention to the textures of interpersonal exchange, that is the act of conversing itself. After all, an offer of conversation does not request answers much less closure or resolution. That the desire to understand that generates these conversations is rarely satiated, puts on display the effort—rather than outcome—of attempts toward empathy. In this sense, Bee and the Carthage townsfolk answer the call posited by one half of Linklater's most celebrated conversationalists, Céline (Julie Delpy) in *Before Sunrise* (1995): "if there's any kind of magic in this world it must be in the attempt of understanding someone, sharing, something. I know, it's almost impossible to succeed ... but who cares, really? The answer must be in the attempt." In *Where'd You Go, Bernadette* and *Bernie*, it is in the attempt—the effort toward empathy—that love and compassion reside.

NOTES

1. Alex Neill, "Empathy and (Film) Fiction," in *Philosophy of Film and Motion Pictures: An Anthology*, edited by Noël Carroll and Jinhee Choi (Malden, MA: Blackwell Publishing, 2006), 247–259.
2. For examples of spectator-character empathy see Neill, "Empathy and (Film) Fiction"; Deborah Knight, "In Fictional Shoes: Mental Simulation and Fiction," in Carroll and Choi *Philosophy of Film and Motion Pictures*, 271–280; Jane Stadler, *Pulling Focus: Intersubjective Experience, Narrative Film, and Ethics* (New York: Bloomsbury, 2012); also Murray Smith, *Engaging Characters : Fiction, Emotion, and the Cinema* (Oxford: Clarendon Press, 1995).
3. Todd Berliner, "Hollywood Movie Dialogue and the 'Real Realism' of John Cassavetes," Film Quarterly 52:3 (1999): 3–5.
4. While closure and resolution should not be conflated, there are clear instances where narrative closure is resisted in Hollywood cinema. I am grateful to Paul Sheehan for his example of the horror genre, in which films are often predicated on the "return of the repressed" and as such end with a hint of the "return of the return." Nevertheless, the dominant conception remains focused on closure. See, for instance, David Bordwell, *Narration in and the Fiction Film* (London: Routledge, 1986) and *The Way Hollywood Tells It: Story and Style in Modern Movies* (Berkeley: University of California Press, 2006); Thomas Schatz, *Hollywood Genres: Formulas, Filmmaking, and the Studio System* (New York: Random House, 1981); Kristin Thompson, *Storytelling in the New Hollywood: Understanding Classical Narrative Technique* (Cambridge, MA: Harvard University Press, 1999).
5. Sarah Kozloff, *Overhearing Film Dialogue* (Berkeley: University of California Press, 2000), 6.
6. Ibid., 33.
7. Ibid., 33–34.
8. See for instance, Timothy Corrigan and Patricia White, *The Film Experience: An Introduction* (5th ed.) (New York/Boston: Bedford/St. Martin's, 2017); and David Bordwell, Kristin Thompson, and Jeff Smith, *Film Art: An Introduction* (12th ed.) (New York: McGraw-Hill Education, 2019).
9. Sherry Turkle, *Reclaiming Conversation: The Power of Talk in a Digital Age* (New York: Penguin Press, 2015), 172.
10. Ibid.
11. Kozloff, *Overhearing Film Dialogue*, 70.
12. Neill, "Empathy and (Film) Fiction," 247.
13. Ibid.
14. Ibid., 257–258.
15. See Martha Nussbaum, *Upheavals of Thought: The Intelligence of Emotions* (Cambridge: Cambridge University Press, 2001), 304–342.
16. Turkle, *Reclaiming Conversation*, 246.
17. See Berliner "Hollywood Movie Dialogue," and Mark Minett, "Elaborate Chaos: Altman and Overlapping Dialogue," in *Robert Altman and the Elaboration of Hollywood Storytelling*, (Oxford: Oxford University Press, 2021), 170–217.
18. Kozloff, *Overhearing Film Dialogue*, 16–18.
19. Bordwell, *The Way Hollywood Tells It*, 28–29.
20. Todd Berliner, "Killing the Writer: Movie Dialogue Conventions and John Cassavetes," in *Film Dialogue*, edited by Jeff Jaeckle (New York: Wallflower Press, 2013), 104.
21. Turkle, *Reclaiming Conversation*, 8.
22. Berliner, "Killing the Writer," 105.

23. Sianne Ngai, *Ugly Feelings* (Cambridge, MA: Harvard University Press, 2007), 10. I have written on the relationship between irony and existential anxiety in American indie cinema at length in *American Eccentric Cinema* (New York: Bloomsbury Academic, 2019).
24. Karel Reisz and Gavin Millar, *The Technique of Film Editing* (New York: Hastings House, 1968), 86.
25. Turkle, *Reclaiming Conversation*, 3.
26. Jeff Jaeckle, *Film Dialogue* (London and New York: Wallflower Press, 2013). Jennifer O'Meara, *Engaging Dialogue: Cinematic Verbalism in American Independent Cinema* (Edinburgh: Edinburgh University Press, 2018).
27. David O'Donoghue, "Richard Linklater and the Power of Conversation," *Cultured Vultures*: https://culturedvultures.com/richard-linklater-power-conversation/ (February 26, 2016); Jason Hellerman, "Three Conversation Writing Tips from the 'Before' Trilogy," *No Film School*: https://nofilmschool.com/How-to-write-a-conversation (May 7, 2019); Manohla Dargis, "From Baby Fat to Stubble: Growing Up in Real Time," *The New York Times*: https://www.nytimes.com/2014/07/11/movies/movie-review-linklaters-boyhood-is-a-model-of-cinematic-realism.html (July 10, 2014) (all accessed June 18, 2021); David T. Johnson, *Richard Linklater*, Vol. 155 (Champaign: University of Illinois Press, 2012); Rob Stone, *The Cinema of Richard Linklater: Walk, Don't Run* (New York: Columbia University Press, 2018).
28. Tim Dean, "The Failure of Reason," 3 (unpublished manuscript, 2020).
29. Jane Stadler, *Pulling Focus: Intersubjective Experience, Narrative Film, and Ethics* (New York: Bloomsbury, 2012), 155.
30. Neill, "Empathy and (Film) Fiction," 252–253.
31. Heinrich von Kleist, "On the Gradual Production of Thoughts Whilst Speaking," in *Selected Writings: Heinrich von Kleist*, ed. and trans. David Constantine (Indianapolis, IN and Cambridge: Hackett Publishing, 2000), 405.
32. Katrina G. Boyd, "'Grief Tragically Becoming Comedy': Time, Tasks, and Storytelling in Linklater's *Bernie*," *Film Quarterly* 68:3 (Spring, 2015): 48.
33. Tanya Horeck, *Justice on Demand: True Crime in the Digital Streaming Era* (Detroit, MI: Wayne State University Press, 2019), 14. See also, Zoë Druick, "The Courtroom and the Closet in *The Thin Blue Line* and *Capturing the Friedmans*," *Screen* 49:4 (2008): 440–449; and Jean Murley, *The Rise of True Crime: 20th-Century Murder and American Popular Culture* (Westport, CT: Praeger, 2008), 2.
34. Horeck, *Justice on Demand*, 2.
35. Nussbaum, *Upheavals of Thought*, 301.
36. Ibid., 321.
37. Ibid., 327, 333.
38. Nussbaum debates the necessity of empathy for compassion.
39. Boyd, "'Grief Tragically Becoming Comedy,'" 48.
40. Nussbaum, *Upheavals of Thought*, 311.
41. Ibid., 313, 314.
42. Ibid., 319.
43. Ibid., 299.
44. David Bordwell, *Narration in the Fiction Film* (Madison: University of Wisconsin Press, 1985), 157.

CHAPTER 10

Richard Linklater's Humanism: Moral Primacy, Recency Effects, and *SubUrbia*

Wyatt Moss-Wellington

In serial memory processing, the first and last items in a memory set are easier to recall than those in the middle; researchers find that people generally recollect details at the beginning and end of lists of information more quickly, and with greater accuracy.[1] This is known as the serial position effect, constitutive of a pair of cognitive biases that together hold implications for our understanding of narrative: privileged recall of "prime" information is known as the primacy effect, while recall of the most "recent" information is known as the recency effect.[2] Information from the beginning and ending of a filmed narrative is similarly privileged in memory due to such a primacy-recency sequencing, and this temporal dimension can inform accounts of a spectator's experience of narrative, implicating the ways in which stories work with our cognitive biases in order to make causal sense.

The relevance of this effect in film studies was noted by David Bordwell in 1985.[3] Bordwell drew from narratologist Meir Sternberg's notion of a reader updating hypotheses, expectations, and anticipation of narrative information to develop his own account of the ways in which audiovisual narratives "reward, modify, frustrate, or defeat the perceiver's search for coherence" in concert with perceptive faculties, and expectations perceivers bring with prior knowledge of narratives in the form of "schemata."[4] Bordwell also borrows from Sternberg's speculations on the narrative relevance of primacy and recency to explain how film viewers privilege different narrative information as it is presented over time; the time at which information is presented affects its salience, and ergo affects the audience's ongoing probabilistic predictions and sense-making throughout engagement.[5] In *Narration in the Fiction Film*, primacy and recency are "reasoning shortcuts" that inform inferences actively made by film spectators as the narrative unfolds.[6] Primacy and recency work together: we bring prime information with us and run it by the most recent information, such that recency qualifies (in some cases negates) prime information.[7] For instance, in his account of forking-path plots, Bordwell notes that:

> the "recency effect" privileges the final future we see. Because endings are weightier than most other points in the narrative, and because forking-path tales tend to make the early stories preconditions for the last one, these plots suggest that the last future is the final draft, the one that "really" happened; or at least they reduce the others to fainter possibilities.[8]

Effectively, filmed media collaborates with our temporal cognitive biases, rather than operating in spite of them, to help us make sense of a narrative (in this case the bias is one in serial information processing).

Primacy-recency is relevant, too, to adaptations of canonical texts, as James H. Lake explores in films of *Hamlet*: audiences remember early, influential texts and tend to judge recent instantiations against a cultural memory that privileges "prime" adaptations.[9] Thus the most recent *Hamlet* is "re-positioned in the memory as simply one of the many Hamlets following Olivier's watershed production."[10] Yet Lake is again more interested in the use of primacy-recency effects within the films themselves, demonstrating how each adaptation of *Hamlet* motivates primacy-recency to craft various kinds of ambivalence and ambiguity—especially around Fortinbras's leadership and Denmark's future at the story's close—from Shakespeare's initial text, which mobilized those same biases to conversely imbue a sense of the new leader's fortitude and Denmark's continuity.[11] The lesson here is that primacy-recency effects can be used to craft quite different conclusions from the same story, the same fabula. This holds importance for moral readings of film.

Recency effects do not only serve the intelligibility of audiovisual narratives, they also influence, subjectively, the kinds of information we deem to be important in a narrative (which can clearly vary between audience members of different inclinations), and what we deem to be important carries ethical weight. Primacy and recency can guide audiences toward the salience of information for ethical effect, and to make moral cases about that which is worthy of our time and deliberation. Richard Linklater tends to make films that are character studies, minimizing plot detail in favor of progressively revealed character details, or implied causal features of a social network those characters exist within. The use of primacy and recency effects across his films reveals some of the ethics of narrative and character emphasis, who and what we privilege in memory, and a morality encapsulated in narrative attention.

Bordwell notes the use of primacy not just in comprehending narrative, but in the moral qualities we attribute to characters, as well: "A character initially described as virtuous will tend to be considered so even in the face of some contrary evidence; the initial hypothesis will be qualified but not demolished unless very strong evidence is brought forward."[12] This effect could also be attributed to an inconsistency discounting bias, whereby we are more likely to disregard information that is not continuous with that previously provided; this bias has been shown to affect assessments of individual likeability and jury decisions.[13] Where narratives offer a midway plot point, a moment of exposition, or an important twist, we might also look for proximate information that confirms what we now know at the expense of remote details.[14] Similar investigations in literary studies, again inspired by Sternberg's use of primacy-recency, note the importance of these biases in guiding reader sympathy toward particular characters.[15] Yet I feel there is more going on here, as foregrounding and backgrounding character details, making them more or less prominent, can dance between emphasizing plot causality, or character trait information, or indicators regarding the story's implication of social causality. Of course, nothing of this information is categorically distinct, as characters and their interactivity are part of understanding stories and how they unfold. However, Linklater's more conversational films demonstrate that audiences can be encouraged to focus on different components of the narrative. Michael Z. Newman, for instance, uses a comparison between *Passion Fish* (John Sayles, 1992) and *21 Grams* (Alejandro González Iñárritu, 2003) to note how primacy and recency can be involved in building more complex characterizations across a film, rather than just frustrating attempts at understanding a causal narrative:

> Characterization in *Passion Fish* relies on a strategic order of exposition for its effects. The first information that a film gives us about a character biases our interpretation of all of the subsequent information, a phenomenon known as the "primacy effect" ... The primacy effect emphasizes certain type assignations, but later on a "recency effect" balances the primacy effect by demanding a revision of our assessment of the characters.[16]

Here, Newman also demonstrates the uses of an audience- and reception-centered understanding of film cognition in revealing, through close hermeneutic readings, what Gregory Currie would call a film's "propositional" content.[17] An understanding of the ways in which films invite our biases not just to make sense, but to make propositional *moral* sense, can enrich any "thick" or phenomenal description of particular films, their particular effects, and how they work together with audience experience to generate their plurality of meanings. In this chapter I investigate the use of similar primacy-recency effects in the works of Linklater, and in particular *SubUrbia* (1996). The following reading focuses on *SubUrbia*, yet also speculates on storytelling techniques that unite this film with Linklater's other features, as well as films by other humanistic filmmakers like John Sayles, who in the past has collaborated with

Linklater as a screenwriter, and directors of earlier youth films, such as Amy Heckerling and John Hughes.[18]

Linklater's films rarely emphasize the work of plot comprehension, and nor do they call on the viewer to morally assess their characters—in some films, like *Bernie* (2011), character judgment is rendered impossible by stressing the unreliability of information all moralistic judgment is founded upon.[19] The same cognitive biases Bordwell was interested in, that help us discern plot points, fill out diegetic understanding, and judge characters, are also important in films that request a different manner of contemplative mental work: to be aware of the meanings we can extrapolate from depicted social lives. Readings of Linklater's films, with his less moralistic interest in characters in various states of relational connectedness and disconnectedness with those around them, reveal something more than simply plot intelligibility or character judgment at work. The depicted transactive cause-and-consequence of his conversational pictures can be less focused upon character virtue, vice, or sympathy, but instead upon understanding models of social causality. Reading implied social consequences is constitutive of the moral "meaning" audiences can draw from such narratives; narratives that request a striving to understand moral behavior given social pressures that are abstracted, and not directly presented in plot detail. Importantly for any theory of the role of memory in narrative engagement, memory studies also find that people group recollected items *thematically*, which can lead to other kinds of meaning-making biases.[20]

A primacy effect is also observed here: when asked to recall a sequential memory set, respondents tend to apply a theme to items at the beginning of a list, and then allocate meanings to later items based on initial expectations of a cohesive theme to reduce the amount of deviation in a list.[21] Obviously we are pattern-seeking, sense-making beings, and storytelling is intrinsic to mutual pattern-seeking and sense-making. Yet the key here is not just that first impressions matter to narrative comprehension or character judgment, the sequencing of information matters too to the broader, thematic meanings we apply to that narrative and to those characters. There is a second order, and perhaps more important processing, that occurs at the level not of understanding a narrative but of personalizing its signifiers as meaning, and that process also works within established cognitive tendencies for attentional and recollective biases. The following reading reveals the importance of those biases in constructing meaning from Linklater's *SubUrbia*.

SUBURBIA'S HUMANISTIC PRIMES

Linklater's multi-character youth philosophy dramedies—what he calls his "hangin' out quintet"—are partially autobiographical works, and he has maintained of these films that "they represent my life at different times."[22] Earlier features like *Slacker* (1991) fashioned a cinematic space to contemplate various overlapping (and often dissident or nonconformist) subcultures, and later works still tended to avoid any normalized, idealistic visions of the situation young Americans found themselves in. Linklater made his hardest hitting of these films with *SubUrbia* in 1996, from playwright Eric Bogosian's script. *SubUrbia* follows characters perhaps familiar from Linklater's teen pictures a little later in life, in their early to mid-twenties: they are flunked out of college or resenting an abortive military career, dreaming of fame or selling notions of social ascendancy to their peers, accepting the aggressive terms of American consumer culture or being injured by them, and here more than Linklater's other films they are emotionally thwarted by their dead-end surrounds, a network of concrete parking lots and strip malls.[23] Linklater mentions in an interview with Marjorie Baumgarten that these characters:

> could be OK, and they're 20—this isn't the end of the world for them. I was really fucked up at 20, just like they are. You kind of find your footing, make your life, and maybe you can get it together . . . and I think a large percentage of them will.[24]

Baumgarten observes: "Bogosian's dark vision of the vile behavior of which human beings are capable seems an odd mix for Linklater's more humanist world view in which every character has his or her reasons for acting as they do," however Linklater counters in the same article:

> at the end of the day, [Eric Bogosian is a] kind of a moralist. Eric is trying to have people treat each other better and right the social ills. He really wants to right wrongs and things like that, much more than I care about in certain character ways.[25]

In one respect, the film's attentional politics move the viewer between perspectives that are binarized here as moralism and humanism, or a tension between moral emphasis on the individual's agency given a troubling context that restricts that agency, or on humanistic understanding of the circumstances that inform behavior. The problem of locating a reliable moral agency that can be pinned to individuals shaped by larger forces is a theme recurring across Linklater's oeuvre, perhaps most explicitly in *Waking Life* (2001). As Bogosian's script also contained autobiographical elements, the resultant film sits somewhere between Linklater's and Bogosian's account of the challenges and responsibilities at the beginning of their adult lives.

The first thing one might note about *SubUrbia* from its opening images is its intervention against the schemata suggested by its title, which may draw to mind inherited images and associations of past filmic suburbias. Popular depictions of suburbia often conjure an upper-middle whiteness, norms associated with a trickle-down economics that presumes a similar suburban dream will inevitably be furnished to all. *SubUrbia* presents an intervention against audiovisual fantasies associated with the suburbs that may recover a sense of many constituents' lived experience of medium density America—one that acknowledges worlds of suburban precarity.[26] In *SubUrbia*, we see instead a "wasteland" of capital;[27] suburban images played over the title sequence before we meet its inhabitants, seemingly filmed from a car window, trace a landscape of grey strip malls and vast parking lots outside megastores, connected by more streets and more bitumen in various stages of development or decay, not the leafy, middle-class, double-story buildings film viewers might associate with American suburban cinema. This is not Hollywood's "suburbia without comment . . . a detached house in suburbia, often larger and somewhat more luxurious than those in which the audience lived."[28] The "symbolic ecology" of mainstream suburban cinema, with its façades and white picket fences concealing darker relational truths, its utopian monument to personal wealth parked alongside a dystopian account of upper-middle domesticity, is replaced here by another suburbia drained of any resources for human flourishing outside of commercially interested spaces, a cement shopping ground that clearly serves dehumanized profitmaking goals more so than offering aesthetic or practical spaces for fulfilling human interaction.[29]

This intervention is presented as a framing device through which audiences might understand many of the character interactions they are about to witness. In terms of prime information, however, it is not expository, but implicatory: the prime implies larger, organizing political structures and commercial forces that we will not bear direct witness to over the course of the film. We instead observe the way the architectural spaces invisibly shaped by those forces guide interactions between characters. Perhaps we could call this a kind of "hostile architecture," then, or "defensive urban design" that funnels youth to materialistic experiences rather than places where they might congregate to interact, where social experiences without economic rationale are not to be trusted.[30] And so *SubUrbia*'s twenty-somethings bring their congregations outside of the home to hostile spaces like the parking lot they call "The Corner," that similarly inform public behavior. As Robert Beuka puts it, "strip mall and convenience store parking lots come to define the boundaries of both environment and experience for a group of young friends."[31] This information is initially conveyed via an aesthetically suggestive primacy effect that frames the ensuing action. With this prime in mind, the behavior we will later witness becomes more intelligible.

In contrast to the utopian/dystopian suburban allegories of 1990s cinema, *SubUrbia*'s priming images attempt to reformulate the image of suburbia and seize it back from its aspirational fantasies. In the tradition of youth rebellion films like *Over the Edge* (Jonathan Kaplan, 1979), this means that *SubUrbia* was also able to reflect genuine concerns in town planning for young and vulnerable constituents and admit failures in (sub)urban design. *SubUrbia* is, as David T. Johnson says, "more critical of the culture as a whole than the suburbs as such," and conveys a care about the emotional needs of the people who live there.[32] Linklater indeed cites *Over the Edge* as an influence on earlier hanging-out picture *Dazed and Confused* (1993):

> I had some exposure to these planned, suburban communities that had been springing up throughout the '70s. The movie is a perfect mix of all the conformity and boredom that goes along with the local geography of these places, and the natural restlessness, anger, and antagonisms of the teenage years.[33]

More so than other teen films that depict youths' struggles against typification inherited from their elders, like *The Breakfast Club* (John Hughes, 1985; the high jinks of which go some way to reinscribing those types by making women's bodily autonomy the object of so many jokes), Linklater was more interested in demonstrating how teen identities are constructed as an induction into (aimless) consumer culture, how one might be symbiotic with an environment that overwhelmingly propels its residents toward hedonistically unenriching norms, and how some smart young people actively struggle against these cultural cues.[34] Yet hanging out, rebuffing consumer norms, chatting, and philosophizing are presented not heroically as such, but as flawed and often equally aimless rebellions.

SubUrbia is perhaps the one Linklater film in which hanging out and talking unequivocally inflames the schisms between its characters rather than bringing them closer together. One could especially contrast its vision with the more romantic *Before* films, the first two of which observe a couple coming together over their philosophic musings. I have written before on the ways in which the *Before* trilogy commits to film a convincing rendition of the emotional space of the D&M, or "deep and meaningful" conversation:

> A film like Richard Linklater's *Before Sunrise* (1995) attempts to demonstrate the similarities between the liminoid space of a story and these exploratory, risk-taking conversations, in which the world seems alive with philosophical possibility while one is unbound. *Before Sunrise* maps the experience of a D&M onto a film narrative.[35]

This unique filmmaking mode is satisfying as it registers a kind of conversational style, and a kind of relational experience, that is familiar to and cherished by many as part of growing up. But it has an intrinsic indulgence, too—perhaps a necessary indulgence that goes some way toward identity formation in concert with peers, and growing together with those peers. (Although late night D&Ms have been some of the most vividly rewarding experiences of my life, I would probably shudder to hear now what seemed like co-discovery and -elaboration of world-opening insights at the time!) *SubUrbia* asks instead when that indulgence might be harmful, when it puts one's self-absorptive identity concerns ahead of care for others, when it refuses not only to see abuses, but rise to challenge them—when it's all just talk. This puts *SubUrbia* in an intriguing position within Linklater's canon of films humanizing young people by committing to screen representations of their "deep and meaningful" conversations.[36]

The *Before* films also map the electric feeling of these conversations onto a city, the layout and culture of which affords the time, cultural events, and public spaces to support joint attention, and thus nurture the sharing of ideas. The comparison, then, is a fruitful one as it provides a clue as to why the characters of *SubUrbia* are not doing so well: Linklater's depressing shots of a concrete suburban jungle at the beginning of *SubUrbia* imply that there aren't really any alternatives to sitting around the parking lot of a convenience store all night. Rob Stone suggests that in Linklater's films "the street is a place and time of visual, auditory, sensual, romantic, spiritual and philosophical encounters,"[37] and these representations meet support in a wealth of sociological writing about teenagers' reappropriation not just of urban streets, but also the hostile architecture and suburban "non-places" under examination.[38] *SubUrbia* is somewhat unique among Linklater's features, then, presenting a street culture that generates precisely the obverse of these boons. As Johnson notes:

> The opening credits are a reversal of *Before Sunrise*'s closing montage; whereas the latter captured aesthetically pleasing locations still resonating with romantic desire, this sequence foregrounds ugliness. Many shots depict nearly empty parking lots in front of strip malls, such as one showing the decaying, broken pavement stretching outward from a PetSmart . . . In many ways, the Corner is the antithesis of social spaces like the Emporium or the Moon Tower in *Dazed and Confused*; whereas the latter provide release, places where differences can be temporarily elided, even if they persist, the Corner serves only to increase the anxiety, frustration, and despair of those who gather there.[39]

Johnson suggests that the characters in *SubUrbia* take the dehumanizing cues of an environment that affords no potential for thoughtful shared attention, and no meaningful future through which to channel their passions. Instead, they are seen to be channeling their dissatisfaction into antagonism and abuse:

at worst, we witness characters assaulting Pakistani shop owners Nazeer (Ajay Naidu) and Pakeesa (Samia Shoaib), and "negging" the film's female characters.[40] The consequences for the victims are dire. It is the only Linklater film that really unambiguously faces the consequences of sexist and racist bullying that is sometimes contained within the putative moral exceptionalism of not-quite-adulthood. As such, *SubUrbia*'s refiguration of Linklater's youthful flâneur figure informs the film's pivotal moral probing: perhaps, as Linklater says, these young adults will be okay, perhaps they *could* appropriate these streets to more collaborative or prosocial ends. But in an inherited America that divides people by land and wealth, and affordances of land and wealth are distributed along ethnic lines, how culpable can youths be for a failure to imagine a less competitive use of space?

After the prime framing of interventionist suburban imagery, the film's dialogue moves the viewer between racist assault and sexist invective, and then characters' musings on their place in the world and the meaning of their lives. Characters are able to use flights of personal philosophy, self-consideration, and grandstanding anti-suburban nihilism to distract one another from the effects they have on their peers as they accept, ignore, or apologize for these abuses. Prior readings of the film have tended to focus on the primary framing of suburban imagery. Perhaps, given it is tacit and visual, it is easier to read than later action and dialogue, in which recency effects modify those earlier images by colliding the descriptively humanist mode with subsequent, more prescriptively moralistic questions about youth agency and accountability. Again, the recency effect that pulls one's considered attention forward to update a sense of the most salient information is not plot focused, and nor is it so much about how we feel about the characters; as in the best humanist filmmaking, assessing characters' virtuous or villainous statuses is decentered. *SubUrbia* instead asks us to be aware of how our attention is directed (both by the "director" and by depicted proselytizers), how that directedness affects what we privilege in memory and what we accept as salient, and how memory and salience are ergo political. This technique might also draw our attention to the ways in which our modeling not just of a fictive world, but of the moral consequences and our implication in that world, is subject to a kind of moral bracketing that is guided by its sequential information, its primacy and recency effects.

SUBURBIA'S MORAL RECENCY EFFECTS

The consequences of bracketing that which should be more important (the generalized effects of sexist discourses borne in silence by those who are implicitly its targets) become clear at the film's climax: during a confrontation between the racist Tim (Nicky Katt) and the Pakistani couple he antagonizes that appears on the verge of gun violence, the unconscious body of recovering alcoholic Bee-Bee (Dina Spybey) is found on the roof of the convenience store, forgotten and near death after a suicide attempt. We might, at this point, think back to reconsider events as clues to the fact that this character was not coping with the abuses visited on her: it might begin with the way Jeff (Giovanni Ribisi) shuts down Bee-Bee's enthusiasm for her friend Sooze's (Amie Carey) feminist performance art at the beginning of the film, or the camera lingering on her mortified reaction as Buff (Steve Zahn), after sleeping with Bee-Bee, sexually objectifies a music publicist from Los Angeles, Erica (Parker Posey). These injuries hiding in plain sight culminate in Jeff and Tim conferring that "women are all whores," while Bee-Bee sits nearby, listening on. Again, the camera lingers and a guitar dirge plays as Jeff makes silent eye contact with Bee-Bee, then leaves her with a bottle of spirits that she will attempt to end her life with. Jeff never says anything sexist to Bee-Bee, but he does say sexist things to her friend, and he does participate in misogynistic conversations when she is nearby. One need not explicitly victimize someone to harm them—perhaps given glimpses of Jeff's capacity for deeper thought and caring about others' well-being, we should expect more of him. And, potentially, of ourselves: the film is more or less focalized with Jeff, following his perspective more so than other characters. Following his earlier diatribe about the Pakistani couple as "humans with feelings," maintaining that global inequality should concern everyone, we hope that his humanist leanings will prevail over the toxic peer pressure of Tim and Buff, over a world that seems to lack care in its very spatial inducements.

They do not. Tim goads Jeff, who feels it is his "duty as a human being to be pissed off" but clearly does not know how to direct that anger, into the view that there is "only one answer" to his discontent, that no one matters so "fuck 'em all." This commitment is the gateway to being goaded further into throwing a box of Chinese takeaway at Nazeer's and Pakeesa's shop window. It is clear that a self-serving nihilism is not only seductive because of the absence of alternatives presented in their world, it also underscores and permits racist abuse. "Nobody's really different, even if they think they're different . . . that's what makes me free," Jeff tells Bee-Bee, using anti-suburban homogenizing rhetoric to justify looking past proximate others' specificity of circumstance, putting his nihilistic soapbox ahead of any careful listening to Bee-Bee's own needs, "as long as I don't care, I can do anything I want." From this, Bee-Bee concludes that every day is the same, so nothing matters in her own life: "here's another day, you know, it's just like the last one," she says, "I mean what difference does it make?" He does not respond, and the consequences are fatal. In the film's closing lines, Nazeer admonishes Jeff for throwing his life away, and the audience is invited too to consider if their own humanist convictions generally prevail over any normalization of the dehumanizing aspects of this culture, one that puts capital before lives, and to question our place within the abuses that become naturalized in that world.

Bee-Bee's fate in *SubUrbia*'s final act may be unexpected, although we realize it should not be, and that we may have been paying attention to the wrong problems—the loudest are not necessarily those in most need of attentive care. The climax of the film may also draw our attention to the role of forgetting in primacy-recency effects, as both the characters and audience are somewhat chided for forgetting Bee-Bee; or at least, the impact of the ending relies upon a prompt to moral re-evaluation. Even while narratives craft emphases for audiences to follow that encourage them to privilege recent information at the expense of prior concerns, narratives at the same time exhort viewers to feel ownership over their response to those prompts. Yet there are other serial processing biases at work, here, too: we may also find it difficult to recall items on a list that are similar or seem synonymous, or simply sound the same.[41] Where a narrative amalgamates characters into a group of similar identities, a comparable effect may be produced in that it can be harder to remember each individual within those groups presented as having collective identity traits. Sometimes this bias is intervened when one such character becomes essential to the narrative in some way, by surprise. In *SubUrbia*, while Bee-Bee's deteriorating mental health is conveyed across both visual and musical cues, these cues are minimized by recency effects, as the camera and dialogue will move swiftly to proximate others, encouraging comparisons but not prolonged attention to her state of mind.

To borrow Margrethe Bruun Vaage's terms, we might call this moment a "reality check" that intervenes against the "fictional relief" of a film that is less implicating in its circuitous brouhaha; depiction of horrific consequences brings moral point to the narrative that calls out to be actively considered and accommodated.[42] These strategies are familiar from the final acts of other famous youth pictures that change their tone from entertaining teen fantasy to a serious consideration of the emotions that can cause young people to act in desperate ways. Consider Cameron's (Alan Ruck) narrative arc in *Ferris Bueller's Day Off* (John Hughes, 1986) as an example. *Fast Times at Ridgemont High* (Amy Heckerling, 1982), on the other hand, punctures fantasy schemata of the teen raunch film in more deflating ways: male fantasies are indulged but then interposed with scenes that collapse the fantasy, and "a proto-feminist perspective in the film's nonchalant treatment of abortion" intercedes against more hysterical polemics on teen pregnancy.[43] The recency in these examples concerns not just our notion of a film's plot, but a diegetic emotional causality: the prime schema is an entertaining fantasy world untethered from lasting consequences, but our notions of consequence must be updated to integrate the moral effects of character behavior, and the emotions that prepare that behavior. In *SubUrbia*, Linklater and Bogosian use the "hanging-out" format, gathering together groups of Gen X individuals around a similar point in their lives, and present louder characters that distinguish themselves from the group often with nascent philosophizing. We are not necessarily thinking about the inner life of peripheral characters as we are asked to focus on more extroverted individuals; introverted characters appear as one of the collective bound to the established "hanging-out" filmic mode. Bee-Bee's final act, in effect, intervenes schemata (and their associated sense-making biases) Linklater had helped establish over prior features. The intervention highlights problems embedded in the narrative structure: a structure of storied, sense-making attentional biases that may have correlates to the ways in which attention is allocated in our daily lives to others' problems, or empathic consideration of their emotional being. It may be, too, that this is a particularly poignant observation to return to in a post-digital era that affords loud, and often hateful, voices a platform by which they seem more substantial and representative of collectives than they really are.[44]

In fact, the film gradually reveals itself to be a consideration of the politics of attention: dialogue often centers on the question of who has a "right" to be heard. When successful singer-songwriter Pony (Jayce Bartok) shows up to revisit his hometown, this dialogue intensifies around class divisions, revealing one of the "hidden injuries of class": resentment at inequities in who is afforded a voice that commands attention.[45] We might, at this point, reframe motivations around the youths' philosophizing as a desire for their experiences to be recognized in an environment that discourages social interest in one another's emotional needs or well-being.[46] At the same time, nihilism and racist and sexist loudmouths grab attention, and pull Jeff's potential for care away from the eminently visible harms of sexism (Bee-Bee's experience) and racism (Nazeer's and Pakeesa's experiences). Thus, the film's attentional politics not only recognize the damage of abuse but the concealed harms of those who accept that abuse, who could but do not intervene.

Yet given that this seductively nihilist self-indulgence emerges from an inherited consumer landscape and a culture that, by enlarging class boundaries and differences between people, forces dehumanization to make horrible naturalized sense, the morality of the film is not open and closed. Audiences still must question how far any agency for resistance extends when young people have little say in urban development, or the identity and career choices it affords. Musing on his interest in characters in their early twenties, Linklater says:

> I keep coming back to it, just because it's such a poignant time in someone's life, and I was amazed at the things you're up against. It was clear to me at the time—when you're a teenager and you're like that [an aimless philosopher], it's kind of charming and people understand, but once you're college age and beyond, society and your parents and everybody

have zero sympathy. The culture has such contempt for some young person who doesn't have it all together, or have a bunch of ambition—sanctioned ambition, you know, that they approve of.[47]

We must question, too, at what point in growing up one assumes the mantle of accountability for the culturally distributed effects of one's actions in a landscape that fetishizes individual responsibility but delimits options for engagement to "sanctioned ambitions" and passive consumption. *SubUrbia* puts the viewer through a similar experience in the use of primacy and recency effects, but also by forcing us to be aware of their politicized directedness: who do our attentional biases ask us to care or not care about, and how are they shaped by the stories told in the environments we inhabit? Linklater is right, the film is not moralistic, but it is morally concerned in its structure of attention that crafts salience from attentional biases bringing our awareness, humanistically, to the situated dilemmas of young people inducted into a politically unfair and unequal America.

PRIMACY AND RECENCY IN LINKLATER'S OTHER WORKS

I have surveyed two filmic narrative strategies that collaborate with our biases to help us make sense of a film like *SubUrbia*: a primacy effect that frames a world not in terms of plot events but in terms of an environment that produces certain behaviors, and a recency effect that politicizes narrative attention. Both effects attempt to produce metacognitive awareness of the moral resonances of world-modeling during fictive engagement. The point is that a film's organization of primacy and recency do not only help us make sense of story fabula, or plots with evaluable characters as was Bordwell's concern, they also help us understand the narrative as an act of communication, how that fictive world comments on our own, and how its moral commentary might implicate the viewer. Before closing, I would like to point out how Linklater's other works employ primacy and recency techniques to ends that demonstrate further humanistic threads across his oeuvre, and connect those techniques back to *SubUrbia*.

One might note, for a start, that primacy and recency can exist within camera movements, and the meanings spectators can draw from those camera movements. Linklater's films recognize social hierarchy, yet at the same time they will often destabilize the supremacy of such hierarchies as his characters move fluidly between contact with different groups. *Slacker*, for example, echoes a similar technique used in John Sayles's *City of Hope* (1991), released the same year and harnessing new steadicam technology into "a long unbroken take meandering from group to group, picking up phrases and showing how all these people connect up."[48] Greg M. Smith elaborates: "The passing maneuver duplicates and extends one of the basic experiences of being in a city: the sideways glance. It is acceptable to look briefly at the homeless guy or the loudly arguing housewives, but one cannot stare without making contact with a stranger."[49] *Slacker* allows the viewer, positioned as flâneur like Linklater's characters, to bounce from group to group in passing, observing the construction of an urban social selfhood. This relies on establishing set-up that presents information about individuals (the prime) that is then modified with new information about the social milieu those individuals exist within as the shot unfolds, an effortful recency that requests the viewer to continue updating a sense of urban, social multi-causality. From that visually represented social detail, we might glean other insights about the film as communication: in using this technique, Linklater's films quietly rejoice the way a desire for connection propels residents to rebel against power structures that reinforce competitive boundaries between people, a "taking back" through exploratory, autotelic conversation. Everyone, popular or unpopular, young or old, disillusioned or accepting of the status quo, is still demonstrated to have the capacity for and interest in all manner of contemplative discourse. Yet again, this resistant philosophizing does not provide all of us the means to resist the damage an uncaring, amoral culture can inflict: "Offices and streets become inhumane when rigidity, utility, and competition rule; they become humane when they promote informal, open-ended, and cooperative interactions."[50]

Fast Food Nation (2006) is another multi-character humanist drama that echoes *SubUrbia*'s concern with the limitations of personal resistance in the face of exploitative industrial norms: in this film, the synchronous exploitation of workers and animals (and by extension customers, who are seen to be eating spit and shit through the course of the film) in the fast-food industry. The characters of *Fast Food Nation* take cues from a different kind of environment of exploitation, albeit connected to that of *SubUrbia* by its normalized network of abuses in a world that puts capital before well-being. Like *SubUrbia*, *Fast Food Nation* is ambivalent about the place of individual agency within the monolithic forces of capital that are upheld among many players; it displaces moral blame to a "machine" that is the sum of the labor and consumer practices it compels. As rancher Rudy Martin (Kris Kristofferson) puts it early on in the narrative, "This isn't about good people versus bad people, it's about the machine that has taken over this country. It's like something out of science fiction. The land, the cattle, human beings, this machine don't give a shit." As in *SubUrbia*, the centrally focalized fast food executive Don Anderson (Greg Kinnear) fails to rise to the moral standards we expect him to by the narrative's close. The moral shock at the end of the film is that despite everything he has learned, Don returns to work as usual. His personal journey is no match for the vast political shifts that would need to take place to challenge fast-food production chains, and he lives in a world in which his job security is contingent upon acceptance of those abuses. This conclusion is all the more impactful arriving as it does after an emotionally climactic, Brechtian narrative break that transposes the film's talk of exploitation with scenes from the kill floor of an abattoir. This new information that is intended to have the audience viscerally feel the horror of animal torture, that "uses the horror of the factory farm slaughterhouse to highlight the evil and absurdity of agribusiness," must be accommodated against the primary commitments encouraged by the earlier narrative.[51] As in other Linklater experiments working between fiction and non-fiction, such as *Bernie*, *Fast Food Nation* sets up primary narrative schemata that are then, by various means, violated with modes of filmmaking that are hard to accommodate against those schemata. Here, the multi-protagonist fictionalization of Eric Schlosser's source text is presented as a journey of discovery for the central character Don, but the norms of that genre are violated when he learns the truth but does not try to change it, and also when we bear witness to real cattle slaughters and feel the worldly consequences of that failure to change. After the film's close, recency modifies the passivity of a genre that proposes a heroic detective figure will seriously challenge "the machine" by revealing its abuses. Its abuses are known; what to do to change those abuses is not.

On the other hand, a major theme in all of these pictures is the unseen and the unknowable. To return to *SubUrbia*, one might note the strategy employed when Tim lies about having killed Erica in a fit of misogynistic rage. While Jeff is recovering from the shock of finding Erica still alive, the audience too goes through Bordwell's process of plot comprehension, updating their version of events with more recent information, what *really* happened. However, adjusting one's sense of narrative events is less instrumental here than noting how willing we may have been to believe Tim's compulsive lying, and in this case a false confessional that paints the worst picture not just of others around him, but of himself as well. Audiences do not only run recent information back against former narrative sequences and update their sense of the film's fabula—that is the easy part. The hard part is updating our sense of what, politically, that fabula might fruitfully tell us, how it exists as communication, and how effective men like Tim can be in selling their dehumanizing vision through deceitful means.[52] A central theme of Linklater's is the unreliability of information on which moral judgment depends (perhaps one reason why he was attracted to adapting the work of Phillip K. Dick, which similarly destabilizes a reliable sense not only of reality but threat appraisal if we do not know who or what is in control of that reality). These storytelling techniques not only put viewers through the strain of piecing together a causal sense of the narrative, they problematize the ways in which we apply that information to a centered moral or political perspective. Tim uses that space of unreliable knowledge to make his case for uncaring and amoral nihilism: if you cannot trust me because I lie, you cannot make consequential decisions. One might wonder, then, at the role of the storyteller or filmmaker who similarly crafts such ambiguities of cause and consequence?

These are all the kinds of moral dilemmas Linklater approaches—and conversationalizes—through his humanistic lens. A filmmaking style that de-emphasizes dramatic action to focus audience attention on the space between people similarly refocuses awareness to all manner of communication that film both presents and represents. Conversations can be artful resistance, and the film can be a conversation; everyday philosophy and everyday film watching are united in their potential for resistance, and in their moral responsibility. Linklater's social studies are moral and political, revealing across all manner of celluloid-facilitated communicative exploits the cognitive biases, those human quirks of memory and attention, that provide our morality and politics their fulcrum.

NOTES

1. Bennet B. Murdock Jr., "The Serial Position Effect of Free Recall," *Journal of Experimental Psychology* 64:5 (1962): 482–488.
2. The first account of the serial position effect can be found in Hermann Ebbinghaus, *On Memory: A Contribution to Experimental Psychology* (New York: Teachers College, 1913).
3. David Bordwell, *Narration in the Fiction Film* (Madison: University of Wisconsin Press, 1985), 17.
4. Meir Sternberg, *Expositional Modes and Temporal Ordering in Fiction* (Baltimore, MD: Johns Hopkins University Press, 1978); Bordwell, *Narration*, 38.
5. Bordwell, *Narration*, 37.
6. David Bordwell, "Cognitive Theory," in *The Routledge Companion to Philosophy and Film*, edited by Paisley Livingston and Carl Plantinga (London; New York: Routledge, 2009), 360.
7. Sternberg, *Expositional Modes*, 90, 98–101; Bordwell, *Narration*, 165.
8. David Bordwell, "Film Futures," *SubStance* 31:1 (2002): 100.
9. James H. Lake, "The Effects of Primacy and Recency upon Audience Response to Five Film Versions of Shakespeare's *Hamlet*," *Literature/Film Quarterly* 28:2 (2000): 112–117. Conversely, Ian Jarvie makes the case for a recency bias when assessing the importance, merit, or value of recent cultural products. Ian Jarvie, "Is Analytic Philosophy the Cure for Film Theory?" *Philosophy of the Social Sciences* 29:3 (1999): 425.
10. Lake, "The Effects," 113.
11. Ibid., 114.
12. Bordwell, *Narration*, 38.
13. Norman H. Anderson and Ann Jacobson, "Effect of Stimulus Inconsistency and Discounting Instructions in Personality Impression Formation," *Journal of Personality and Social Psychology* 2:4 (1965): 531–539; Patricia G. Devine and Thomas M. Ostrom, "Cognitive Mediation of Inconsistency Discounting," *Journal of Personality and Social Psychology* 49:1 (1985): 5–21.
14. This can be associated with another contiguity effect known as lag recency: Marc W. Howard and Michael J. Kahana, "Contextual Variability and Serial Position Effects in Free Recall," *Journal of Experimental Psychology* 25:4 (1999): 923–941.
15. Howard Sklar, "Narrative Structuring of Sympathetic Response: Theoretical and Empirical Approaches to Toni Cade Bambara's 'The Hammer Man,'" *Poetics Today* 30:3 (2009): 561–607.
16. Michael Z. Newman, "Character and Complexity in American Independent Cinema: *21 Grams* and *Passion Fish*," *Film Criticism* 31:1/2 (2006): 89–106.

17. Gregory Currie considers the distance between propositional inferences in fiction and in life in *Imagining and Knowing: The Shape of Fiction* (Oxford: Oxford University Press, 2020).
18. Correspondence between Richard Linklater and John Sayles, "Scripts, Rewrites," Box 19, *John Sayles Papers*, University of Michigan Library (Special Collections Library), Ann Arbor, Michigan, United States.
19. Wyatt Moss-Wellington, "Affecting Profundity: Cognitive and Moral Dissonance in Lynch, Loach, Linklater, and Sayles," *Projections* 11:1 (2017): 53–55.
20. Michael J. Watkins and Zehra F. Peynircioğlu, "Determining Perceived Meaning During Impression Formation: Another Look at the Meaning Change Hypothesis," *Journal of Personality and Social Psychology* 46:5 (1984): 1005–1016.
21. Ibid.
22. Marjorie Baumgarten, "Subdividing *subUrbia*: Richard Linklater Discusses His New Movie," *The Austin Chronicle*, February 21, 1997: http://www.austinchronicle.com/screens/1997-02-21/527433; Kevin John Bozelka, "An Interview with Richard Linklater," *Velvet Light Trap* 61:8 (2008): 54.
23. Contrast this especially with those pictures depicting the city as a facilitator of enrichingly philosophic experiences for flâneur protagonists, such as the *Before* films.
24. Baumgarten, "Subdividing *subUrbia*."
25. Ibid.
26. While not unique specifically to this film—one might consider Hal Hartley a contemporaneous figure making similar interpolations—these depictions of suburban youth experience could still be considered atypical. *SubUrbia* marks a significant point in a continuum toward what Timotheus Vermeulen explores as the "teen noir" film, with its roots in pictures like *Rebel Without a Cause* (Nicholas Ray, 1955), eventuating in millennial instantiations including *Alpha Dog* (Nick Cassavetes, 2006), *The Chumscrubber* (Arie Posin, 2005), and *Brick* (Rian Johnson, 2005), reclaiming the meaning of the suburban street by admitting teenagers' use of its socio-spatial affordances. Likewise, *SubUrbia* takes its place in a history of shifting cinematic depictions of a diversity lives intersecting across suburban geographies—a diversity that would be central to millennial suburban ensemble cinema two decades hence. Timotheus Vermeulen, *Scenes from the Suburbs: The Suburb in Contemporary US Film and Television* (Edinburgh: Edinburgh University Press, 2014), 154; Wyatt Moss-Wellington, *Narrative Humanism: Kindness and Complexity in Fiction and Film* (Edinburgh: Edinburgh University Press, 2019), 129.
27. C.f. Henri Lefebvre, *Pyrénées* (Lausanne: Éditions Rencontre, 1965), 121.
28. David E. Wilt, "Suburbia," in *The Columbia Companion to American History on Film*, edited by Peter C. Rollins (New York: Columbia University Press, 2003), 484.
29. For a historicization of these filmic tropes, see David R. Coon, *Look Closer: Suburban Narratives and American Values in Film and Television* (New Brunswick, NJ and London: Rutgers University Press, 2014); see also Albert Hunter, "The Symbolic Ecology of Suburbia," in *Neighborhood and Community Environments*, edited by Irwin Altman and Abraham Wandersman (New York: Plenium Press, 1987), 191–221.
30. Cara Chellew, "Defending Suburbia: Exploring the Use of Defensive Urban Design Outside of the City Centre," *Canadian Journal of Urban Research* 28:1 (2019): 19–33.
31. Robert Beuka, "'Cue the Sun': Soundings from Millennial Suburbia," *Iowa Journal of Cultural Studies* 3:1 (2003): 166–167.
32. David T. Johnson, *Richard Linklater* (Urbana, Chicago, and Springfield: University of Illinois Press, 2012), 42.
33. Mike Sacks, "Over the Edge," *Vice*, September 1, 2009: https://www.vice.com/en_us/article/wdz5bb/over-the-edge-134-v16n9

34. As Lesley Speed points out, Linklater's work had moved on from the John Hughes model to more equalizing concerns, with egalitarian coverage and space in the script's expository dialogue provided to people from varied generations, established intellectuals and contemplative amateur storytellers, and all manner of character types resisting their typification. Lesley Speed, "The Possibilities of Roads Not Taken: Intellect and Utopia in the Films of Richard Linklater," *Journal of Popular Film and Television* 35:3 (2007): 102.
35. Moss-Wellington, *Narrative Humanism*, 96.
36. Note that 2013's *Before Midnight* would also puncture the romance of these earlier films by making characters' gendered behavior toward one another more potent than the romance of idealistic chatter.
37. Rob Stone, *The Cinema of Richard Linklater: Walk, Don't Run* (New York: Columbia University Press, 2013), 74.
38. For a fascinating union of discussions across sociology and film theory considering teenaged lived experience of suburban sites, see Vermeulen, *Scenes from the Suburbs*, 149–151, 155–159.
39. Johnson, *Richard Linklater*, 40–42.
40. Kathleen Green, Zoe Kukan, and Ruth J. Tully, "Public Perceptions of 'Negging': Lowering Women's Self-esteem to Increase the Male's Attractiveness and Achieve Sexual Conquest," *Journal of Aggression, Conflict and Peace Research* 9:2 (2017): 95–105.
41. Elizabeth L. Bjork and Alice F. Healy, "Short-term Order and Item Retention," *Journal of Verbal Learning and Verbal Behavior* 13:1 (1974): 80–97.
42. Vaage uses these terms to discuss antiheroic TV shows; however, it is more broadly applicable in other media contexts, as well. Margrethe Bruun Vaage, *The Antihero in American Television* (New York and London: Routledge, 2016).
43. Frances Smith and Timothy Shary, "Introduction to Part I," in *ReFocus: The Films of Amy Heckerling* (Edinburgh: Edinburgh University Press, 2016), 15.
44. Robert B. Talisse, *Overdoing Democracy: Why We Must Put Politics in Its Place* (New York and Oxford: Oxford University Press, 2019).
45. Richard Sennett and Jonathan Cobb, *The Hidden Injuries of Class* (New York: Knopf, 1972).
46. Jonathon I. Oake writes that the encounter sets up a "dialectic of 'popularity' and 'authenticity'" familiar in representations of Gen X, however this is not really true of a film that makes no space for assessments of its characters on a continuum of "authenticity," who are all simply responding to their environment in a variety of ways. Jonathon I. Oake, "Reality Bites and Generation X as Spectator," *Velvet Light Trap* 53 (2004): 89.
47. Qtd. in Johnson, *Richard Linklater*, 134.
48. Philip Kemp, "Limbo," in *American Independent Cinema*, edited by Jim Hillier (London: British Film Institute, 2001), 223.
49. Greg M. Smith, "Passersby and Politics: *City of Hope* and the Multiple Protagonist Film," in *Sayles Talk: New Perspectives on Independent Filmmaker John Sayles*, edited by Diane Carson and Heidi Kenaga (Detroit, MI: Wayne State University Press, 2006), 119.
50. Richard Sennett, "Humanism," *The Hedgehog Review* 13:2 (2011): 27.
51. Alison E. Vogelaar, "Fatal Abstractions: A Reflection on Cinema, Suburbia, and Slaughter," *JAC* 32:1–2 (2012): 343.
52. Of course, not all of Linklater's films are motivated by a "message" as such, some are very much about following an idea through to see what insights develop along the way—*Boyhood* (2014), for instance.

CHAPTER II

Keeping Time in *Dazed and Confused*, *Everybody Wants Some!!*, and *Boyhood*

Bruce Isaacs

For those of us who had followed the stories about its production across a twelve-year period, *Boyhood* (2014) was one of Richard Linklater's most anticipated film releases. It screened at a range of festivals, as was common with Linklater's work, and arrived at the Sydney Film Festival in June, 2014, where it sold out at the State Theatre. I was at that screening. Knowing Linklater's earlier films (and having a special fondness for *Slackers* [1990] and *Dazed and Confused* [1993], shared by almost every one of my social circle), I found *Boyhood* deeply moving, calling to mind my own memories of boyhood in a striking filmic experiment about the way in which time is, in a sense, always part of our lives, and always present to us. It is a classic Bergsonian idea that has been brought to several analyses of Linklater's work: that our pasts remain steadfastly present to us, always enmeshed in present experience.[1] We can then also say that when reflecting on the past, rather than departing for a distant mental place constituted by vague images in the mind, we actively call the past *to the present*, to our present attention and awareness, not as it was, but as a reinvigorated image of that (once present) moment in time. This condition of pastness allows Bergson to suggest that, for example, "states of consciousness, even when successive, permeate one another, and in the simplest of them, the whole soul can be reflected."[2] We see this interlacing of pasts and presents in many beautiful moments in *Boyhood*; I remember being awed by the cut from a sequence in which Mason's (Ellar Coltrane) sister, Samantha (Lorelei Linklater), performs Britney Spears's "Oops! . . . I Did It Again" (2000) to an unspecified, unmarked future, with the little Samantha now visibly aged, a fully embodied older being, having leapt (but fully lived) through the intervening time. A hard cut from one image to the next in which Mason's mother, Olivia (Patricia Arquette), has aged in wrinkles surrounding her eyes was profoundly affecting; that materiality of changed flesh—across a single cut—constitutes, in formal and phenomenological terms, such an affront to our traditional experience of film time.

This notion of time as something important, or mysterious, or more than we can understand—which is the starting point for Bergson's complex meditation—has been explored so frequently in Linklater's work as to become a standard approach.[3] His films are often expressly *about time* in a broader philosophical sense; their stories trace the passing of time, or reflect on times past, or examine the character of "a time" in period pieces. And yet, in viewing his body of work again for the writing of this chapter, I kept asking myself: what do his films say about the experience of time, if anything at all? What do they reveal about its intricate modulations of selfhood or consciousness in time, or the vitalism of temporal experience, which is the bedrock of Bergson's ideas?

I find Mason's zesty proclamations in *Boyhood* about wishing to understand the purpose of all things, or Mason Sr.'s (Ethan Hawke) instruction to shut out that impulse, trite, simplistic, and familiar. The weakest parts of the film are the moments in which Linklater attempts to articulate in words the mystery of cosmic time and space. At a critical moment of Mason's coming-of-age, frustrated with the institutional barriers of convention, he says: "I don't usually even try to, like, vocalize my thoughts or feelings or anything. Just—I don't know, it never sounds right. Words are stupid." In a similar fashion, characters in *Dazed and Confused* and *Everybody Wants Some!!* (2016) learn that life is lived in the moment, as a perpetual "now," and characters iterate and reiterate this essential lived condition. But my sense is that, in the context of Linklater's desire to explore the potentiality of lived time, words are, in films like *Dazed and Confused*, *Everybody Wants Some!!*, and even *Boyhood*, "stupid," or at least grossly inadequate. And Linklater seems to understand this. Words are not adequate to the task of creating a cinematic experience of time within the straightjacket of a familiar coming-of-age narrative. His films are also explicit genre pieces, and have propulsive narratives of episodic peaks and troughs that reveal a strange tension between straight-ahead classical storytelling and the aimless narrative wanderings that mark so much of the output of the American Independent cinema of the 1990s.[4] Spoken words in Linklater's films thus tend to function as a literalized, deterministic (story)telling. Which is to say that, in Linklater's coming-of-age films, the model for coming-of-age—or "becoming", if we adopt Bergson's philosophical framing—is uniform and perspectivized through a lens of social, political, and ideological norms. The narrative image "of time" tends toward simplicity, uniformity, and universality.

In this chapter, I want to argue that, in spite of such generic coming-of-age narrative conventions, *Boyhood* nonetheless represents Linklater's most significant philosophical and poetic achievement in relation to an explicitly Bergsonian ontology of temporal experience. Further, I argue that *Boyhood* represents a decisive philosophical and poetic break from the model of temporal experience narrativized in *Dazed and Confused* and *Everybody Wants Some!!*. In making this claim, I want to uphold an important distinction for both Bergson and Gilles Deleuze (who adopts the Bergsonian model in framing a taxonomy of cinematic images) between time *as an image*—the image of time that is lived and immersive—and time as a concept or thematic idea that finds expression in the words, narrative tropes, character arcs, and chains of events that constitute many of Linklater's stories.[5] In my estimation, Linklater's films frequently thematize the experience of lived time without revealing the potential of the image to *show* time and *live* time within the Deleuzian philosophical schema. However, in the unique temporal experiment of *Boyhood*, Linklater's philosophy of time leaps across an ontological divide between idea and image, making of the image something more than the purveyor of words and ideas. Deleuze reserves a very special place for the time-image in his extensive analysis of a history of montage, tracing it through auteur-focused studies from the neo-realists to the European "new wave" works, to filmmakers like John Cassavetes in the American tradition.[6] And yet, in all of Deleuze's time-images of the great auteur filmmakers and their experimental works, I can't recall feeling the intensity of lived time as a cinematic image that I felt in the State Theatre that night, when the end credits rolled, and I beheld what happened next.

As happens at the end of all festival screenings, the audience offered a final round of applause. And at that precise moment, the film's protagonist, Mason Evans, appeared from behind a curtain. I had been deeply moved by the story of Mason, despite the relatively formulaic narrative of his lived boyhood and adolescence. When re-viewing the film for this chapter, after the final cut to black, I immediately started the film again, to try to capture the effect of such an abrupt cut to a childhood, shot twelve years before the closing scene, in which Mason explains the provenance of wasps to his mother; in this way, I forced myself into a contemplation of *Boyhood*'s expansive time. But it is far more difficult to capture in words the effect of Mason's appearance on the stage of the State Theatre. If all of Linklater's films are studies of time passing, to my mind, nothing in his corpus had achieved the philosophical and affective jolt of this figure suddenly materializing before me as a 19-year-old when he had been a flesh and blood 6-year-old earlier that evening. In this moment, Linklater seemed to have realized what Buster Keaton had projected in *Sherlock Jr.* (1924), or Woody Allen in *The Purple Rose of Cairo* (1985): Mason had walked *out of the screen* to inhabit my space and my time, to address me as a spectator from the diegetic world contained within the image, which was until a moment before hermetically sealed off from the non-diegetic space of the theatre. Of course, on one level I knew the figure to be Ellar Coltrane, the actor who had spent twelve years of his boyhood in the production of the film. But

I was compelled into an awareness of a figure in excess of Coltrane, inhabiting that material body to which I was now present.

The applause from the audience gained in volume, even as Coltrane seemed uncomfortable in his exhibition. As Mason moved awkwardly in the harsh spotlight, I felt a level of intimacy with that body and how it moved, and how it shirked the gaze of the spotlight in the same way that Mason had shirked the gaze of school friends, or a love interest, or a drunken, violent stepfather. I recognized and felt those movements as fully the movements of Mason rather than Ellar Coltrane, who seemed a paltry, insignificant, dwarfed figure on stage. I suspect that the applause from the audience was less about the appearance of the film's star than about the magic and allure of the cinematic illusion Linklater had foisted upon us. My sense then was that the illusion constituted the most direct time-image I had encountered in the cinema.

SISYPHUS AND PINK FLOYD: FROM HOMOGENOUS TO HETEROGENEOUS TIME

Dazed and Confused and *Everybody Wants Some!!* are composed of highly ordered narrative segments, strung in rational progression, with an effortless drive that takes the spectator from frame one to the close of the film. Each film is set to time, with *Dazed and Confused* riffing on the generic familiarity of the last day of high school film, and *Everybody Wants Some!!* counting down to the commencement of college classes on the weekend before semester begins. Each narrative is therefore a coming-of-age less as an open exploration of time's potentiality than as a predetermined, closed set of temporal coordinates designed explicitly by Linklater to map a narrative toward personal maturation and enlightenment, usually of a young male protagonist. It is thus a curious challenge to fit Linklater in the Deleuzian schematic of movement-images and time-images, which are built so explicitly out of Bergson's architecture of "heterogeneous" experience.[7] All of Linklater's characters seem in one way or another to lose a sense of volition and personal agency, but each seems reassured by the knowability of structures to point the way ahead, to formulate trajectories of discovery that reach an endpoint. Linklater's stories of personal becoming, against the model proposed by Bergson, have always seemed to me steadfastly teleological.

The story of becoming (and change) in Linklater is therefore less an open-ended process (as it is for Bergson) than a "becoming something," and if it is a "becoming something," it is always a becoming something in relation to a projected endpoint. Of characters divested of action and the goal-centric coordinates of a classical cinema, Deleuze suggests that the cinema of the neo-realists represents a kind of occlusion of action, and the incapacity to stitch one action to another through rational sensory-motor communication.[8] But can we say the same of the protagonists of *Dazed and Confused* or *Everybody Wants Some!!*? Against the potentiality of lived time, Linklater presents generic coordinates, and even concrete dichotomies of ideologically coded experience in the 1970s and 1980s. Linklater's corpus doesn't feel like a philosophical statement or even a statement of philosophical intention in the same way that filmmakers like Jean-Luc Godard or Michelangelo Antonioni used cinema for overt philosophical ends. As Stone argues, there is a curious regionalism in Linklater that seems to create a hermetic world around his films, both containing them and intensifying the things they wish to communicate.[9] In *Dazed and Confused*, Mitch Kramer (Wiley Wiggins) comes of age by learning to break from the institutional bulwarks of school, family, and the grand narratives of a conservative Austin, Texas political identity. This involves an engagement with an experimental aesthetics in progressive rock and pop soundtracks that challenged a rock 'n' roll conservatism that was increasingly viewed as old fashioned and quaint. At a critical moment in Mitch's integration into a world of freer experience—which is less a break from tradition than an emphatic upholding of a prior tradition—we hear a refrain from Bob Dylan's "Hurricane," an anthem from 1976 that, for Dylan, marked a return to a politically oriented folk-rock form. In every sense, Mitch's coming-of-age is generic, familiar, predictable, and more affecting for its appropriation of a teen coming-of-age genericity familiar to mainstream audiences. Linklater apparently sought to overturn the John Hughes coming-of-age story as self-realization and affirmation, and yet, in my viewing of *Dazed and Confused* the clean political and ideological dichotomies that give the narrative shape, poise, and affective import recall the classical generic trajectory of conflict resolution and self-realization. *Dazed and Confused* finds affirmation in the stupidity of a past generation: and Randall "Pink" Floyd (Jason London) may not know precisely what he is at the film's conclusion, but he knows with absolute clarity what he is not. Randall is not the exhausted protagonist Christian Keathley reads through a Deleuzian paradigm, tracing it to the postclassical American cinema.[10] Rather, he is exhausted with the inadequacy of others and their intent to silence his voice, which is always proudly and profoundly expressive. These are characters who speak and act in the space and time of high school in Austin, Texas 1976, with a stunning sense of purpose and enviable self-confidence. Mitch's coming-of-age in *Dazed and Confused* is less a Bergsonian becoming than an act of conforming to a narrative pre-ordained by a prior and generically familiar ideological fantasy. In the film's symbolically-laden scene that takes place on the halfway line of a football field, Randall and his friends articulate the central narratives they are to take from their individual and collective comings of age. Each character is confident, verbose, precise, and clear-eyed in the projection of the pathway ahead. Even if Linklater suggests that coming-of-age is an empty fantasy, nonetheless each character is resigned to the fullness of the experience and its metaphysical import. As Wooderson (Matthew McConaughey), one of the film's perennial high schoolers, proclaims: "The older you do get, the more rules they're gonna try to get you to follow. You just gotta keep livin', man. L-I-V-I-N!"

In *Everybody Wants Some!!* Linklater traces a very similar teleology of coming-of-age. The film was broadly described by Linklater as a spiritual sequel to *Dazed and Confused*, and it maps almost precisely the same trajectory of ideological maturation in late 1970s and early 1980s America, except now the high school narrative is transposed to the beginning of the college year.[11] Mitch Kramer (who played high school baseball in *Dazed and Confused*) metamorphoses into Jake Bradford (Blake Jenner), a baseball player who has graduated high school to join one of the leading college teams in the country. In one of the film's pivotal Linklateresque scenes, Jake explains the curious congruence between Sisyphus's eternal struggle and baseball:

> The point of the whole thing is the gods intend for Sisyphus to suffer, right? Well, my point was that they've actually blessed him with something to focus on. Something that he could potentially find meaning in. And it's a gift to be striving at all, even if it looks futile to others . . . And yeah, it's ridiculous to roll a boulder up a mountain over and over and over again, but so's everything else in life . . . especially a game.

Jake's coming-of-age is wrapped up in a highly idiosyncratic interpretation of the myth of Sisyphus, which is traditionally read, as Jake admits, as a metaphor for suffering in life in a way Albert Camus would describe as "the absurd."[12] We see ample evidence here of Linklater's model of time bereft of the weight of time upon the individual, and of the suffering that weight of time bears. Jake does not inhabit the existential anomie of radical indeterminacy, but the affirmative cosmos that encompasses one's aging as projected fulfillment, a literal coming-of-age as finite, deterministic becoming something more than what once was.

Linklater's concept of time in these coming-of-age narratives in large part conforms to what Bergson describes as the "homogenous" image of time, which broadly refers to a time that is spatialized, measurable, and abstracted from pure experience.[13] We see this tension between homogenous and heterogeneous time played out in the juxtaposition of two scenes in *Everybody Wants Some!!* The first scene depicts the essential competition that organizes the baseball characters into a community. The further the film progresses, the more we are reminded that these characters are in fierce competition with each other for limited places in the team. There is a clear implication that several of the players that constitute the makeshift community will fail and return to a life of relative anonymity. Tyler Hoechlin (Glen McReynolds), one of the senior players, loses a ping pong game to Jake (a rookie), and in a fit of fury at having lost the game, breaks the ping pong bat and storms out of the room. "That dude needs to relax," murmurs Jake off-screen; he understands that this is a lesson that demonstrates the encroachment of institutional constraints and impediments to what he had thought was a free-spirited (if hedonistic) community.

The film then cuts to a separate commune of several players broken off from the competitive environment. Jake sits in Charlie's (Wyatt Russell) room with a bunch of the other rookies and one senior player, smoking pot, listening to a Pink Floyd record, "Fearless" (*Meddle*, 1971). As the progression moves up the scale, Charlie, sounding very much like Mason Sr. in *Boyhood* waxing lyrical on Wilco's "Hate it Here" (*Sky Blue Sky*, 2007), implores the others to

> Listen to this song. Listen to this progression here, okay? Listen to how it goes up. It steps up from one moment to another, and leads you there, just . . . Finding the tangents within the framework, therein lies the artistry, man . . . Guys, it's about finding out who you are in the space in between the notes that they're offering you.

This is a sophisticated reading on Charlie's part of the complex temporality of musical form, both rhythmically and harmonically. The notion of a space between the notes may not be a direct quotation of Bergson, but it is at this moment that Linklater sounds as if he is channeling a Bergsonian model of *lived* time, and something quite unlike the more conventional coming-of-age fable. The spaces between notes, Charlie suggests, are not mapped, or regulated, or abstracted from the whole, or commoditized by corporate America; instead, the spaces between notes are the in-between of movement and time as experience. In its ideological import, the Pink Floyd sequence presents an ideological corrective to what is represented in the ping pong game, which Linklater suggests is an ethically and existentially destitute form of capitalist competition and patriarchal repression. While the coming-of-age narrative of *Everbody Wants Some!!* communicates a homogenous time, Charlie's musical metaphor of experience takes us nearer to a Bergsonian experience of heterogenous time, or duration, and thus to the ontological break signaled by the experiment in cinematic time of *Boyhood*.

In a famous passage in *Time and Free Will*, Bergson contrasts a dominant model of deterministic time (or the "homogenous" time previously discussed) with a far more eccentric model he wishes to propose. Of homogenous time and experience, Bergson writes: "it is true that when we make time a homogenous medium in which conscious states unfold themselves, we take it to be given all at once, which amounts to saying that we abstract it from duration."[14]

But what, exactly, is duration? Even in this somewhat vague formulation, there is a clear distinction between the way Bergson suggests we conceive and model time—the way we abstract it in "words," to recall Mason's rejection of words as "stupid"—and *lived time*. It also helps to think about this distinction in the context of the phenomena of movement and change. If we are to ask ourselves "what is movement?" we fumble with words that extract from the phenomenon of movement to formulate the concept of movement. When we attempt to engage the *experience* of movement and change, words tend to be inadequate, or "stupid."

Against this homogenous, abstracted, spatialized time, Bergson attempts to explain how we might consider lived time as duration:

> Pure duration is the form which the succession of our conscious states assumes when our ego lets itself *live*, when it refrains from separating its present state from its former states . . . [forming] both the past and the present states into an organic whole, as happens when we recall the notes of a tune, melting, so to speak, into one another. Might it not be said that, even if these notes succeed one another, yet we perceive them in one another, and that their totality may be compared to a living being whose parts, although distinct, permeate one another, just because they are so closely connected?[15]

I find this a challenging passage in Bergson because one senses Bergson wishing to show the fullness of lived time, but constrained by words. Lived time, while conceptualized as a break from homogenous time, is nonetheless formulated in words and necessarily abstracted from experience into a cluster of static, unchanging concepts. Words are stuck on Bergson's page, and thus bereft of the vitality of movement. Bergson himself understands the inadequacy of words to do the job of revealing the experience of duration, and so prompts the reader to consider the relationship between an experience of time and an experience of the temporality of musical form. And it's at this point that Bergson's music metaphor makes explicit contact with Charlie's quest to discover the "space in between the notes" in *Everybody Wants Some!!* Melody, for Bergson, bears a fascinating relationship to time: it is both a sequential series of separate notes (such as the ascending G major scale of Pink Floyd's "Fearless" in *Everybody Wants Some!!*) and the spontaneous opening, stretching, and perpetually changing whole. Each note thus articulates its melodic pitch (say, the root "G") while configuring spontaneously a relation to each other intervallic position (say, from the opening of the root "G" to the fifth, "D"). For Bergson, the majesty of melodic form stems from the infinitely divisible space between the notes that, once laid open, constitute the fullness of the whole. It is then a small leap to suggest that such intervals (spatialized in the division of the whole into intervals) function primarily as regulatory divisions, setting up formal regimes of order, convention, genericity, common practice, and even hard-wired evolutionary ways of listening.[16] Linklater's mouthpieces—in this case Charlie, as he tokes on a bong—reject the constraints of institutional order and convention, and thus seek self-knowledge and self-identity in the space between the notes. For Charlie, these are not intervallic spaces but the sensed indivisible openness and infinite creative possibility of the experience of the whole.

Linklater deploys narrative tropes and the image iconography of a long history of films that take unassuming protagonists and attempt to forge counter-identities; *Easy Rider* (Dennis Hopper, 1969) and *The Last Picture Show* (Peter Bogdanovich, 1971) seem overt touchstones for the way in which Charlie rejects the mechanization of regulated time, or the constraints of social, governmental, and civic institutions. Linklater also channels an anti-Reaganite, anti-consumerist ideology in his images of young men who search for some elusive purpose by breaking from the regulation of institutional time and place. The Pink Floyd sequence provides Linklater with a metaphor that encompasses and extends across the cinematic word, concept, and experience, bridging that chasm between the narratives encompassing homogenous time in *Dazed and Confused* and *Everybody Wants Some!!* and the time-image of *Boyhood* that displays the radical potential of lived time as creative and constant *change*.

STEPPING FROM BEHIND THE CURTAIN

> "It's like it's always right now."
>
> Mason, *Boyhood*

It's unclear to me whether Linklater wishes the audience to take Mason's declarations about society's inadequacies seriously. In his most patronizing moment, he admonishes his then girlfriend with "We're being chemically rewarded for allowing ourselves to be brainwashed." In a later scene that reflects on the failure of his relationship with that girlfriend, Mason Sr. admits his own cluelessness: "We're all just winging it, you know?"; in the sequence, Linklater explicitly reveals that Mason Sr. has a deeply antiquated view of desire and human relationships. In the film's final scene, Mason, on a chemical high staring at the generic image of nature Linklater employs throughout his films, muses: "It's like it's always right now." The image is held in an extremely intimate two-shot, lending a special *gravitas* and solemnity to the moment. Linklater amplifies the atmospherics and sounds of nature that bring the characters into direct contact with the lived environment. The set-up for the conclusion of a twelve-year duration is profound. And yet, I'm not quite sure what Mason means beyond the platitude of living each moment as if it has intrinsic value in and of itself, as if it is special and segmented from all other moments. My sense is that this living in the moment—"like as if all of time is unfolded before us so we could stand here and look out and scream 'fuck you!'"—is very far from a Bergsonian ontology of duration. Linklater may be subtly alluding to Mason's *unlived* experience: that experiencing all moments as "right now" is a material luxury not afforded many others, and certainly not his own mother, who concludes her twelve-year narrative of becoming with "I just thought there would be more." Olivia's realization channels a Sisyphean reading that wisely (and with the benefit of lived time) overturns Jake's sophomoric reading of the meaning of Sisyphus's suffering in *Everybody Wants Some!!* At this moment in *Boyhood*, Olivia takes her place as Camus's figure outside the phone booth watching the "meaningless pantomime," brought into contact with the cosmic absurdity of temporal experience.[17]

In what way, then, does *Boyhood* incarnate the image of radical, heterogenous, *lived* time? The critical leap for Linklater is to incarnate lived time within the cinematic image, and through the technological apparatus of the cinema. The production lasted twelve years, with Linklater casting and beginning shooting in 2002, when Ellar Coltrane was six years old. By shooting the film over twelve years, in effect stretching the time of the film lived by characters, actors, and crew in duration rather than the forced artifice of classical montage, Linklater brings cinematic time into a proximate relationship to non-cinematic time. Yes, there are cuts throughout *Boyhood* that conform to a classical montage schema. But each cut is an expanse of lived time rather than a spontaneous leap *over time*, as we would see in a conventional narrative coverage of twelve years in a feature film. *Boyhood* pins us to the flow of time as whole. Throughout the twelve years of the film, we are brought into direct relation to the spaces between events, such as the stretch of time that marks Mason's change of middle school and his high school graduation, as if the two events are in perfect, constant communion, or Olivia's metamorphosis from student to teacher, as if the process is part of the natural flow of time. Olivia's aged visage when we first see her in front of a class is therefore not a denotational sign of time passed but a time-image encapsulating the flow of her experience enmeshed in the flow of the subjective experience of the spectator.

In *Boyhood*, the spectator feels the enveloping presence of time—a constant Sisyphean ordeal for character, actor, and spectator—in the growing of children toward adolescence and adulthood, and the aging of parents toward middle age and then death. Each character is stretched, traumatized, and enriched by the burden of time, as if moulded and kneaded by a sculptor. The effect of the palpable duration within the image is not dissimilar to Kubrick's aging astronaut in the final sequence of *2001: A Space Odyssey* (1968), for whom lived time is an opening of the whole toward an infinitely heterogenous, cosmic consciousness. Olivia acknowledges the burden of time at the moment of Mason's departure for college:

> You know what I'm realizing? My life is just gonna go, like that. This series of milestones. Getting married. Having kids. Getting divorced. The time that we thought you were dyslexic. When I taught you how to ride a bike. Getting divorced, again. Getting my master's degree. Finally getting the job I wanted. Sending Samantha off to college. Sending you off to college. You know what's next, huh? It's my fucking funeral!

Olivia's milestones map neatly to Charlie's false intervals, these markers of homogenous, spatialized time we all chronicle as past events. But the image of an exhausted, burdened, aged, and lived Olivia (who has expunged the flesh and blood of Patricia Arquette) contains the cumulation of lived moments as a phenomenological whole. The transformation of Olivia as an embodied, aged, lived being, who has not leaped over time through montage but has been forced to live that time in a cumulation of infinite moments, brings Olivia and the spectator into what Bergson might call a shared duration. And this is a stunning example of cinema's unique capacity to incarnate time within the image.

In a contemporary review of the film, Matt Pais of the *Chicago Tribune* criticizes the film for being, merely, "a concept." For Pais, *Boyhood* is a "dramatization of life, not an authentic portrait," and I take Pais to be levelling the same criticism at *Boyhood* I've levelled at *Dazed and Confused* and *Everybody*

Figure 11.1 Olivia: the unbearable burden of time

Wants Some!! and the narrativization of coming-of-age that underpins so many of Linklater's stories.[18] And yet, for its familiar story and ideas and words about time and living in the moment, my deep sense in experiencing the film is that the time-image presented in *Boyhood* establishes a unique regime of temporal experience that contains, as Bergson suggests, "an interconnexion and organization of elements, each one of which represents the whole, and cannot be distinguished or isolated from it except by abstract thought."[19] Against Pais's notion of the film as concept, I read the *Boyhood* time-image as an opening into a Bergsonian whole, a glimpse or fleeting sensation of time incarnated within the duration of the film image, infinite in its creative potential and indivisible into Charlie's discrete segments broken from the whole.

CONCLUSION: THE PROXIMITY OF CINEMATIC TIME TO NON-CINEMATIC TIME

Deleuze begins his massive study of the kinds of montage that produce movement and time in *Cinema 2* by channeling the ontology of the film image in the work of André Bazin. Against the simplistic readings of Bazin that marked a lot of film theory, Deleuze says that for Bazin, the film image was "a matter of a new form of reality."[20] I want to close this chapter by suggesting that Linklater, channeling Bazin's vaunted assessment of neo-realism's dialectical leap in the history of the film image, brings the American Indie film image into a special relationship to the real. This relation is a function of time within the matter of the image. In a famous reading of the achievement of the neo-realist image in Vittorio De Sica's *Ladri di biciclette* (*Bicycle Thieves*, 1948), Bazin says that the film image displays the "disappearance of the actor, disappearance of *mise en scene* . . . The very principle . . . is the disappearance of a story."[21] The proximity of the subjective time of the spectator to the subjective time of character in *Boyhood* is such that, following Bazin, mise-en-scène or performance, or the diegesis of story itself is, if not effaced, forcibly subordinated to the real of the cinematic image. All of Linklater's generic tropes of coming-of-age feel subordinated to the magnitude of the time-image of becoming. It's not that the cinematic image takes over the real in the kind of fantastical virtuality we see in Woody Allen's *The Purple Rose of Cairo* (1985), but that the real (which is to say the subjective temporality of the spectator) is in every way and in each moment contaminated by the cinematic image and expanded into a field of cumulative duration.[22] The duration of the conventional feature film is distended, absurdly, into the duration of "my time"; each duration represents a creative opening of the whole, and in concert, an extension of that process of creative change. Time is not explicitly marked by signs or segmented into intervals; there is no "three years later" intertitle to demonstrate time's close-off *pastness*.

And, in fact, the gratuitous signs of Mason's change in hairstyle marks time too emphatically, forcing time into its abstracted intervallic form required of Linklater's generic coming-of-age narrative. But if we take Mason's insight—"it's like it's always right now"—as the expansion of the whole, that is, a Bergsonian ontology of temporal experience that encompasses pastness within the present—we have a sense of the scale of Linklater's achievement that exceeds Mason's capacity for understanding: the moment is not a fetishistic high, but a cumulative, lived part of the whole.

The 1990s and early 2000s were the mainstream studio and independent era in which time was reconceptualized, reordered, non-linearized, and exploded in terms of imagistic potential.[23] Some experiments with time were more exploratory and philosophically adventurous than others. Alexander Sokurov's *Russian Ark* (2002) marvellously captures centuries of time in a single long take to extract some sense of the felt duration of historical change. But it is still an artificial history, and its long take is, while logistically intricate and spectacular, and even philosophically rich, a transparent contrivance of montage. David Fincher's *The Curious Case of Benjamin Button* (2008) attempts to imagine radical time through recently developed digital technologies to de-age the central character, but the experiment fails and reveals instead the contrivance of a false duration. The effect is cloying and a constant affirmation of the artifice of melodramatic narrative form. Even Martin Scorsese's recent *The Irishman* (2019), in spite of its majesty as a chronicle of Scorsese's history of gangsterism, fails as a digital contrivance of lived time. Robert De Niro's uncanny eyes enforce a temporal, intervallic artifice over the duration of narrative time, affirming the unreality of diegetic form.

Attaching the money to the *Boyhood* production was its own Sisyphean ordeal, as recounted by Linklater.[24] In its unique production experiment, Linklater provides a more direct, intense, and real access to time and its flow. There are no make-up contrivances, or actor substitutions, or digital renderings that attempt to convince us of time's indexical realness. Time simply *is*. Twelve years pass as lived time within the diegesis. Each episode within the narrative functions elegantly as Bergson's melodic duration: intervallic and progressive, and yet always in relation to the fullness of the whole. These are twelve years that register the full indexicality of time's effect—from a minute change, such as a facial mark that marks time, or Mason's camping trip with Mason Sr., at which point I first realized that Mason's voice had broken.

Time-images vary in Deleuze's examination of the European auteur cinema, and one time-image—say the long take in Antonioni's *The Passenger* (1975) in which the protagonist transforms from a living to a dead body off-screen—is not equivalent in its durational import to the long take in *Russian Ark*, or indeed the long take coverage of a conversation between Mason and a friend as he walks home from school. Thus, we can say that Deleuze's notion

Figure 11.2 Mason and the spectator in a knowing, collusionary exchange

of the time-image in Antonioni is provocative and confronting, but it is special and specific to a film and its diegesis, a filmmaker's philosophical disposition, and the context in which Deleuze reads it. My sense is that, even in Deleuze's most emphatic time-images, we are imaginatively and existentially broken from a direct experience of time; this is obviously not Deleuze's position, but I can't help feeling that *Boyhood*'s forced temporal experiment opens the spectator to some other *proximity* to time and duration. There is a directness in the opening of the time-image, and a freedom of access to the intensity of that image. And this has nothing to do with a forced aesthetic realism in the progression of time, nor the fact that characters are always reminding us to be aware of time and its effect, but in the imaginative way in which the naturally unfolding image of time brings the spectator into proximity with the real. Can we say that Mason, at least in my own viewing of the film in the State Theatre, was fully incarnated *in* time in the moment of stepping from behind the curtain? My own sense was that Mason's materialization from behind the curtain was not an affirmation of the artifice of the screen, but a natural, intuitive expansion of the real. And we can then also speculate that Mason's stepping from behind the curtain collapses the seam that has traditionally marked a boundary between diegetic and non-diegetic cinematic experience.

A direct address of the camera is usually an explicit marker of the artifice of the diegesis, a so-called collapse of the fourth wall. In a fleeting moment before we cut from the image to the closing credits of *Boyhood*, Mason's eyes hold the camera's gaze—and our eyes—almost casually, and it is only for a very brief moment before we cut away. But it is a knowing look. Mason regards the spectator in a kind of collusionary exchange. The exchange is less the product of a look down the barrel of the camera than a Bergsonian elemental connection in time between character and spectator. The acknowledgment is therefore not a direct address of the camera at all, but the expression of a lived relationship between Mason and the spectator unencumbered by screen, montage, or any part of the cinematic apparatus.

NOTES

1. Henri Bergson, a leading French philosopher of the late nineteenth and early twentieth century, articulates this influential formulation in *Time and Free Will: An Essay on the Immediate Data of Consciousness* (Abingdon, U.K. and New York: Routledge, 2013 [1910]). For one of the most lucid explanations of what Bergson precisely means by this intricate and somewhat counter-intuitive position, see Suzanne Guerlac, *Thinking in Time: An Introduction to Henri Bergson* (Ithaca, NY: Cornell University Press, 2006), especially chapters 2 and 3.
2. Bergson, *Time and Free Will*, 98.
3. For two of the best studies reading Linklater in relation to time and experience, see Rob Stone, *The Cinema of Richard Linklater: Walk, Don't Run* (New York: Columbia University Press, 2018), especially chapter 4; and Ellen Grabiner, "The Holy Moment: *Waking Life* and Linklater's Sublime Dream Time," *Film Quarterly* 68:3 (2015): 41–47. Stone's analysis is especially detailed and insightful in applying Linklater to a Bergsonian model of temporal experience.
4. For a persuasive reading of the "American Indie" protagonist appropriated from the postclassical "unmotivated hero," see Kim Wilkins, *American Eccentric Cinema* (New York: Bloomsbury, 2019), 10–14.
5. Deleuze builds his taxonomy of cinematic images explicitly through a Bergsonian ontology of space, movement and time, and consciousness. See Gilles Deleuze, *Cinema 1: The Movement-Image*, trans. Hugh Tomlinson and Barbara Habberjam (Minneapolis: University of Minnesota Press, 1997), especially the three theses on movement, 1–11.
6. Deleuze explicitly relates the evolution of montage systems to the emergence of the time-image. See Gilles Deleuze, *Cinema 2: The Time-Image*, trans. Hugh Tomlinson and Robert Galeta (Minneapolis: University of Minnesota Press, 1997), 34.
7. Bergson, *Time and Free Will*, 97.
8. Deleuze, *Cinema 1*, 205–215.
9. Stone, *The Cinema of Richard Linklater*, 8–20.
10. Christian Keathley, "Trapped in the Affection Image: Hollywood's Post-traumatic Cycle (1970–1976)," in *The Last Great American Picture Show: New Hollywood Cinema in the 1970s*, edited by Thomas Elsaesser, Alexander Horwath and Noel King (Amsterdam: Amsterdam University Press, 2004), 293–308.
11. Russ Fischer, "Interview: Richard Linklater Talks 'Everybody Wants Some!!,' Spiritual Sequels, Music in His Films, & More," *IndieWire*, April 15, 2016: https://www.indiewire.com/2016/04/interview-richard-linklater-talks-everybody-wants-some-spiritual-sequels-music-in-his-films-more-292510/
12. Albert Camus, *The Myth of Sisyphus and Other Essays*, trans. Justin O' Brien (Harmondsworth: Penguin Books, 1979).
13. Bergson, *Time and Free Will*, 97–98.
14. Ibid., 98.

15. Ibid., 100, italics in original.
16. For an awe-inspiring demonstration of the deep embeddedness of melodic intervals of the major scale in human beings, see "Bobby McFerrin Demonstrates the Power of the Pentatonic Scale," YouTube, July 24, 2009: https://www.youtube.com/watch?v=ne6tB2KiZuk
17. Camus, *The Myth of Sisyphus*, 20–21.
18. Matt Pais, "*Boyhood* is Only Impressive in Theory," *Chicago Tribune*, July 17, 2014: https://www.chicagotribune.com/redeye/redeye-boyhood-is-only-impressive-in-theory-20140715-column.html
19. Bergson, *Time and Free Will*, 100.
20. Deleuze, *Cinema 2*, 1–3.
21. André Bazin, "Bicycle Thief," in *What is Cinema? Volume 2*, trans. Hugh Gray (Berkeley and Los Angeles: University of California Press, 1971), 58.
22. In her excellent and succinct reading of the way in which cinema "does" time, Lee Carruthers similarly reads Bazin and Deleuze in concert for their "shared commitment to the phenomenon of filmic duration." See Lee Carruthers, *Doing Time: Temporality, Hermeneutics, and Contemporary Cinema* (Albany: SUNY Press, 2016), 6.
23. Todd McGowan, *Out of Time: Desire in Atemporal Cinema* (Minneapolis: University of Minnesota Press, 2011).
24. Tatiana Siegel, "*Boyhood*: Why Richard Linklater Owns His New Movie," *The Hollywood Reporter*, June 19, 2014: https://www.hollywoodreporter.com/news/general-news/boyhood-why-richard-linklater-owns-712427/

CHAPTER 12

Rhythm and the Rotoshop: *Waking Life*, *A Scanner Darkly*, and Rhythmanalysis

Christopher Holliday

INTRODUCTION

While it is commonplace to find "movement" and "motion" as vital principles within definitions of animation's affective power and unique form of representation, discourses of "rhythm" offer potentially illuminating ways of framing the medium's ability for endowing objects and characters with life and expressiveness. Rhythm is foremost an elusive concept that may be initially constituted by and through individual objects or audiovisual forms exhibiting *a* rhythm (music, poetry, language). However, since the early 1990s it has also emerged as a distinct interdisciplinary methodology in the form of rhythmanalysis, which interrogates specific natural, cultural, and technological processes of existence through their connections to rhythm. The conflict between what Henri Lefebvre and Catherine Régulier term *cyclic* rhythms (natural, biological, cosmic rotations = fundamental) and *linear* rhythms (timetables, schedules, calendars = quantified) structures our involvement with advanced industrial capitalism, as we become subject to "the perpetual interaction of these rhythms with repetitive processes linked to homogenous time."[1] Our everyday engagement with such micro and macro cycles of experience—from seasonal "earthly" variations in organic rhythms to the institutionalization of monotonous repetition via the segmentation of labor—ultimately frames rhythm as an increasingly socio-political problem because "everyday life remains shot through and traversed by great cosmic and vital rhythms."[2] However, Ryan Pierson also speaks to animation's potential for "rhythmic relations," patterns and figures, asking of rhythm why it might be so "capable of containing the potential for chaos in deformation."[3] Indeed, for many animators, artists, and practitioners "all animation and action are based on rhythm," particularly given the ways that time and duration are managed and measured as part of cartoon production.[4] Yet if the default understanding of animation is that it persuasively presents images of life, force, and motion, then a turn to rhythm and its analysis can potentially help to organize and further elaborate upon the medium's defining preoccupation with movement, but also the interaction between characters and the variant energy of their sentient animated bodies.

This chapter observes the implications of thinking through rhythm in relation to animation by examining filmmaker Richard Linklater's animated feature films *Waking Life* (2001), a series of vignettes following the dreamlike wanderings of an unnamed young man; and *A Scanner Darkly* (2006), an animated adaptation of Philip K. Dick's 1977 science fiction novel set in a dystopian future America struggling under the weight of a drugs epidemic and invasive surveillance technologies. Both films have come to occupy an intriguing footnote within recent histories of popular Hollywood animation, as they present a distinct visual style created using the digital tool Rotoshop. Developed by American artist and computer programmer Bob Sabiston in the late 1990s at the MIT Media Lab, Rotoshop technology involves a process whereby pre-existing live-action footage is painstakingly overlaid with digital paint, creating a modulating effect to the resultant images that appear to "move and slide incessantly."[5] This graphic peculiarity fully serves and intensifies the central narrative premise of both *Waking Life* and *A Scanner Darkly*, whose dreamlike stories are in different ways structured by themes of fragmented identities and fractured perceptions. However, the Rotoshopped software equally suggests and invites a more "rhythmical" understanding of computer animation, and the possible set of relationships that digital technology can have with animation and live-action cinema. Sabiston's Rotoshop offers images that appear to be "animated in rhythms and patterns," as the digital paint achieves a fluid graphic motion that seemingly sits on top of the film's indexical "surface."[6] In this way, the use of Rotoshop intensifies the visibility of rhythm, sharpening the complex interactions "between a place, a time and an expenditure of energy" that constitute the rhythms of everyday life, and accentuating precisely the *cyclical* and *linear* ritual forces that converge to underwrite human activity.[7] Each film's particular application of digital aesthetics therefore draws on the Rotoshop to augment their reflexive interrogation of the political siting and institutionalizing of bodies according to "lived" social rhythms. Sabiston's technology functions to effectively articulate the coexisting spatial and temporal relations described by Lefebvre and Régulier that likewise shape the experiences of protagonists Wiley Wiggins in *Waking Life* and Bob Arctor (Keanu Reeves) in *A Scanner Darkly*, particularly in the latter's "arrhythmic" alignment of mind, body, and environment. The outcome is that Linklater works both with and against rhythm to present his figures as abstracted, displaced, and highly fragmented intersections of competing rhythms, cycles, and powers. By identifying the many rhythms of *Waking Life* and *A Scanner Darkly*—alongside Rotoshop's vexed relationship to agency and liveliness—this chapter ultimately uses rhythmanalysis to examine the "rhythmed" identity of Linklater's animated bodies and the styles, performances, and labor of his digitized images.

THE RHYTHM OF LIFE

Animation has typically been understood as a medium of rhythm. It is certainly not uncommon to find references to rhythm among historical-critical explorations of animation's diversity of processes, forms, and modes, alongside more instructional accounts of its fundamental principles and elements of creative practice. In its guise as both a shorthand descriptor of aesthetics and as a practical concept supporting the industry of animation, rhythm has proven to be particularly durable in sharpening the legibility of character, identified by (and for) artists and animators as a way of registering the animated figure's uniqueness of movement, pose, and action. For Leslie Bishko, an animated character and its qualities of life must incorporate specific "movement phrases" or "individualized rhythmic patterns and preferences" that connote the labor and effort of an animated body moving in, through, and across graphic space.[8] In these terms, rhythm defines animation because animation requires choreography as part of its precision of imagery, typically in cases where animators are driven by a desire for heightened graphic verisimilitude and more realistic forms of representation. Yet in also divulging how time and space are coordinated and managed in character animation, rhythm is a term that immediately begins to suggest how the animator's organization of bodies-in-motion might intersect with the intentions of rhythmanalysis, which as Lefebvre and Régulier make clear is a methodology that seeks to locate the shifting natural rhythms of existence and socially embedded sensations of everyday synchronicity and expenditure. To animate, then, is to conduct an analysis of the rhetoric and effects of rhythm. Movement and motion must be carefully mapped out, and "key positions hit the timing of a catchy rhythm," allowing the resultant imagery to register as coherent, believable, authentic, and enchanting.[9]

Best remembered for his character animation at the Walt Disney Studio and under Tex Avery at MGM (though he began under Walter Lantz at Universal), artist Preston Blair suggests that "rhythm and design" were, in fact, the "secret formulas [. . .] behind the appeal and charm of great cartoon art."[10] The frame-by-frame action analysis and motion studies conducted at Disney during the 1930s and 1940s reflected something of this industry desire to continually re(de)fine cartoon movement in support of a particular kind of hyperrealistic visual orthodoxy. The synchronization of sound and image developed at

Disney was certainly part of this pervasive agenda of pictorial realism, involving "the close association between screen-rhythm and musical-rhythm" and leading to the "mickey-mousing" technique that matched character action with the rhythm of music.[11] Yet beyond Disney's notational organizing of character timing and speed (that nicely evokes Lefebvre and Régulier's rhythmanalytical approach to the impact of diverse temporalities upon and through the body), more experimental and non-figurative "characterless" forms of animation have equally been conceptualized as highly rhythmical in their audiovisual operations. This is because, as Bishko argues, "Movement is the raw material of animated film. Through movement we can read an animated film, just as we can 'read' music through its melody or rhythm, or a painting through color, line and shape."[12] Such an equation between the fundamental principles of movement (in animation) and rhythm (of music) was explored most forcefully in the European visual music and "absolute film" tradition of filmmakers Walter Ruttmann, Viking Eggeling, Oskar Fischinger, and Hans Richter during the 1920s, which conveyed the art of rhythm and counter-rhythm through sensorial abstraction-in-motion. For Paul Wells, "abstract films are more concerned with rhythm and movement in their own right as opposed to the rhythm and movement of a particular character."[13] Mary Allen Bute's five-minute short *Rhythm in Light* (1934) that refracted light through a prism; Len Lye's *Rhythm* (1957) intended as a promotional film for the Chrysler motor corporation; and the "pure abstract visual rhythm" of Richter's own series of animated *Rhythmus* (1921–1924) shorts inspired by Cubist precisionism, all demonstrate how even non-figurative animated traditions have explored the medium's defining rhythmical form.[14]

It comes as little surprise, then, that Steve Roberts has claimed that "All animation has rhythm," largely because the medium across a spectrum of techniques and production processes operates "like a dance or a poem" in how its beats of action are carefully choreographed, rehearsed, and animated.[15] However, among animation's variant styles of image-making, the specific industrial and aesthetic properties of Rotoshop's innovative digital paint system used for Linklater's *Waking Life* and *A Scanner Darkly* seem to invite particular consideration of animation's potential rhythms of movement and motion, as well as enforcing its broader ties to the flows and forms of technics and society that so interested twentieth-century rhythmanalysts. Both films represent the mainstreaming of a digital technology that, up to 2001, had been largely the preserve of animated shorts in the years following its invention in 1996 when Sabiston was an MIT graduate. After seeing its application in the shorts *Project Incognito* (Bob Sabiston and Malissa Ryder, 1997), *Roadhead* (Sabiston, 1998), *Snack and Drink* (Sabiston, 1999), and *Grasshopper* (Sabiston, 2004), Linklater hired a team of artists to employ the system for *Waking Life* as a way of creating a specific "painterly" quality to the animated images achieved by a computer that essentially "paints" over live-action footage. One the one hand, Rotoshop maintains the act of drawing as fundamental to the act of Rotoshop's production processes even though, as Paul Ward explains, "the digital basis of the live action meant that the footage could be converted to Quicktime files and worked on in a computer program using Wacom pads and pens."[16] Yet on the other hand, and as part of Rotoshop's heavily digitized production, there are clear divergences from more traditional animation techniques and practices. Ward further notes that:

> Sabiston's innovation was to develop an "interpolating" feature where the software would automatically "in-between" certain lines, removing the need for the artist/animator to trace every line. This interpolation is one of the things that gives Rotoshop its much remarked-upon "floating" aesthetic.[17]

Despite connections to the inbetweening (or "tweening") of cel-animation that similarly involves the creation by artists (known as "tweeners" in the production workflow) of intermediate frames, Rotoshop's technological capacity for "automatic" digital interpolation between key frames hints quite strongly at the specter of automation and image generation that has increasingly enveloped a number of computerized processes in the digital era, and in particular those that (like the Rotoshop) capture human movement as either source material or data set. The very "liminal status of Rotoshopped material" in Linklater's work as simultaneously animation and/or live-action on account of its conjunction of both has meant that "What is interesting about films like *Waking Life* and *A Scanner Darkly* is that we do not really know how to categorize them."[18] Such a convergence of moving images types has been used to place the technique in close proximity to other "ambivalent" technologies that have historically pushed at the limits of what might define as "pure" animation, as well as complicating their categorization as live-action. Sabiston's Rotoshop tool has—alongside motion-capture technology—thus been positioned as a digital descendent of the rotoscope, a tracing technique patented by Max Fleischer in 1917 and pioneered by the Fleischer studio throughout the 1930s in their Betty Boop and Popeye cartoon shorts. In fact, Ward argues that as a digital tool, "Rotoshop follows some of the same principles as ordinary rotoscoping in that it traces over live-action footage," despite Sabiston's technology involving "a number of different animation principles" than the typically cel-based rotoscoping technique.[19] When taken together, these three processes (rotoscoping, Rotoshop, motion-capture) seize and rework live-action footage as an ontological "template" in their transcription of bodily movement and interpretation of performance, yet in doing so enforce something of their marginal place that challenges their very identities as animation at all.[20] If animation is a category that has historically troubled, expanded, and contracted our understanding of cinema, then the Rotoshop digital paint system has come to exert a similar pressure on definitions of both animation and live-action cinema too.

Rotoshop's digital tracing of live-action footage shot in-camera has, ultimately, sharpened the technology's fractious relationship to animation, in much the same way that "mo-cap" image processing has encountered both industrial and critical resistance as an alleged shortcut that circumvents the labor of traditional animation production. But the Rotoshop's unique surfacing of the visual-indexical trace of real bodies and backgrounds that lie behind the digital paint crafts a signature aesthetic that sits squarely at the heart of its intermediary state. It is, in turn, precisely this formal ambivalence that generates a new kind of audiovisual rhythm to the animated image, and that opens up the technology to more rhythmanalytical understanding of competing physiological and psychic patterns of the "lived" body suddenly made animate via technological intervention. The slippery, sliding animated images in *Waking Life* and *A Scanner Darkly* certainly seem to hover over their filmed origins, as characters (and even landscapes) continually throb and undulate with a latent energy between and within frames. In *Waking Life*, for example, animated bodies are seemingly made the victim of colliding rhythmical forces formed and reformed by the Rotoshop digital tool. Buttons float to the edges of the very clothes they supposedly fasten; hair shifts in style and cut in a matter of seconds; and eyes seem to extend beyond the physiognomies of the computer-animated characters they define. The arrival of protagonist (unnamed in the film but played by Wiggins) at a busy train station in *Waking Life*'s opening sequence is particularly demonstrative of the distortive visual effects enabled by the Rotoshop system, and the ways in which the graphic style employed by Linklater operates in service of actualizing certain subjective experiences. As the disoriented Wiggins walks through the station's corridors, each consecutive arch that comprises the building's ceiling design flexes and strains as if unmoored from one other, while the lights hanging down shift impossibly their positions from left to right (and back again) (a similar flexibility to architecture occurs later in the film when Wiggins meets poet Timothy "Speed" Levitch on a bridge, and the structure veers back and forth as if on the verge of collapse) (Figure 12.1). When Wiggins next stops to make a call at a row of payphones at the station in the hope of "bumming a ride" off a friend, his clothes now appear to ripple independently from his body while the nearby telephone kiosks similarly move in and out of focus. Resigned to catching a cab to continue his onward journey, Wiggins soon glimpses of a young woman opposite him at the transport depot, and as the shot cuts to the female object of his momentary affections, the woman's fixed and seated position is again challenged by the pulsing tiled floor and wooden door that begin to float and drift around her. *Waking Life*'s style follows this pattern throughout, the Rotoshop technology crafting a perceptible energy to the unstable animated

Figure 12.1 Wiley Wiggins at the train station in *Waking Life*

images that appear highly malleable, but which function as a suitable accompaniment to the wanderings and serendipitous activity of its central protagonist who may (or may not) be dreaming. As the driver (played by Bill Wise) of Wiggins's unexpected ride explains when discussing the pleasures of travel as a window on the world, "I accept it, and sort of glide along."

Similar, then, to the inevitable independence of oil and water, the rhythms of live-action and the digital in Linklater's Rotoshopped films mix in ways that are not entirely commensurate or resolvable. They likewise "glide along" to match their characters' nomadic lack of fixity, seeming to operate on different planes that render unsteady distinctions between foreground and background. Yet it is in this tension that new modes of animated rhythm can, perhaps, be located, and in ways that usefully offer up Linklater's films to rhythmanalysis's defining investment in embodiment and culture through their joint focus on collective and individual bodily rhythms under the experience of modernity. For Émile Benveniste, to analyze rhythm via rhythmanalysis is to identify a typology of individual and collective human behavior and experience, of the "durations and the repetitions that govern them, and also when, beyond the human sphere, we project a rhythm into things and events."[21] The Rotoshopped style of *Waking Life* and *A Scanner Darkly* prioritizes discordance in intensity, and in their graphic variation allows an exploration of sensation and of the transactional relationship between screen bodies and their energetic animated patterning. Maja Manojlovic argues that in the case of *Waking Life*'s digital aesthetics, "The pulsating images create rhythms within the image, where the animated spatial layers float and undulate almost independently from one another, indicating the dissonance and heterogeneity inherent to the apparently homogeneous movement of the whole."[22] The narratives of both *Waking Life* and *A Scanner Darkly* share an intensely reflexive discussion of lucid dream states, shifting consciousness, and perceptual processing, themes that are highly conducive to precisely this signature "floating" style and peculiar indeterminacy of the Rotoshop tool. In *Waking Life*, Wiggins's failure to get a secure fix on his true awakened state throughout his multiple encounters—as he continually lapses into dreams, wakes, yet finds himself still dreaming—serves as a partner to a style that equally plays with the legibility of perception. Even Wiggins's own facial features remain "figured through a mesh of shapes and lines; he is recognizable, but malleable, and the solid structure of his actual human form is thrown into question."[23] *A Scanner Darkly* adds to *Waking Life*'s psychological limbo and spectacle of bodily fracture a narrative focusing on drug-induced paranoia, charting the acceleration of (and addictions to) "Substance D" in Anaheim, California seven years in the future. Just as characters—including protagonist and addict Bob—struggle to own their identities as lives become progressively unfixed and illusionistic due to the rise in hallucinogens, the slippery live-action coated on its surface with digital paint (now functioning as apt metaphor) provides the film's narrative of duplicity, delusions, and double lives with clear stylistic substance.

A THEORY OF MEASURE

In Linklater's digitally animated films, then, the variance of rhythms contained within the attractive self-conscious surface play of the Rotoshop creates bodies and identities that are constantly in flux, supporting their respective narratives with images that seem to consistently "struggle" for (and labor over) their complete graphic form. Many critical accounts of *Waking Life* and *A Scanner Darkly* have discussed this visible energy of Linklater's Rotoshopped images, and the combination between self-conscious shaky style produced by Sabiston's digital paint system and the instability of identities that thematically structure the dreamlike quality to Linklater's two films.[24] However, discussing the wavering bodies of both *Waking Life* and *A Scanner Darkly*, Caroline Ruddell begins to draw on more philosophical understandings of rhythm in describing how "the visuals are disrupted and 'heightened', [and] gestures become markedly more noticeable and skewed" through the Rotoshop technique.[25] Turning to the writing of contemporary thinkers like Giorgio Agamben and Pasi Väliaho (who has himself expanded Lefebvre's theorization of rhythm and rhythmanalysis), Ruddell positions Linklater's animated features against Väliaho's claim that "cinema realizes a certain kind of modulation of bodily dynamics and also generates dislocated and erratic gestures in focus, a serious alteration of our corporeal rhythms."[26] If the gesture, as Väliaho suggests, "is imperative to understanding the moving image generally," then the energizing and erratic force of the Rotoshop enables a visibility of movement that dually covers *and* intensifies the very footage upon which the animation is effectively mapped.[27] Such rotoscoped material in both *Waking Life* and *A Scanner Darkly* "allows and revels in this 'seeing under' and encourages viewers to see both under and between," which is different to other forms of digital image-making whereby such effects are traditionally driven by a desire to "hide their derivation, or the fact they are effects at all."[28] In this way, the rhetorical excess of the Rotoshop style stakes out new territory for the application of digital effects technologies within Hollywood feature film production, which is typically driven by a desire for a seamless photorealistic synthesis of live-action and virtual components. In contrast to the pristine visual illusionism of much mainstream VFX imagery, Linklater's Rotoshop style in both *Waking Life* and *A Scanner Darkly* serves to broaden the expressivity and creative possibilities of digital animation technologies. This is despite the industry's progressive shift toward non-photorealistic rendering (NPR) that has ushered in a "new painterly direction for computer graphics."[29] Yet both *Waking Life* and *A Scanner Darkly* pose a challenge to this uniform visual approach and stylistic "self-similarity" that has traditionally guided commercial three-dimensional computer animation, instead presenting new realisms and constantly morphing images afforded by this digital "painting" process.[30] Aylish Wood discusses the Rotoshop's introduction of a "visible digital inscription to the interface, which disturbs the conventional spatio-temporal dynamics of the imagery."[31] This disruptive inscription serves as the foundation upon which accusations of the Rotoshop's troubling of (and relationship to) live-action and animation as discrete categories have been levelled. But it also further strengthens the link between the Rotoshop and earlier pre-digital animated technologies on account of its painterly visual style, and the ways in which rhythm functioned as a defining principle of hand-drawn cartoon technique.

The pulsating images of *Waking Life* and *A Scanner Darkly*'s unique painterly style and mode of production approximate what Dan Torre has termed the characteristic "boiling" effect of earlier hand-drawn animation (prior to the popularization of cel production), whereby the (over)layering of disparate drawings provides slight discrepancies or flickers between the individual frames. As Torre argues:

> Boiling is an animated process that also involves tracing. In order to create the boiling effect, an original drawing is made and then a number of tracings (normally somewhere between three and eight) are prepared. These tracings are then played back cyclically for as long as necessary

and, depending upon how carefully the images are traced, the resulting animation will have either less or more quivering movement.[32]

Such "boiling" effects bring to the fore "a unique dichotomy of movement and stillness" whereby such incremental divergences in otherwise identical image are amplified by the rapid frame-by-frame process of animation, which illuminate in their now quickfire sequential movement the imperceptible fluctuations in form, shape, and composition.[33] However, although Torre's conclusions are intended to register the formal particularities of early animation production and the graphic inconsistencies latent within images that are required to be drawn and redrawn or traced by hand, the "quivering movement" that materializes such artisanal labor is a clear precursor to the rhythms of the Rotoshop digital painting system developed by Sabiston. This is because "boiling" has been understood in relation to the very aesthetics of rotoscoping, which in the 1930s and 1940s stood out against the logic of standardization that defined the U.S. Golden Age animation industry. The mass production cycles of studio animation pivots—as it still does today—on the consistency of form, with character boards, motion studies, and model sheets acting as reference points to regulate the behavior, appearance, pose, and gesture of characters for communities of animators who may be working across separate spheres of cartoon labor. Within this industrial production pipeline, and notwithstanding the rotoscope's "obvious and direct connection to a live-action referent," there still exists "considerable latitude for individual interpretation in the way that the lines might undulate or seem out of control."[34] In the case of the Rotoshop, Sabiston's system maintains a similar "latitude," as the practical tracing over the live-action footage to distort and magnify character and environment evokes the "traced-over still images (thus with quivering 'animated' lines)" described by Torre as a fundamental technique of animators as wide-ranging as Winsor McCay, Bill Plympton, and Joanna Priestley.[35] Despite Rotoshop's digital interpolation whereby the graphic lines are drawn manually on set key frames only (ready for the computer to "smoothly fill in the lines that have not, literally, been drawn"), the natural variance or fluctuations between painted frames provide a latent rhythmical movement to the Rotoshopped action similar to the effects of "boiling."[36] The discontinuous and fragmentary graphic style of computer animation in both *Waking Life* and *A Scanner Darkly* brims with energy and, in excess of the "underlying rhythm" immanent to animation's properties as a medium, invites a particular kind of visual experience.[37] It is in Linklater's highly rhythmical "boiling" style, coupled with the wavering oneiric qualities of the narratives, where connections to the constitutive forces that drive rhythmanalysis (and its methodological isolation of rhythms felt both inside and outside the body) can be found.

The power of rhythms among the social and spatial sciences had already been taken up in the writing of Émile Durkheim, Marcel Mauss, Lúcio Alberto Pinheiro dos Santos, Gaston Bachelard, and Walter Benjamin, though perhaps it has been best understood through the work of Lefebvre. Receiving its fullest expression in Lefebvre's *The Production of Space* (1991)—the English translation of which coincided with the philosopher and sociologist's death in the early 1990s—and then in the collection of essays *Rhythmanalysis: Space, Time and Everyday Life* (originally published in 1992 as *Éléments de rythmanalyse*, but again translated posthumously in 2004), rhythmanalysis for Lefebvre presents an understanding of subjective struggle through imposed spatio-temporal conditions and endogenous eruptions felt due to seasonal and cultural cycles. In *The Production of Space*, he proposes that a turn to rhythmanalysis would:

> seek to discover those rhythms whose existence is signalled only through mediations, through indirect effects or manifestations. Rhythm analysis might eventually even displace psychoanalysis, as being more concrete, more effective, and closer to a pedagogy of appropriation (the appropriation of the body, as of spatial practice).[38]

There are again immediate clues to a possible association with animation's labor of movement and principles of rhythm and motion—including the "floating" Rotoshop—found within Lefebvre's descriptions of both objects *in* space and time and of the political and ideological constructions *of* those same spaces and times. Rhythm is a measure of energy and, as such, logically overlaps with popular conceptions of animation (to be excessively "animated"), though Gordon Walker cautions that "it is not enough though to understand rhythm only as movement, flow or animation."[39] However, Lefebvre and Régulier provocatively note that rhythmanalysis is a conceptual ability to perceive and register a "current" of energy whereby "a few solid objects [are] animated by a movement of their own."[40] Lefebvre says elsewhere in his work too that "Energy animates, renders time and space conflictual."[41] This language of vitality, sensitivity, and control begins to qualify rhythmanalysis's implications for animation, including the Rotoshopped aesthetics of *Waking Life* and *A Scanner Darkly*, given the medium's unique mode of production and illusion of objects and figures seeming to move of their own volition. Adam Whybray, for example, has connected Lefebvre's writings on rhythm to Czech stop-motion animator Jiří Barta, who like his contemporaries Jiří Trnka, Jan Švankmajer, and Russian animator Yuri Norstein remains invested in the vitalism of humble yet exquisite everyday objects (made from wood, metal, ceramics). If cinema is a "temporal-spatial medium, structured according to the rhythms of editing," then rhythmanalysis is equally suited for analyzing the aesthetics and labor of animation and the incremental movement of three-dimensional objects seemingly without human intervention.⁴² For Whybray, Barta's animated objects express the "rhythmic difficulties" and politicized struggle of experience that underpin Lefebvre's Marxist praxis. The Prague-born animator's films illustrate

> that only though better acquainting themselves with the variegated, heterogenous rhythms of natural time might citizens of Czechoslovakia (or, indeed, any society) free themselves from the stifling structures of human-centered time, whether rational clock time under capitalism or charismatic time under socialism.⁴³

However, the stakes of rhythm are not only present in the narratives of Barta's films that "interrogate the notion that space and time are non-political."⁴⁴ Rather, rhythm can be located in the broader links to a stop-motion process—as with all frame-by-frame animation—that is predicated on a language and labor of frequency, temporality, and sequences of activities created through the metrical structure of accent and phasing.

Rhythmanalysis is, perhaps, also a good fit for thinking through animation's illusion of movement because it is an approach invested in subjectivity, space, and nature as rhythmical elements (organized by biological, physiological, social/cultural, and organic regularities, patterns, and cycles). Given Linklater's application of the Rotoshop within metaphysical narratives exploring existence and consciousness too, it seems further useful for sharpening the ways which the individual's vexed relationship with the world in the filmmaker's work takes the form of a rhythmical connection. Indeed, at the center of Lefebvre's materialist approach to the "rhythm of daily life" lies the contrast between cyclical and linear principles of rhythm that play a constitutive role in the broader felt rhythms that are encoded into our spaces and times.⁴⁵ Such rhythms function as two coexistent temporalities held in tension, which continually maneuver and mobilize to impact our experience of and with the world. These "long and short times" are part of a recurring series of "stops, silences, blanks, resumptions and intervals" that "must appear in a movement" for there to be rhythm.⁴⁶ Cyclic rhythms are more natural, biological, or cosmic in their relationship to human experience, relating to movements "from the microscopic to the astronomical, from molecules to galaxies."⁴⁷ Such cyclic rhythms include those of solar frequencies, sunrises/sunsets, cosmic rotations, seasonal change, tides, and similar forms of interval that alternate across the spans of day and night, month and year. However, linear rhythms are successive and perpetual encounters, typically institutionalized through cycles of habit and metronomic reproduction in a capitalist society (Lefebvre tellingly explains such variations in intensity and amplitude through a highly industrial language, likening linear rhythms to "blows of a hammer, the noise of an engine").⁴⁸ Such routines and repetitions of human activity are therefore more mechanical accents of rhythm, rather than organic, because they involve a continuous direction of forward motion that is both interrupted and structured by time as it is itemized and qualified (watches, clocks, calendars, alarms, timetables, and schedules). This ongoing exchange between cyclical and linear rhythms to which individuals are subject may operate as multiple and interrelated (polyrhythmia); in harmonious symbiotic accordance (eurhythmia); or else become catastrophically discordant (arrhythmia). In whichever configuration, their modes of interaction consistently "regulate movement through time" and are marshalled by "agents of the ideological superstructure (the police, law courts)" as much as the broader natural times of the cosmos that determine an environment's "operations."[49]

As a theory of "measure," rhythmanalysis is therefore aimed at the critical awareness of the siting of the individual as fundamentally located between the politics of such biological/physiological/cyclic and social/cultural/linear forces. We experience a spectrum of "movements, undulations, vibrations, returns and rotations," as well as the "antagonistic unity" that marks the "interminable struggle" between cyclical and linear processes that repeatedly traverse each other to politically construct the body as an "intersection of internal and external rhythms."[50] As Gregory Minissale notes, the category of the everyday must be understood to function "as an embodied and social attunement to the clockwork rhythms structured by family, school, consumerism and work."[51] The rhythms of lived spaces therefore require an understanding of their lack of political neutrality. Environments are "rhythmed" in ways that invite an ideological understanding of this energetic charge as a material construction. Even struggles over time have prompted a shift in social practices, which as Lefebvre and Régulier note, "eats into the hours of darkness" as rituals of drinking and clubbing "burst out" in the form of a "Saturday night fever" that 'disrupts circadian rhythms."[52] From the planning of entertainment leisure according to "holiday season," to the cohesive rhythms of a religion, there are many other technological and socio-economic forms of rhythm and rhythmical activity that interfere and arbitrate into our embodied experience of social, political, and cultural spaces, often in their accumulation and alliance. Sue Middleton argues that in educational institutions, for example, more linear

> imperatives of the conceived – deadline, appraisals, standards – "colonise" cyclic pulses of the lived (pregnancy, sickness, childrearing, tribal obligations). The physical, psychological/intellectual or emotional growth of a child may be "arrhythmic" with linear (conceived) institutional "levels", "stages" or "standards".[53]

Yet despite the increased visibility of rhythmanalysis across social and urban studies as a way of sharpening the rhythms of capitalist production, environment, and routine, it is a mode of investigation that also provides an opportunity and vocabulary to comprehend the illusions and vitality of the Rotoshop as a particular form of animated media, and the arrhythmic bodies such a technology generates.

SCRAMBLED BODIES AND ANIMATED ARRHYTHMIA

Although avoiding any direct reference to rhythmanalysis as a methodology, Manojlovic's examination of the "hypnagogic" in-between digital aesthetics of *Waking Life* and the "sense of drowsiness" that such a formal style can induce connects Linklater's use of the Rotoshop to Lefebvre's ideological reading of the rhythms of a city, place, or space.[54] She argues that, for Lefebvre, "abstract space is produced by capitalism, as the effect of the independence of abstract productive activity from reproductive processes and labour."[55] In *The Production of Space*, Lefebvre would term this the "modification" of "natural rhythms" and "their inscriptions in space by means of human actions, especially work-related actions," leading to the "spatio-temporal rhythms of nature as transformed by a social practice."[56] The vignette structure of *Waking Life* (and the film's cumulative focus on time, including one of Wiggins's conversation that mentions film theorist André Bazin and cinema's temporality) certainly supports its interrogation of habits and daily rhythms. Recalling Linklater's earlier *Slacker* (1990) that self-consciously meanders between multiple lives and conversations in Austin, Texas—as well as the monologue structure of the filmmaker's *Before* trilogy (1995–2013) and coming-of-age rhythms of *Boyhood* (Richard Linklater, 2014)—*Waking Life* is likewise supported by Linklater's signature "long takes, fluid camerawork and evocative rhythms of the dialogue."[57] However, the distinct spatial politics and reorganization of the image's planes of action available in Rotoshop cut across the film's engagement with the linear rhythms of the environment by delivering a more disembodied notion of rhythmical energy. The Rotoshop is a technology that, for Manojlovic, articulates our "embodied urban experience in which we are continuously required to interact with the electronic screens of ATMs, cell phones, and computer screens of various sizes or to orient ourselves within a maze of decentered postmodern urban geography and flat, reflective architectural surface."[58] In *Waking Life*, the Rotoshop aesthetic with its interpolated floating rhythm helps to animate such a politics of modern dislocation, visualizing the scrambled experience of electronic spaces and infrastructures (the internet, communication/information technologies) and the broader assimilation of such technologies into our cultural experience. Yet the very rhythms of the Rotoshop in Linklater's animated films bring with it an opportunity to reflect on the relationship between the technology's interpolated processes and rhythm, and in particular how this unusual graphic style conjures rhythmical environments and bodies structured by specific forms of interaction.

Toward the beginning of *Waking Life*, and after obtaining a lift into town from the train station, Wiggins is unexpectedly struck by a car, warned of the oncoming vehicle by a note laying on the road that reminds him to "Look To Your Right." As the car approaches (as predicted, from the right), the impact marks a perceptible shift in visual style with the block colors of the preceding scene now replaced by a stark black and white sequence depicting Wiggins slowly waking from his sleep. Beyond confusing the spectators's registration of narrative chronology (given that Wiggins appears to suffer no physical effects of the crash as he stirs), *Waking Life*'s shift in the spatial organization of its Rotoshopped graphics also enforces the technology's connections to the "boiling" style of pre-digital animation, as the oscillating black lines that shimmer against the white background evoke the unstable ink-on-paper drawing of early animators and their imperfectly traced frames. Yet the lethargy of Wiggins's slumber is immediately placed at odds with the seemingly unruly Rotoshopped bedsheets and pillow that swirl around him as he moves (or, perhaps, not) into consciousness. Once the shot of Wiggins waking has been returned to color, the camera follows him as he moves through his apartment toward the fridge and eats his breakfast as part of his daily routine. The style of animation noticeably shifts again as Wiggins moves from room to room, this time more closely approximating the rough edges, raggedy scratched lines and "compositional looseness" that defined the cel-animated style of Warner Brothers' *Looney Tunes* series (1930–1969), the mid-century modernism of the United Productions of America (UPA) studio, and even Disney animated features of the 1970s that employed the Xerox photocopying technique to ink and color cels by machine.[59] *Waking Life* then jumps again from Wiggins's domestic space to a lecture hall, and a college class given by an unnamed scholar (played by philosophy professor Robert Solomon from the University of Texas) that deals with existentialism, curiosity, passion, responsibility, and knowledge. Wiggins converses with the lecturer, who informs his student (via a turn to French philosopher Jean-Paul Sartre) that a person's identity is often understood as a "social construction," or as a "confluence of forces" (though he later changes this to a "victim of various forces").

This encounter is one of many experienced by Wiggins in *Waking Life* that reflexively acknowledges the abstract, intangible, and transient nature of existence, and the unspeakable nature of perception. Indeed, soon after his exchange, Wiggins meets yet another intellectual Eamonn Healy, chemistry professor at Texas, who enthusiastically explains:

> If we're looking at the highlights of human development, you have to look at the evolution of the organism and then at the development of its interaction with the environment. Evolution of the organism will

begin with the evolution of life perceived through the hominid coming to the evolution of mankind. Neanderthal and Cro-Magnon man. Now, interestingly, what you're looking at here are three strings: biological, anthropological—development of the cities—and cultural, which is human expression.

Though firmly in the realm of evolutionary biology rather than the social sciences, Healy's summation of the "strings" that support human development (biological, anthropological, cultural) recalls how in rhythmanalysis, "the body becomes a metronome, with the intersection of internal and external rhythms complicating the exchange."[60] As Lefebvre and Régulier put it, the body marks "the intersection of the biological, the physiological (nature) and the social [. . .] where each of these levels, each of these dimensions, has its own specificity, therefore its space-time: its rhythm."[61] The addition of the unique Rotoshop animated style again strengthens this framing of the body as a collision of rhythms. The fact that Healy's body contorts uncontrollably in both size and shape as he explains the path towards a "neo-human [. . .] with a new individuality and a new consciousness" provides an appropriate visual counterpoint to his reflective monologue. The tone of the exchange also anticipates Wiggins's later conversation in the film with philosophy professor David Sosa, who similarly describes bodies as "just physical systems" built from "complex arrangements of carbon molecules" so that there is "not a lot of room left for freedom." But as Healy reflects on "two types of information: digital and analogue" as part of this explication of what he terms the "evolutionary paradigm," his Rotoshopped body marks the very convergence of such digital and non-digital/analogue modes of image-making. The animated style digitally painted over the live-action footage recorded by Linklater stabilizes the creation of a new individuality now charged with its own excessive rhythms (Figure 12.2).

The many animated bodies that inhabit the Rotoshopped world of *Waking Life* are sites of interrelated rhythms and co-presence. Linklater's animated characters are placed in the crosshairs of cyclic and linear rhythms, whose interference becomes manifest as both "compromise" and "disturbance" in the animated articulation of bodily form.[62] In their pulsing movements, these animated figures appear to function as examples of the polyrhythmic mode of engagement, a rhythmic order described by Lefebvre that encompasses both eurhythmic and arrhythmic states. Polyrhythmic is a term that captures the general manner in which multiple rhythms move in a variance of flow, are overlaid, and become superimposed over each other to create shifting, complex experiences of the everyday that traverse scales of the corporeal (local) and cosmological (global). Rhythmanalysis is aimed at understanding what is intuitively felt as a "polyrhythmic field," and "the relations between complex

Figure 12.2 Wiggins encounters Eamonn Healy

processes and trajectories, between bodies and waveforms."[63] The flows and intermingling of "bodies" and "waveforms" that become surfaced by rhythmanalytic frameworks are made clear in the form and content of *Waking Life*. Wiggins's engagement with the features that constitute linear rhythms—from everyday repetitions (traveling, sleeping, learning, eating, consuming media, shopping, dancing) to the complexity present in everyday spaces (train station, home, school, restaurant, petrol station, cinema, supermarket, dance hall)—are figuratively "shot through" by the Rotoshop system, which adds yet another linear rhythm rooted in technology to provide a bundling collision and interaction between complementary rhythmic fields. The rational, structural rhythms experienced by Wiggins as he navigates through the urban environment are therefore entirely supported by the Rotoshop, which in its practical and formal abstraction of the real visualizes the simultaneous experience (and fragmentation) of bodies via social rhythms that are institutionalized through cycles and powers.

Such bodily dislocation is, however, further intensified in Linklater's *A Scanner Darkly*. Shot in twenty-three days but animated via the Rotoshop over a period of eighteen months (at a cost of US$8.7 million), the film again explores the subjective experience of urban space through rhythmic cycles of existence, albeit disrupted by a nationwide drugs epidemic. However, while the film's narrative of addiction—set against the backdrop of Californian drug culture—anchors and qualifies much of its Rotoshopped visual delirium, it also provides the dramatization of more frictional arrhythmic relations that are animated into life by Sabiston. Whereas polyrhythmic mobility defines the multiplicity and interrelation of the linear and the cyclic as simply coexistent, arrhythmic rhythm is actively rooted in experiences of precariousness and disturbance. It is understood by Lefebvre as a rhythm that relates to a more "pathological" framing of disruptions as threatening (insomnia; irregular heartbeat or murmur; mood disorders). Just as it does when it describes an abnormal heart rhythm, a socio-cultural experience of arrhythmia is one that is highly discordant, produced by a "garland of rhythms" that ultimately involves suffering "that sooner or later become[s] illness."[64] Arrhythmic rhythm is therefore a term that sharpens the fragmentation of phenomena that might be "out of step," or those who feel intensely incongruous or dysfunctional, manifesting on a spectrum from low-level "jet lag" to feelings of social alienation and radical psychological/physiological disassociation. Drug addiction is, then, arrhythmia made toxic. In *A Scanner Darkly*, the wave of "Substance D" is a signal of this dangerous arrhythmic identity collapse, as its narrative presents characters who cannot get a fix on themselves because their behavior is increasingly fueled by their "fix" on narcotics. For Bob, the "D" in "Substance D" stands for "dumbness, and despair, desertion. The desertion of your friends from you, you from your friends, everyone from everyone." There are several sequences that creatively show the characters' experience of dependence and dislocation (in the film, we are told that nearly 20 percent of the population is classified as addicts). The opening sequence, for example, depicts an imagined infestation of aphids as a way of communicating the paranoia of Charles Freck (Rory Cochrane) due to the epidemic (Charles imagines his own death in a subsequent hallucination). Later, Bob is asked by a psychologist whether he has experienced any "cross-chatter" between the left and right hemispheres of his brain. Clues to his drug-induced functional impairment are presented again via a series of fantasies showing a bucolic family life, which may or may not be traces or memories of his past, and more sinister visions where housemates James Barris (Robert Downey Jr.) and Ernie Luckman (Woody Harrelson) mutate into giant bugs (Barris had earlier described how "seeing and feeling buggy bugs" were side-effects of "Substance D" addiction). Other sequences in *A Scanner Darkly* are sped up as if viewed through the staccato rhythms of a security camera, anticipating a later scene where Bob attentively watches back footage—set to fast-forward—of himself as part of his covert investigation. If central to the rhythmanalytical project is a preoccupation with "temporalities and their relations within wholes," then Linklater's manipulation of duration sharpens our awareness of the concrete social, cultural, and political reality of rhythms experienced by a damaged Bob.[65] When paired with the disorienting spatio-temporal relations enabled by the Rotoshop style, such formal devices create a further arrhythmic alignment of rhythm, speeds, and temporalities as part of its reflexive interrogation of displacement.

Bob's identity as an undercover narcotics agent certainly provides *A Scanner Darkly* with the opportunity to further "rhythm" the actions of his body and physicality. To maintain the integrity of his covert investigation (and hide his true self to professional colleagues), Bob must wear a "scramble suit" that disguises his facial features and clothing by preserving his anonymity as an undercover operative, allowing him to perform under the assumed name of "Fred." This deception leads to Fred's latest mission given to him by his superior, "Hank" (also a codename), to investigate and observe Bob, with Bob (as Fred) essentially turning in information on himself in ways that evoke the 1970s Nixon-era paranoia that enveloped U.S. culture at the time of Dick's original novel. In addition to such looped identities (Hank is further revealed to be Bob's girlfriend Donna Hawthorne [Winona Ryder], itself a pseudonym for police officer Audrey), the scramble suit as a cloaking device reprises animation's long-standing relationship to metamorphosis and transformation. Indeed, the medium's spectacular culture of quick change can be traced as far back as the early twentieth-century cartoons that gave rise to the medium's "boiling" aesthetic. When Bob (as "Fred") therefore gives a talk to the Anaheim 709th chapter of the Brown Bear Lodge early in the film, the scramble suit moves between a spectrum of genders and generations as part of his necessary disguise. The host of the fraternity gathering further explains that the suit is comprised of approximately 1.5 million "fraction representations of men, women and children in every variant," transforming the wearer into a "constantly shifting vague blur" (Figure 12.3). With its "mosaic of shifting colours, shapes and lines," the fluctuations and "fractions" of

Figure 12.3 Bob's shifting physiognomy and composite form as he wears the scramble suit in *A Scanner Darkly* contrasts with the uniformity of the audience

Bob's suit capture and reflect back the digital Rotoshop style, and the kinds of rhythmic orders Sabiston's technology is able to award the very animated bodies it overlays.[66] With Rotoshop, "the body and its every move waver, are shaded, outlined, and highlighted," all actions that are intensified by the scramble suit's aptitude for multiple physiognomies that move in and out of visibility as part of its project to make the wearer undetectable (it also incorporates a vocal modulator into its design).[67] Bob's scramble suit in *A Scanner Darkly* therefore raises to a higher pitch of emphasis the intense mutability of the Rotoshop technology, operating as a partner to Bob's fractured psyche and "bilateral dysfunction" (as he terms it) that is addled by his addiction to "Substance D."

As a narrative device, the scramble suit also serves to further intensify the lived body as the site of competing rhythms and multiple forces. Whybray argues that "the rhythmanalyst's body acts like a reference oscillator, through and against which external rhythms are processed and defined."[68] The tension between inner/Bob and outer/Fred prompted by the agent's use of the scramble suit magnifies his alienated and isolated identity in flux. Navigating a double life, his heterogeneity constructs a body where linear and cyclic rhythms are traversed. As the psychologist states in a consultation with Bob, his "competition phenomenon" in the brain shows "two signals that interfere with each other by carrying conflicting information." Bob's addiction causes him to become increasingly out of step with his environment and his body, and comprised, according to Hank, of "short circuits" and "sparks," which lead to a complete collapse in identity. Lefebvre similarly argues that "In arrhythmia, rhythms break apart, alter and bypass synchronization."[69] For Bob, his arrhythmia reaches its peak when he succumbs to his addiction, renamed once more as "Bruce" at the film's climax as part of his rehabilitation at a clinic, despite his overwhelming cognitive deficiencies. The outcome in *A Scanner Darkly* is a doubly-mediated form of arrhythmia, where Bob/Fred/Bruce's alienated body becomes further animated by the Rotoshop in ways that amplify its lack of rhythmic synchronicity. Ian Garwood levels charges of creative conflict and dissonance between rhythms in his analysis of Rotoshop, noting that the technology is able to shift from tight audiovisual synchronization toward more expressive possibilities in coordination between voice (sound) and body (image) (what he terms "Slip-sync").[70] Both *Waking Life* and *A Scanner Darkly* are more conventional in their audiovisual synchronicity than in the "free-floating undulation" of speech in Sabiston's Rotoshopped compilation of shorts *Figures of Speech* (2000).[71] However, the scramble suit in Linklater's film is where identity in the film is at its most fractious, precarious, tested, and jeopardized, transforming the body into a space where the collision between rhythms, bodies, and voices is felt and "lived" by Bob most acutely.

CONCLUSION

Rhythmanalysis is highly generative for thinking through animation's broader qualities of representation, sharpening an understanding of both its various styles, forms, and processes, and the medium's hidden labor and routines of production that occur between the frames. However, the many animated energies and frequencies created by Sabiston's unique Rotoshop digital paint system—in evidence throughout Linklater's *Waking Life* and *A Scanner Darkly*—present a particular opportunity to connect digitally animated media to Lefebvre's rhythmanalytical approach. As a social and political project, rhythmanalysis seeks to make sense of the discordant rhythms held both in tension and opposition that structure our involvement with the everyday, itself recoded by Lefebvre and Régulier as the "theatre" for "a conflict between great indestructible rhythms and the processes imposed by the socio-economic organisation of production, circulation and habitat."[72] In Linklater's animated features, the Rotoshop digital tool overlays the live-action body with new modes of rhythm, which refine the characters' movements through (and experience of) the monotonous "quantified" linear rhythms and time scales of capitalism and industrial labor. Engineered by the digital, such mechanical Rotoshopped rhythms become fully intertwined with the many other linear rhythms that shape bodies, providing a visible energy to Linklater's films that approximates the kinds of linear times imposed by technology that challenge, disrupt, and fragment more physiological or natural cycles. But the Rotoshop tool's defining intermediary position caught between image-making technologies equally secures its place within contemporary convergence or remix culture, where the digitization of media has presented combinatory ways of seeing and a "rhythmed" media ecology rooted in questions of audiovisual hybridity and appropriation. As Carol Vernallis argues, "contemporary digital media present forms of space, time, and rhythm we haven't seen before," which in turn mirror "contemporary experiences like work speedup, multitasking, and just-in-time labor."[73] These new audiovisual configurations encompass the unique stylistic qualities of the rippling, slipping, and sliding Rotoshop that defines *Waking Life* and *A Scanner Darkly*, two films that in their highly rhythmed and rhythmical form appear pleasurably and powerfully off-beat.

NOTES

1. Henri Lefebvre and Catherine Régulier, "The Rhythmanalytical Project," in Henri Lefebvre, *Rhythmanalysis: Space, Time and Everyday Life*, trans. Stuart Elden and Gerald Moore (London: Continuum, 2004), 73.
2. Ibid.
3. Ryan Pierson, *Figure and Force in Animation Aesthetics* (New York: Oxford University Press, 2020), 44.
4. Angie Jones and Jamie Oliff, *Thinking Animation: Bridging the Gap Between 2D and CG* (Boston, MA: Thomson, 2007), 119.
5. Caroline Ruddell, "'Don't Box Me In': Blurred Lines in *Waking Life* and *A Scanner Darkly*," animation: an interdisciplinary journal 7:1 (2011): 8.
6. Aylish Wood, *Digital Encounters* (London: Routledge, 2007), 15.

7. Henri Lefebvre, "The Critique of the Thing," in Lefebvre, *Rhythmanalysis*, 15.
8. Leslie Bishko, "The Uses and Abuses of Cartoon Style in Animation," *Animation Studies* 2 (2007): 27.
9. Steve Roberts, *Character Animation Fundamentals: Developing Skills for 2D and 3D Character Animation* (Boca Raton, FL: CRC Press, 2012), 298.
10. Preston Blair, *Cartoon Animation with Preston Blair, Revised Edition!: Learn Techniques for Drawing and Animating Cartoon Characters* (Laguna Beach, CA: Walter Foster Publishing, 2020), 70.
11. Roger Manvell, *The Animated Film* (London: Sylvan Press, 1954), 32.
12. Bishko, "The Uses and Abuses of Cartoon Style in Animation," 34.
13. Paul Wells, *Understanding Animation* (London: Routledge, 1998), 43.
14. Dan Bashara, *Cartoon Vision: UPA Animation and Postwar Aesthetics* (Berkeley: University of California Press, 2019), 31.
15. Roberts, *Character Animation Fundamentals*, 298.
16. Paul Ward, "Independent Animation, Rotoshop and Communities of Practice: As Seen Through *A Scanner Darkly*," *animation: an interdisciplinary journal* 7:1 (2011): 61.
17. Ibid.
18. Ibid., 60; Ruddell, "'Don't Box Me In,'" 8.
19. Paul Ward, "Rotoshop in Context: Computer Rotoscoping and Animation Aesthetics," *Animation Journal* 12: 32–34.
20. Wood, *Digital Encounters*, 160.
21. Émile Benveniste, "The Notion of 'Rhythm' in its Linguistic Expression," in *Problems in General Linguistics*, trans. Mary Elizabeth Meek (Miami: University of Miami Press, 1971), 281.
22. Maja Manojlovic, "'Dream Is Destiny': *Waking Life* and the Digital Aesthetics of the In-between," *Discourse* 33:2 (Spring, 2011): 198.
23. Ruddell, "'Don't Box Me In,'" 12.
24. See K. L. Walden, "Double Take: Rotoscoping and the Processing of Performance," *Refractory: A Journal of Entertainment Media* 14: http://refractory.unimelb.edu.au/2008/12/24/double-take-rotoscoping-and-the-processing-of-performance-%E2%80%93-kim-louise-walden; Ian Garwood, "Roto-Synchresis: Relationships between Body and Voice in Rotoshop Animation," *animation: an interdisciplinary journal* 7:1 (March 2012): 39–57; Rob Stone, *The Cinema of Richard Linklater: Walk, Don't Run* (New York: Wallflower Press, 2013). Linklater has since revisited the Rotoshop technology for his recent animated feature film *Apollo 10½: A Space Age Childhood* (2022).
25. Ruddell, "'Don't Box Me In,'" 9.
26. Qtd. in ibid. See also Julian Henriques, Milla Tiainen, and Pasi Väliaho, "Rhythm Returns: Movements and Cultural Theory," *Body & Society* 20:3/4 (2014): 3–29.
27. Qtd. in ibid.
28. Ibid., 12.
29. Christopher Holliday, *The Computer-Animated Film: Industry, Style and Genre* (Edinburgh: Edinburgh University Press, 2018), 16.
30. Ibid., 36.
31. Wood, *Digital Encounters*, 60.
32. Dan Torre, "Boiling Lines and Lightning Sketches: Process and the Animated Drawing," *animation: an interdisciplinary journal* 10:2 (2015): 149.
33. Ibid., 50.
34. Ward, "Independent Animation, Rotoshop and Communities of Practice," 69.
35. Torre, "Boiling Lines and Lightning Sketches," 149.
36. Ward, "Rotoshop in Context," 33–34.
37. John Halas, *Film Animation: A Simplified Approach* (Paris: UNESCO, 1976), 45.

38. Henri Lefebvre, *The Production of Space*, trans. Donald Nicholson-Smith (Oxford: Blackwell Publishing, 1991), 205.
39. Gordon Walker, *Energy and Rhythm: Rhythmanalysis for a Low Carbon Future* (Lanham, MD: Rowman & Littlefield, 2021), 19.
40. Lefebvre and Régulier, "The Rhythmanalytical Project," 79.
41. Lefebvre, "Music and Rhythms," in Lefebvre, *Rhythmanalysis*, 60.
42. Adam Whybray, *The Art of Czech Animation: A History of Political Dissent and Allegory* (London: Bloomsbury, 2020), 10.
43. Ibid., 133.
44. Ibid., 11.
45. Lefebvre, *The Production of Space*, 31.
46. Ibid.
47. Ibid., 76.
48. Ibid.
49. Whybray, *The Art of Czech Animation*, 128.
50. Gregory Minissale, *Rhythm in Art, Psychology and New Materialism* (New York: Cambridge University Press, 2021), 67–68.
51. Ibid., 67.
52. Lefebvre and Régulier, "The Rhythmanalytical Project," 74.
53. Sue Middleton, "Henri Lefebvre on Education: Critique and Pedagogy," *Policy Futures in Education* 15:4 (2017): 415.
54. Manojlovic, "'Dream Is Destiny,'" 195.
55. Ibid., 191.
56. Lefebvre, *The Production of Space*, 117.
57. Stone, *The Cinema of Richard Linklater*, 54.
58. Manojlovic, "'Dream Is Destiny,'" 191.
59. Chris Pallant, *Demystifying Disney: A History of Disney Feature Animation* (London: Bloomsbury, 2011), 69–70.
60. Minissale, *Rhythm in Art, Psychology and New Materialism*, 68.
61. Lefebvre and Régulier, "The Rhythmanalytical Project," 81.
62. Lefebvre, "The Critique of the Thing," 8.
63. Lefebvre and Régulier, "The Rhythmanalytical Project," 79.
64. Lefebvre, "The Rhythmanalyst: A Previsionary Portrait," in Lefebvre, *Rhythmanalysis*, 20.
65. Ibid., 23–25.
66. Ruddell, "'Don't Box Me In,'" 16.
67. Ibid., 10.
68. Whybray, *The Art of Czech Animation*, 128.
69. Lefebvre, "Conclusions (Résumé)," in Lefebvre, *Rhythmanalysis*, 67.
70. Garwood, "Roto-Synchresis," 51–52.
71. Ibid., 54.
72. Lefebvre and Régulier, "The Rhythmanalytical Project," 73.
73. Carol Vernallis, "Accelerated Aesthetics: A New Lexicon of Time, Space, and Rhythm," in *The Oxford Handbook of Sound and Image in Digital Media*, edited by Carol Vernallis, Amy Herzog, and John Richardson (Oxford: Oxford University Press, 2013), 707.

Index

$5.15/Hr (2004), 39–41
9/11, 101, 107, 108, 112

activism, 43, 45, 46–8, 106
  activist filmmaking, 35, 46
aesthetic experience, 211, 215
Akin, Fatih, 150
American Dream, 85–7, 89, 91, 96
American Graffiti (1973), 102, 127
American individualism, 16, 30, 57, 91–2, 96, 98, 129, 188
animal-industrial complex, 35, 41, 44–5
animation, 47, 210–15, 218–21, 224, 228, 230–1
Aristotle, 110, 137, 169
Arlington National Cemetery, 119
Arquette, Patricia, 115, 204
art-house cinema, 17, 35, 37, 48
Ashby, Hal, 50–9, 61–2, 64–5, 117
Austin (Texas), 15–30, 55–6, 67–71, 73, 76, 78
Austin Arts Council, 22
Austin Film Society (AFS), 15, 17, 18, 22–3, 28, 55–6
Austin City Limits (ACL), 17

Austin Studios, 23
auteurism
  authorship and film, 6, 79, 103, 165, 196
avant-garde, 91–2

Bad News Bears, The (1976), 85, 97
Bad News Bears (2005), 85, 87, 89–92, 96, 97, 103, 118
baseball, 85–98, 118, 199
Baudrillard, Jean, 70, 75, 77
Bazin, André, 205
Before Midnight (2013), 61, 86, 136–51
Before Sunrise (1995), 50–2, 61, 69, 70, 103, 136, 140–1, 146, 173, 182–3
Before Sunset (2004), 52, 69, 141
Benjamin, Walter, 220
Benning, James, 85, 92
Bergson, Henri, 194–201, 203–6, 208
Berliner, Todd, 158–9, 162–4
Bernie (2011), 58–9, 157–8, 166–73, 179, 190
Bakhtin, Mikhail, 139
Bildungsroman, 100, 118

Bishko, Leslie, 212–13
Black, Jack, 59, 79, 157, 168
Blake, Jenner, 85, 117, 199
Bogosian, Eric, 180, 186–7
Bonnie and Clyde (1967), 17
Bordwell, David, 158, 172, 176–7, 179, 188, 190
Bound for Glory (1976), 58
Boyhood (2014), 47–8, 61, 88, 100–13, 115–17, 129–30, 194–7, 200–8
Breaking Bad (2008–13), 120, 123
British Broadcasting Corporation (BBC), 37
buddy movie/film, 116–17, 119, 122, 125–7
Bruno, Giuliana, 72–4
Buñuel, Luis, 91
Burger King, 40, 47
Burns, Ken, 85

capitalism, 24–6, 41–5, 210, 221–3, 231
Carrell, Steve, 62
Cassavetes, John, 162, 196
child actors, 115
cinephilia, 70
civil rights, 55, 96
Coltrane, Ellar, 100, 105, 113, 196–7, 203
comedy (genre), 35, 39, 79, 122, 125–8, 130, 136–40, 146–51, 161–2
  comic worlds, 137–43
  comic space, 137–43, 145–6, 149–51
Coming Home (1978), 58
coming-of-age, 79, 87–8, 95, 100, 117–19, 195, 197, 198–200, 204–6, 223
conversation, 73, 75, 86, 138, 158–73, 178, 183, 189, 191
corporate interest, 21, 24, 29–30, 40–3
Coupland, Douglas, 19, 68

counterculture, also counter-culture, 55–7
commercialism, 29–30
community, 15–27, 86, 89, 92, 169–70, 172–3, 199–200
conspiracy theory, 75–6
Cranston, Bryan, 120, 123, 224
CreateAustin, 22
creative class, 16, 19–23
critical animal studies, 35

Da 5 Bloods (2020), 62–3
Daniel, Lee, 16–17, 18
Davies, Jeffrey, 92
Dazed and Confused (1993), 25, 30, 60–1, 88, 91, 103, 119, 120, 127–8, 130, 182, 183, 195–9, 202, 204
Deleuze, Gilles
  action-image, 53–5, 57–8, 61
  time-image, 196–7, 202, 203, 205–7
  affection-image, 51–8, 60–5
Deleuze, Gilles and Félix Guattari, 68, 71, 78
Delpy, Julie, 137, 142, 148–50
Detour Filmproduction, 23
Deutch, Zoey, 94
dialogue, 41, 53, 122, 126, 127, 158–9, 162–7, 172, 187
Dick, Philip K., 34, 190, 211, 228
digital formats, 104
Disney, 212–13, 224
documentary, 26, 37–8, 47–8, 144, 168
dreamstates (also dream states), 217
drugs, 43, 211, 227
duration, 104, 139, 140, 146, 202–7, 210–11, 216, 228

Easy Rider (1967), 106, 202
ecofeminism, 35
Elsaesser, Thomas, 54, 60

empathetic effort, 157–73
empathy, 92, 157–60, 162, 167–9, 172–5
ethics, 177
European influence, 70, 91, 92, 137–45, 151
European integration, 137, 140–9
Everybody Wants Some!! (2016), 85, 87–91, 93–4, 97, 115–18, 120, 122–3, 126–31, 195–9, 201–3
exclusivity, 98
existentialism, 56, 86, 199–200

family resemblance, 2
Fast Food Nation (book), 34, 36–8, 46, 47, 190
Fast Food Nation (2006), 34–48, 189, 190
fast-food industries, 34, 37, 39–41, 45, 46, 47
feminism (also feminist), 45, 115, 186
   feminist cinema, 55
   feminist critique, 35, 147
Film Festivals, 18, 194
Fincher, David, 206
Fishburne, Laurence, 62, 115, 166
Five Easy Pieces (1970), 55
flâneur/flânerie, 51, 184, 189
Florida, Richard, 21, 22
Foucault, Michel, 20
Fox Searchlight Pictures, 47
Freud, Sigmund, 139

gender, 96, 106, 115–31, 147
genre, 77, 85, 96–8, 106–7, 115–31, 137–8, 169, 190, 195
Gen X, 15, 19
globalization, 19–20, 24
Godard, Jean-Luc, 198
Greece, 142–7
Guattari, Pierre-Félix, 68, 71, 77, 78
guilt, 63, 95, 172–3

Hamlet, 177
hanging out, 53, 182, 186–7
Harold and Maude (1971), 56–9
Harrelson, Woody, 228
Harrod, Mary, 41
Hawke, Ethan, 123, 142, 144
Hawks, Howard, 165
HBO (Home Box Office), 19, 39
Heckerling, Amy, 179, 186
Hellman, Monte, 57
heteronormativity, 108, 168
historiography of the West, 121
Hoak, Jim, 39
homogenous time (Bergson), 197–202, 204, 210
Hooper, Tobe, 17
humanism, 53, 91, 176, 180

idleness, 53–4
immigrants, 40, 43–4, 46, 95
In the Fade (2017), 150–1
Inconvenient Truth, An (2006), 38
independent cinema/independent film, 15–16, 18, 25, 28, 30, 35–6, 48, 50, 53, 55, 104–5, 126, 165, 195
Independent Film Channel (IFC), 105
Independent Spirit awards, 3
Inning by Inning: A Portrait of a Coach (2008), 86, 90
intersectionality, 35, 41–6, 108
interstitial space, 71
intimacy, 149, 160, 197
Iraq War (film genre), 117, 122–5
itinerant (iterance), 1–11
It's Impossible to Learn to Plow by Reading Books (1988), 15, 17, 35, 70, 165

Jameson, Fredric, 73, 91
Jenner, Blake, 127
Johnson, David T., 1–3, 90, 121, 183

Keathley, Christian, 54–8, 60, 64, 198
"Keep Austin Weird," 16, 19–20, 22–4
Kerouac, Jack, 130
Kinnear, Greg, 40, 89, 189
Kozloff, Sarah, 158–60, 162, 168
Kristofferson, Kris, 41, 189

Last Detail, The (1973), 50–2, 61–5
Last Flag Flying (2017), 52, 61–5, 115–29, 157
Last Picture Show, The (1971), 202
Lee, Spike, 62
Lefebvre, Henri, 139, 210–13, 217, 220–3, 225, 227, 230, 231
Levitch, Timothy "Speed," 215
Linklater, Lorelei, 88, 109, 194
Lucas, George, 102, 103, 127
Lyotard, François, 58, 68, 77

McConaughey, Matthew, 29, 168
McDonald's, 47
MacDowell, James, 146, 147
MacLaine, Shirley, 59, 157, 168
McLaren, Malcolm, 38
Man Who Shot Liberty Valance, The (1962), 121
masculinity (also manhood), 87, 89, 93, 95, 116–31
Massey, Doreen, 139, 142, 144
Me and Orson Welles (2009), 4, 5
meat industry, 45–7
melodrama, 137, 138, 146, 148
memory, 75, 96, 101, 126, 176–9, 184, 191
Merrily We Roll Along, 1
Mexico, 42, 45, 46
MGM, 212
military, 62–4, 116, 117, 120–5, 129
monologue, 75, 159, 166–8
Moore, Michael, 37, 39

moral recency, 176–91
motion, 69–72, 210–31
movement, 54–5, 69–74, 91, 200–1, 210–31
MTV, 67–8
Myth of Sisyphus, The, 199

narrative, 35, 40–2, 54–5, 68–72, 74–9, 100–2, 119–20, 129, 159–60, 162, 164, 165, 167, 172, 176–9, 186–90, 195–202, 206, 217, 219, 221, 227, 230
National Endowment for the Arts, 22
Neill, Alex, 157, 159–60
Nelson, Willie, 17
neoliberalism, 16, 20–2, 25, 30, 55
New Hollywood, 53–5
Newman, Michael Z, 36, 178
Newton Boys, The (1998), 58, 103, 121
Night Moves (1975), 55
Nixon, Richard, 53, 58, 64, 228
nomadism, 69–71, 78
non-fiction filmmaking, 34, 45, 190
nostalgia, 15–16, 24, 27–30, 74, 96–7, 120, 129
nostalgia film *see* Fredric Jameson
Nussbaum, Martha, 169–72

Obama, Barack, 101, 106, 112
Ophüls, Max, 91
Orion Classics, 18–19
Oscars, 115

pandemic (also COVID-19), 29, 68
Paramount Pictures, 35–6
Paris, 69, 70, 136, 137, 141, 142
Participant Productions, 37–8, 47
patriotism, 64, 91
PBS, 37, 40
Peloponnese, 137, 142–5

People for the Ethical Treatment of Animals (PETA), 46, 48
Pick, Anat, 45
Pierson, John, 18, 91
Pink Floyd, 130, 197, 200–2
populist nationalism, 142
postmodernism, 69, 78–9
post-Vietnam, 53–5
post-traumatic cycle *see* Keathley
post-war malaise, 53–5
primacy effect, 176–9, 181, 184, 186, 188–91

queer fat, 128

racism, 42, 62, 184, 185, 187
Radwan, Jon, 73–4, 76
Reaganism (also Reaganite), 55, 202
Reaganomics *see* trickle-down economics
Rebel Without a Cause (1955), 103
recency effect, 176–9, 181, 184, 186, 188–91
Reeves, Keanu, 211
Régulier, Catherine, 210–13, 220, 222, 225, 231
Reichardt, Kelly, 55
relational discourse, 165
rhizome, 78
rhythm
  arrhythmic rhythm, 211, 222, 223, 225, 227–8
  cyclic rhythm, 210, 211, 221–2, 225, 227, 230
  rhythm of daily life, 221
rhythmanalysis, 212, 216–17, 219–23, 225, 230–1
Rise of the Creative Classes, 22
rite of passage, 88, 118
road movie, 70, 116–17, 119, 121–4
rock 'n' roll (also rock and roll), 198
Rohmer, Eric, 149

Romanticism, 69
romcom/romantic comedy, 136–8, 146–9
Roth, Philip, 91
Rotoscoping, 128, 214, 219
Rotoshop, 210–31
Ryder, Winona, 228

Sabiston, Bob, 211, 213–14, 219, 230–1
Sayles, John, 165, 178, 188
Scanner Darkly, A (2006), 34, 41, 129, 130–1, 211–20, 227–31
Schlosser, Eric, 34, 36–8, 40, 46, 190
School of Rock, The (2005), 35–6, 58, 103, 105, 115
Sconce, Jeffrey, 68, 74
Scorsese, Martin, 79, 206
scramble suit, 228–30
Second World War, 62, 151
sentimentality, 100
Seurat, Georges-Pierre, 70, 141
sexism, 140, 187
Shakespeare, William, 137, 138
Shampoo (1975), 55, 60, 61
Shaviro, Steven, 131
Sight & Sound, 128
Simulacra and Simulation, 77
Singer, Peter, 46
Slacker (1990), 15–19, 24–30, 41, 57–8, 67–79, 103, 142, 165, 180, 188–9, 194, 223
slacker ethos, 16, 23, 68
slaughterhouse, 40, 42–7, 190
small-town, 38, 59–60, 158
Smith, Kevin, 28, 103
South by South-West (SXSW), 17, 24
space (concept), 50–4, 56–7, 59, 61, 64–5, 70, 71–6, 136–46, 141, 149–51, 163, 173, 181–4, 200–3, 212, 220–5, 227, 230–1
speciesism, 46

spectatorship, 69, 72, 136, 139, 141–2, 146, 147, 149, 176, 197, 203–8
Speed, Lesley, 91
Spielberg, Steven, 103
Stevens, George, 17
Stone, Rob, 24, 36, 70, 74, 91, 96, 146, 183, 198
SubUrbia (1996), 69, 103, 178–91
suburbia (idea of), 178–91
Sundance Film Festival, 18, 28, 55
sympathy, 157, 159–60

Tape (2001), 34, 58, 103, 104, 105, 165
tech sector, 15–16, 20–2
temporality, 126, 142, 149, 200–1, 205, 221
Texan identity, 35, 165
Texas Film Commission, 17, 28
Texas Film Incentive Program, 28
That Animal Rescue Show (2020), 48
time
   aging, 59, 61, 65, 100–4, 199, 203–5
   heterogenous time (Bergson), 204
   homogenous time (Bergson), 199–202, 204, 210
   lived time, 195–6, 198, 200–8
topophilic filmmaking, 68, 71, 73, 74, 79
transnational Europe, 140–5, 149, 151
transnational space, 136–7, 139, 140–5, 149, 151
trauma-induced deferral, 59
traveler, 70–1
travelogue, 68, 70, 79
trickle-down economics, 181
Trouble in Paradise (1932), 138
Tuan, Yi-Fu, 73
Turkle, Sherry, 159–60, 162–4
Turner, Lynn, 4
TV screen, 75, 76–7

Two-Lane Blacktop (1971), 57
Tyson, Cicely, 53

University of Texas at Austin's Radio-Television-Film (RTF), 17–18
urban environment, 76, 223
U.S. Library of Congress's National Film Registry, 15

vegetarianism, 35, 46
veterans, 62, 115–16, 123
Viaggio in Italia (1971), 150–1
Vienna, 69, 70, 136, 137, 141
Vietnam War, 52–5, 62–5, 102, 116, 117, 120–3
von Kleist, Heinrich, 167

Waking Life (2001), 34, 69, 70, 103, 131, 165, 180, 211–13, 215–19, 220, 223–6, 230–1
Wall Street, 55
Walt Disney (corporation), 37, 40, 212–13
Warner Brothers, 224
Weber, Max, 91
Where'd You Go, Bernadette (2019), 61, 157–8, 160–8, 173
whiteness, 97, 181
Whole Shootin' Match, The (1977), 17
Wiggins, Wiley, 211, 215–17, 223–7
Wings (1927), 17
Wittgenstein, Ludwig, 2, 5
Wolfe, Tom, 54
Wood, Robin, 4
World Trade Center, 64

youth cinema/film, 102–3, 105, 106, 116–17, 122
youth culture, 85, 101, 103, 107–9

EU representative:
Easy Access System Europe
Mustamäe tee 50, 10621 Tallinn, Estonia
Gpsr.requests@easproject.com

www.ingramcontent.com/pod-product-compliance
Lightning Source LLC
Chambersburg PA
CBHW070340240426
43671CB00013BA/2382